KIM

Also by Sean Smith

Tom Jones: The Life
Kylie
Gary
Alesha
Tulisa
Kate
Robbie
Cheryl
Victoria
Justin: The Biography
Britney: The Biography
J. K. Rowling: A Biography
Jennifer: The Unauthorized Biography
Royal Racing
The Union Game
Sophie's Kiss (with Garth Gibbs)
Stone Me! (with Dale Lawrence)

SEAN SMITH

KIM

HarperCollins*Publishers*

HarperCollins*Publishers*
1 London Bridge Street
London SE1 9GF

www.harpercollins.co.uk

First published by HarperCollins*Publishers* 2015

1 3 5 7 9 10 8 6 4 2

A catalogue record of this book is
available from the British Library

HB ISBN 978-0-00-810449-8
TPB ISBN 978-0-00-810453-5
EB ISBN 978-0-00-810450-4

Printed and bound in Great Britain by
Clays Ltd, St Ives plc

MIX
Paper from
responsible sources
FSC® C007454

To Rodney and Nicky

CONTENTS

CONTENTS

PART THREE: KIM KARDASHIAN WEST

INTRODUCTION

A DAY IN CALABASAS, 4 JUNE 2015

It's a scorchingly hot Thursday in Calabasas. A helpful guy in the sushi bar told me it was 100 degrees outside. In the middle of the day, even the shade is too warm. The old cliché that you could fry an egg on the pavement certainly applies; in fact, you could cook a full English breakfast. No wonder you are unlikely to see Kim Kardashian West in her new custom-designed silver Rolls-Royce Phantom before the sun has cooled in the late afternoon or early evening.

Calabasas is in what's known in Los Angeles as 'The Valley'. More accurately, this is the San Fernando Valley or the West Valley. Locals reckon it's at least 10 degrees warmer here than in the fashionable beach areas of Santa Monica, Venice and Malibu. Calabasas, though, is becoming just as desirable, thanks to an influx of the rich and famous who realise a 40-minute crawl along the Ventura Freeway (Route 101) is a small price to pay for getting so much more bang for your buck. A $1 million property here might cost $10 million in Beverly Hills. That value for money won't last forever. The Kardashians have made Calabasas famous, thanks to their reality show and the number of times they are photographed apparently living their lives in a normal way.

Other than Kim and her family, the most famous current resident is probably Drake, the phenomenally successful Canadian rapper, who immortalised the place in his song '2 On/Thotful': 'Crib in Calabasas man I call that shit the safe house. Thirty minutes from LA man the shit is way out.'

Local legend has it that Calabasas owes its unusual name to an incident in 1824. A rancher from Oxnard, 60 miles north, was on his way to Los Angeles when he crashed his wagon, spilling a load of pumpkins along the track. The next spring, hundreds of pumpkins or gourds started to grow by the road-side. As a result, the area was called Las Calabasas – the place where the pumpkins fell – after the Spanish word for pump-kin, *calabaza*.

Technically, Calabasas is a city that became part of Los Angeles County in 1991. It doesn't feel remotely like Los Angeles here. The great Hollywood stars of the past didn't live in Calabasas. Instead, they came to work here, although some would take Valley vacations away from the bustle of LA.

In 1935, Warner Brothers bought an estate near Calabasas Creek, which became known as the Warner Bros Ranch. Many classic films were shot there: in *The Adventures of Robin Hood*, starring Errol Flynn, the dusty terrain doubled for Sherwood Forest. Flynn travelled out to the Valley to shoot a number of movies, including the Western *Santa Fe Trail*, which co-starred a future President of the United States, Ronald Reagan. The Hollywood great, Gary Cooper, won an Oscar for his portrayal of Sergeant York fighting in the (Calabasas) trenches in the story of the First World War hero. Most famously, *Casablanca*, the wartime romance that features on almost every list of all-time best movies, was partly shot at the ranch.

Nowadays, classic movies have given way to reality shows, although the Valley has also long been a favoured setting for porn flicks. *Keeping Up with the Kardashians* is by no means the first reality show to be shot at a house in Calabasas. The best known was probably *Newlyweds: Nick and Jessica*, which began in 2003 and followed the embryonic marriage of boy band vocalist Nick Lachey and the blonde bombshell singer Jessica Simpson. The dumb blonde antics of Jessica were quite amusing, but the show had nowhere to go after three seasons, when she filed for divorce. Real life ruined the reality show.

The Kardashians aren't seen in town as much these days, especially after moving their boutique, DASH, to West Hollywood in 2012. The original store, I discover, was in a small parade in Park Granada, just across the road from a large shopping complex called The Commons, the central point of Calabasas. A few years ago, the Kardashians were genuinely out and about every day, as they sought to build their business before the store became little more than a film location. It was pleasant enough, but nothing special – the sort of place you might find in a thousand small towns across America.

In the Shibuya sushi bar, a few yards down from DASH, they used to see the Kardashians every other day. The Kardashian women have always tried to keep their voluptuous figures in check by eating healthily. The chef preparing my tasty lunch of seared toro and peppered tuna at the counter told me that Kim had been to the restaurant lots of times, but Kanye West had joined her on only one occasion.

Shibuya is small and fills up quite easily, so when Kim and Kanye turned up on an evening in late April, they were made to wait in line and sat on a bench outside for half an hour until a table became available. Kim had just appeared on the talk show *Jimmy Kimmel Live!* and this proved to be a convenient photo opportunity on their way home. A photographer was able to shoot some very clear shots. Kanye looked miserable and scowled, as he always does for the cameras. Kim, elegantly made up and revealing her considerable cleavage, smiled happily.

Kim always favours the house sushi roll when she visits Shibuya. In actual fact, they had no need to stop off at all, because they employ a full-time chef. My own chef was not so absorbed in news of the Kardashians. He was extremely interested in Manchester United, however, and dreams of the day when Wayne Rooney pops in for a sashimi snack.

In and around the exclusive little shops, ice cream parlours and health food stores, you are far more likely to see Kim's younger half-sisters, Kendall and Kylie Jenner, who, as teenagers do, prefer to hang out in the mall with their friends than in the fur-lined prison of their gated community.

Round the corner for coffee at the Blue Table deli, a young woman, who was working in Calabasas while she waited for her break as a singer, told me that she had seen Scott Disick the day before. The long-standing boyfriend of Kim's sister Kourtney, and the father of her children, has become a well-known face from his regular appearances on the TV show. 'What does he actually do?' asked my companion. I had to admit I had no idea and made a mental note to find out.

Having celebrities pop in does wonders for local trade. A few hundred yards away, in yet another shopping centre, El Camino, is a 'homey café for health-conscious bites' called Health Nut, which has become celebrated as the place where the Kardashian girls buy the salads they are always munching on TV. I pop in to grab a takeaway of Kim's favourite salad, whatever that might be.

'No problem,' said the man at the counter, bashing my order into the till and taking the money.

'What's in it?' I asked.

'No idea,' he responded smilingly. 'I just hit a button marked "Kardashian".'

It turns out to be a pretty dull chicken salad with a pleasant tangy dressing – nothing the chef couldn't run up in five minutes at home.

For a while, the Kardashians had a major rival as the most famous faces in the neighbourhood when Justin Bieber bought a house in a gated Calabasas community called The Oaks for $6.5 million in 2012. These days it's a Kardashian enclave. Justin tired of life in the suburbs after two years and sold his five-bedroom mansion, complete with pool, hot tub, movie theatre and skateboard ramp, at a $1 million profit to Kim's sister Khloé. She can easily walk round to see their elder sister Kourtney, who also lives there.

Khloé's mansion is relatively ordinary compared to the extraordinary palatial luxury enjoyed by Drake. He is one of the biggest stars in the US, although he has yet to cross the Atlantic with similar success. His best-known British hit was as the featured artist on Rihanna's number one 'What's My Name?'.

He lives in an outrageously opulent home in Hidden Hills, which was originally on the market for $27 million in 2009, but he was able to pick it up for the knockdown price of $8 million after the property market collapsed. It has a cinema, wine cellar, stables, volleyball court, Olympic-sized pool, stables, wet-room bar and so on. Drake once sang on a number called 'Versace' by the hip-hop group Migos: 'This is a gated community, please get the fuck off the property.' He may rap the language of the street, but I don't suppose he wants to live anywhere near one.

Hidden Hills is the gated community that attracted Kris and Bruce Jenner when they were looking to move from Beverly Hills while Kim and her siblings were still at school. Kris was first introduced to the neighbourhood by a friend after her marriage to Kim's father, Robert Kardashian, had collapsed.

There's rumoured to be more money in Hidden Hills than in Bel Air. Kim and Kanye have now bought an estate there with an estimated value of $20 million. I heard they are going to turn it into a palace and it's going to make Drake's property seem like a terrace.

It's supremely ironic that gated communities don't just keep the public out, they fence the residents in. You can't get past the guards without an appointment or, it seems, an E! Entertainment Television identification badge. At least for the famous people who live here, it means the paparazzi aren't looking over the garden fence.

Hidden Hills has a number of entrances and exits, so the photographers split up and wait at each one. Kim will leave eventually, but they won't know in advance which exit she is going to use. When she is spotted, the photographer stationed at that particular gate texts everyone else that she is on the move. By clubbing together in this way, they ensure that they all have the opportunity to get a picture. It is reminiscent of the days when squadrons of paparazzi used to hang around outside Kensington Palace in the hope that Princess Diana would go out. A Kim picture guarantees a sale in much the same way as one of the adored royal icon did.

I popped into a hotel in Calabasas to ask for some directions and told the receptionist, probably a resting actress, that I was writing a book about Kim Kardashian. She volunteered, 'I don't really like her. I don't see what her point is.' It reminded me of local hostility against Britney Spears when I visited McComb, Mississippi, where she was born. Perhaps it's the way people always feel about the most famous face in their midst.

I enjoyed my day in Calabasas, but I needed to beat the traffic on the freeway to return to downtown Los Angeles and civilisation. Before I left, there was time to ask an elegant woman shopping for clothes in a boutique very similar to DASH what she thought of the Kardashians: 'You don't get anywhere in that family without a vagina. Bruce has realised that …'

PART ONE

KIMBERLY

1

MOTHER ARMENIA

———

Kim Kardashian West demonstrated to the world the global power of her celebrity when she arrived at the Armenian Memorial Complex in that obscure country's capital of Yerevan in April 2015. The pictures of her, solemnly carrying a bunch of bright red tulips that matched the colour of her dazzling jumpsuit, went round the world.

After she had laid the tribute at the eternal flame, bedlam broke out as TV cameramen and photographers – and the public brandishing phones – battled for pictures of Kim and her family. It had been the same story ever since she had touched down in Mother Armenia, as she calls the land of her ancestors.

'Armenia, we are here!!!!!' She posted to her then 30 million Instagram followers when she arrived. 'We are so grateful to be here and start this journey of a lifetime. Thank you to everyone who greeted us. I can't wait to explore our country and have some yummy food!'

On the flight from Los Angeles International Airport (LAX), Kim had slept completely hidden from prying eyes by a blanket. She always does this on planes so nobody can snap an unglamorous shot of her snoring with her mouth open. They flew the last part of their journey economy class, much to the amazement of other passengers.

When she arrived, she appeared completely refreshed, in ripped white jeans and a tight white top, although she hid her eyes behind a huge pair of sunglasses, in case the ravages of jet lag had caught her before her make-up artist, who always travels with her, could step in.

The visit saw Kim, and her younger sister Khloé, give an object lesson in how to combine glamour with tasteful respect. For their audience with the prime minister, they wore figure-hugging outfits that showed off all their curves. Kim chose beige and combined it with killer heels. Yet for their trip to the sacred Geghard Monastery, a World Heritage Site, she chose understated black.

Kanye West was on hand to secure his wife's veil affectionately, although her wardrobe assistant took over to make the necessary adjustments for the perfect picture. Arguably, Kim has never looked lovelier than in this respectful homage to the country's tradition. She looked very Armenian, with her coal-black eyes, long black hair and curvaceous silhouette.

This was Kim's first visit to the land of her father's family. Inevitably, there was nothing low key about it, especially as the plan was to feature her journey to the homeland in her long-running reality show, *Keeping Up with the Kardashians*. The television crew from E! tried to look as inconspicuous as possible – as if carrying around a large boom microphone were the most natural thing in Armenia.

A stills man from the Splash News & Pictures Agency, Brian Prahl, a sort of unofficial official photographer at the court of Queen Kim, travelled with them to record the trip, ensuring that the pictures taken were pin sharp and of the highest quality. Brian did his job well and everyone looked their best.

Wherever she went, the streets were lined with hundreds of people anxious to get a glimpse of her or, most prized of all, a selfie with the most photographed woman in the world. It was like a boisterous royal tour, with Kanye and Kim in the role of Prince William and 'Princess Kate'. Their little daughter, North, captured hearts with an array of cute expressions, just as the baby Prince George had on his first overseas trip to Australia a year earlier.

Even Kanye broke into the occasional smile, usually when playing with North. He stayed a pace behind his wife, much in the manner of William with Kate, or Prince Philip accompanying the Queen. The men understand that they are not the focus of attention on these occasions.

Kanye did have his moment in the spotlight, however, when he gave an 'impromptu' concert for thousands of excited Armenians and was able to display some rock 'n' roll behaviour by jumping fully clothed into Yerevan's romantic-sounding Swan Lake. Apparently, he made the decision to go out and sing for the people only that night, although it's doubtful if his Armenian security detail would have allowed such spontaneity. It proved to be good fun.

He had just started singing 'Good Life', when he took everyone by surprise by leaping into the water, which, a little undramatically, only came up to his knees. He managed to get his microphone wet, which brought the song to an abrupt halt. That didn't bother his audience, who began to jump in and splash around as well. Kim, who, dressed in sweats, was looking about as casual as she ever gets, explained that he wanted to be closer to the fans on the other side of the lake. 'It was an exciting, crazy night!' she said. After he had been firmly helped out of the water by guards, Kanye sang another five songs: 'Stronger', 'Jesus Walks', 'Power', 'Touch the Sky' and 'All of the Lights'.

His escapade lightened the mood of what could have been a very sombre few days. Despite the excitement her journey to Armenia generated, there was a serious point to it all. Kim wanted to draw attention to what many – and certainly all of the Kardashians – regard as the first modern genocide.

She had flown in just before the one hundredth anniversary, on 24 April, of the slaughter of more than 1.5 million Christian Armenians by Muslim Ottoman Turks. It preceded the Holocaust in Nazi Germany by a generation, but became a footnote in the history of the twentieth century, scarcely covered in school history lessons. Kim was determined to change that. She blogged, 'Every year, I honour the memory of the martyrs who were killed during the 1915 Armenian Genocide.'

This didn't sound like the sort of issue that might concern a woman posting selfies to her Instagram followers or sharing information online about her favourite salad or how to bleach your eyebrows. She explained, 'So many people have come to me and said, "I had no idea there was a genocide." There aren't that many Armenians in this business. We have this spotlight to bring attention to it, so why would we just sit back? I will continue to ask the questions and fight for the genocide to be recognised for what it was.' There are a few household names from Armenia: Cher, Andre Agassi and the popular French singer Charles Aznavour were three of the best known before the Kardashians became so famous.

Not only is their country a fleeting presence in history lessons, it doesn't feature largely in geography classes either. The Republic of Armenia is a landlocked, mountainous country wedged between the Black Sea and the Caspian Sea. Turkey is to the west, Georgia to the north, Azerbaijan to the east and Iran to the south. Since it achieved independence from the Soviet Union in 1991, Armenia has relied on tourism to the beautiful country to bolster a struggling economy still reliant on Russian gas. An estimated third of the 3 million-strong population live in poverty.

The premier, Hovik Abrahamyan, welcomed Kim and Khloé with open arms, realising they were putting Armenia on the map for millions of people around the world. The sisters were joined by two previously unheralded Armenian cousins, Kourtni and Kara Kardashian, who hadn't shared the limelight with their famous American relatives until now.

Prime Minister Abrahamyan praised the Kardashian contribution to the 'international recognition and condemnation of the Armenian genocide'. Kim, in turn, repeated her pledge to campaign for worldwide acknowledgement of the atrocity.

She apologised for not being able to speak Armenian and said she and her sisters were intent on learning the language, which doesn't feature in the curriculum of the exclusive private schools of Beverly Hills and Bel Air. Even her father, Robert Kardashian, so proud of his heritage, wasn't a fluent speaker.

Kim's efforts to reveal a more serious side to her public image received an unexpected boost when Pope Francis condemned the cruelty of the genocide during a service at St Peter's in Rome. Many commentators acknowledged that the combination of Kim Kardashian and the Pope was a PR disaster for Turkey.

After the family left Armenia, there was one more important stop to make before they flew home. They travelled to Jerusalem for North to be baptised into the Armenian Apostolic Church. The hour-long ceremony at the Cathedral of St James in the Old City was conducted in both Armenian and English, and ended with North being anointed on the head with holy water.

Kim followed the custom of these occasions by wearing a striped wraparound floor-length dress and flat shoes and covering her head with a white shawl. Kanye looked relaxed and happy in white trousers and sweater. North, in a white christening gown, went to sleep. It had been a long trip for a little girl but, as a reward, she was treated to a day out in Disneyland on her second birthday in June.

The 'state visit' to Armenia was a triumph for Kim, although her one disappointment came when President Obama failed to use the 'g word' (genocide) in a speech marking the anniversary. He couldn't risk antagonising Turkey, an important ally in the ongoing fight against terrorism. Kim, who doesn't blame modern-day Turkish people, observed, 'It's very disappointing he hasn't used it as a president. We thought it would happen this year. I feel like we're close …'

When she had first arrived in Armenia, Kim made a point of saying that her father and his parents, now all dead, would have been hugely proud of the visit and what she was trying to achieve. Like her, they had been born in the United States. It was the previous generation of Kardashians, Kim's great-grandparents, who preserved the family line by fleeing Armenia just before the mass slaughter of their countrymen.

In leaving the remote village of Karakale, where the family originated, they were heeding an extraordinary warning made by an illiterate and sickly boy who had visions about the future. Efim Klubnikin predicted, 'Those who believe in this [prophecy] will go to a far land, while the unbelievers will remain in place. Our people will go on a long journey over the great and deep waters.'

Although he made the prophecy first as an 11-year-old boy in the 1850s, he repeated his warning 50 years later, just in time for some 2,000 Armenians to leave before the nation's holocaust. Kim's forebears were among the lucky ones. Accounts testify that 'every soul' in Karakale was murdered. The village is now an entirely Muslim settlement, near the city of Kars, in the harsh, snow-covered environment of eastern Turkey.

In an extraordinary twist, Klubnikin urged his 'believers' not just to flee to the United States, but to settle specifically in Los Angeles. Kim's great-grandparents sailed independently to a new life, and met and fell in love on the boat from Germany. They were among some of the last to flee, not setting sail until 1913.

At the time of the massacres, Armenia was still in Russia. The First Republic of Armenia was formed in 1918 and became a founding member of the Soviet Union four years later. Strictly speaking, the Kardashian ancestors were of

Russian-Armenian stock and the family name was Kardashcoff, which doesn't trip off the tongue as well as Kardashian, although they could still have called their famous boutique DASH.

By the end of the First World War, the Kardashian family was beginning to establish itself at the centre of the new Armenian community in Los Angeles. Many had settled in a poor, slum-like neighbourhood known as 'The Flats' in Boyle Heights, East LA. The area was a gateway to the city for newcomers, and one that they aspired to leave. The Kardashians were no exception.

The displacement of some of a nation's finest men and women bred great spirit and a desire for achievement. Friendships forged in adverse circumstances would last a life-time, binding successful Armenian families together. A fierce loyalty was the hallmark of the community.

The rise in fortunes of the Kardashians began with a rubbish collection business and moved on to hog-farming. From there, it was a natural progression to opening a slaughterhouse for meat processing, as an outlet for their livestock concern. The Great Western Meat Packing Company started up in 1933 in the city of Vernon, 5 miles south of downtown LA. It's a very unprepossessing, almost exclusively industrial area, full of warehouses and plants – and slaughterhouses. Vernon is not a place where you would want to live.

Arthur Kardashian, Kim's grandfather, was born in Los Angeles in 1918 and married her beautiful grandmother, Helen Arakelian, who was a year older, when he was 20. He took over the family business with his brother Bob when their father retired and built it into one of the most successful

Southern Californian enterprises, with a turnover of more than $100 million.

Art and Helen became pillars of a new prosperous Armenian community, settling in the affluent suburb of Baldwin Hills, a million miles away from The Flats. Former California Senator Walter Karabian, a frequent guest, described their home as 'beautiful' and 'upscale'. In the space of a generation, the Kardashians had risen from hard-working immigrants to millionaires. They possessed an ideology of success and how to achieve it that they would pass on to their children and grandchildren.

Kim adored her grandparents. Particularly, she was close to Helen, who died, aged 90, in 2008. 'Nana was seriously so much fun,' she said. 'She was your typical Armenian grand-mother and always cooking the best Armenian meals. Our favourite when we visited was a breakfast dish called *beeshee*, which is a pancake topped with lots of sugar.' Her grand-parents eventually retired to Indian Wells, near Palm Springs, where they originally had a holiday home. When Helen died, she and Art had been married for 70 years.

The biggest influence in Kim's life was her beloved father, Robert Kardashian, who was born in Baldwin Hills in 1944. She observed, 'My father always taught us never to forget where we came from. We grew up learning so much about our Armenian ancestors that we will teach to our own kids one day.' She is clearly giving North a head start in that regard.

2

TOWER OF STRENGTH

———

Robert Kardashian is a name that sounds as if it belongs to a very serious person. In reality, Bob, or Bobby as he was known, was funny and fun-seeking, a young man with a reputation as a practical joker, who never wanted to be tied to the family meat-packing business. It didn't suit his style at all. He would leave that responsibility to his elder brother, Thomas, known as Tommy, who was four years his senior. An elder sister, Barbara, pursued a successful career as a dentist.

He followed them both to USC – the University of Southern California – in Los Angeles where he studied business administration from 1962 until 1966 and, like his brother, was the senior manager of the student American football team, the formidable USC Trojans. Both brothers were keen on sport, particularly football, and could play to a high, if not professional, standard.

Robert decided to continue his education at the University of San Diego, where he graduated in 1969 with a law degree. Tommy observed that his younger brother went to law school to avoid going into the family business. The elder Kardashian already had a Rolls-Royce and Robert was determined that he would have one too. On his return to Los Angeles, aged 25, he joined the firm of two USC law graduates, Richard Eamer and John Bedrosian. After two years, he became a named partner in Eamer, Bedrosian and Kardashian of Beverly Hills.

Bedrosian, a fellow 'hye' (the Armenian word for an Armenian), developed the firm's interest in healthcare, while Robert found entertainment law more to his taste. One of his friends, George Mason, who founded the Armenian newspaper *The California Courier*, observed, 'He's not the kind of man who wants to be chained to a desk and take a briefcase full of work home with him every night.'

If Robert had stuck with his partners, he would have ended up considerably wealthier. They established National Medical Enterprises, which became one of the top healthcare providers in the US before it was sold in the 1990s. As a result, they moved into the realms of the super-rich.

Robert, though, enjoyed the world of celebrity more than the boardroom. He met the man who would change the future for him and his family on a tennis court in Beverly Hills one Sunday morning in the spring of 1970. A game of doubles was set up by the maître d' at the Luau, which was a popular local place for young playboys on the prowl.

Robert and his brother Tommy were a formidable pairing, but they were concerned they had met their match in O. J. Simpson and Al Cowlings. These two had both won sporting scholarships to USC, but did not enrol there until after the Kardashians had left. Orenthal James Simpson, known as 'The Juice', was the most famous college footballer in the US and the winner of the prestigious Heisman Trophy as the most outstanding player of the year. In UK terms, it would be the equivalent of discovering that your weekend tennis game was against David Beckham.

O. J. was already a celebrity. Robert and Tommy were well known in the fashionable bars and restaurants of Hollywood, but they mixed more with professional people. O. J. would change that.

To their surprise, experience narrowly won the day for the Kardashian brothers. The four all became friends and the one-off game became a weekly ritual. Robert and O. J. got on particularly well, despite their very different backgrounds. O. J. had been brought up in a poor area of San Francisco, belonged to a street gang and served time in a youth detention centre. When he moved from college into the professional game, he became one of the most sought-after names in the celebrity world and, by 1971, was said to have earned enough money from endorsements to retire.

Robert recognised the selling potential of his new friend. O. J. would be perfect as the public face of some business ventures. Robert had the ideas and O. J. had the fame, and together they started several stores and restaurants.

They both still had a strong affinity with USC and one of their more successful enterprises was a fashion boutique on the campus called jag O. J. – a play on the popular student cocktail of orange juice and Jägermeister. It sold top-of-the-range jeans and casual wear and they made a tidy profit when they sold the shop after a couple of years.

One of Robert's policies where his start-ups were concerned was not to hang on to a business for too long, whether it was successful or not. He formed a corporation with O. J. called

Juice Inc. and opened a frozen yoghurt shop in Westwood Village, which they called Joy and, once again, sold after a couple of years.

The association with O. J. opened up a new world for Robert Kardashian and his brother. They moved into a house in Deep Canyon Drive, Beverly Hills, which they turned into a bachelor's playground. O. J. was always around, helping to attract a constant stream of guests for tennis and pool parties. In the mid-seventies, he even stayed with the brothers for six months during an off-season as the star running back of the Buffalo Bills. There were three Rolls-Royces parked in the driveway then. Robert had finally acquired one – and he was still in his twenties. O. J. also rented space in Robert's offices to oversee his growing business concerns away from football. Robert's legal secretary, Cathy Ronda, became O. J.'s personal assistant. The connection between the two men was a very strong one.

Robert wanted to pursue interests in music, one of his great loves. His fortunes were transformed in 1973, when he set up a magazine, *Radio & Records*, with his brother Tommy and a new partner, Robert Wilson, who had many music contacts. They had spotted a gap in the market for a weekly trade publication for radio and the music industry in general. At least a third of the pages were charts and statistics. Record company executives could see what radio stations in Alabama or Iowa were playing that week. The idea was to turn it into something that was an essential read for anyone working in the world of music and, to that end, it succeeded brilliantly. It became widely known as *R&R*, a sister to the famous *Billboard*, and an industry bible.

Eventually, the success of this and some of the ventures with O. J. allowed Robert to reduce his law commitments until, in 1979, he was able to stop practising altogether. By that time, he had fallen in love.

When Robert George Kardashian met Kristen Mary Houghton, he was a lawyer, an entrepreneur and a very eligible bachelor living in Los Angeles. She was an 18-year-old girl from San Diego growing accustomed to the finer things in life, thanks to a relationship with a professional golfer 12 years her senior.

They bumped into each other at the renowned Del Mar Thoroughbred racetrack, which boasted the famous slogan 'Where the Turf Meets the Surf'. In the summer months, Hollywood stars would mingle with the cream of moneyed society in a beautiful setting by the ocean. A consortium of famous actors from the golden age, including Gary Cooper and Oliver Hardy of Laurel and Hardy, had clubbed together to build the course. They were led by Bing Crosby, who was on the gate greeting racegoers when it opened in 1937.

The meeting in July was a little like Royal Ascot, in that the wealthy and well-connected would travel from San Diego, 20 miles south, or Los Angeles, 100 miles to the north, to be seen and to show off their new hats. It was definitely a place to interest an aspiring socialite.

According to Kris, Robert barrelled up to her outside the exclusive Turf Club and said that she was someone he knew, even though he kept getting her name wrong, insisting she was called Janet. She thought he bore a striking resemblance to the pop singer Tony Orlando, who memorably sang 'Tie a

Yellow Ribbon Round the Ole Oak Tree'. With his big, heavy moustache and slick black disco hair, he might also have been mistaken for a seventies porn star. She was a shapely brunette with great sex appeal. She had oomph.

He persisted with his corny chat-up lines and asked for her phone number, which she refused to give him. He trailed after her for the rest of the day and even introduced her to his elder brother Tommy, who was with him that afternoon. Naturally, her reluctance to give him her number lit the blue touch paper of his enthusiasm. At the time, she thought he was too old, although, at 30, he was four months younger than her boyfriend.

In her autobiography, she refers to the golfer only as Anthony. That wasn't his name, of course. Much later, he was revealed to be a forgotten, if handsome, face on the PGA tour called Cesar Sanudo, who was from a modest Mexican family. He had been a caddie before graduating to playing golf himself. He was on the tour for 14 years at a time when great names like Jack Nicklaus, Arnold Palmer and Tom Watson ruled the fairways. The irrepressible 'Super Mex', Lee Trevino, was one of his best friends on tour.

Although Cesar won only one tournament, the 1970 Azalea Open Invitational at the Cape Fear Country Club in North Carolina, he was a popular figure, always at ease with ordinary golfers and film stars like Bob Hope and Clint Eastwood. He also played golf with presidents, including Richard Nixon, Gerald Ford and George Bush, Sr.

After they started dating, when she was just 17, he gave Kris the perfect introduction to the world of celebrity, and took her to golf tournaments all over the world. His brother Carlos maintained that it was Cesar who provided Kris with the connections she was able to use throughout her life.

Cesar installed his teenage girlfriend in his townhouse near the ocean in Mission Beach, an area of San Diego rather similar to Malibu or Santa Monica. Kris moved in, with her best friend from high school, Debbie Mungle, for company, as Cesar spent so much time on the road at golf tournaments. It wasn't Beverly Hills, but it was a step in the right direction.

Kris may not have enjoyed the privileged upbringing that plenty of money gave Robert Kardashian, but she was comfortably middle class. Her father, Robert Houghton, had a good job as an engineer with the now defunct aircraft company Convair in San Diego. Her grandparents ran a candle store called Candelabra in fashionable La Jolla and her mother, Mary Jo, was their part-time assistant. When she was old enough to be a help and not a hindrance, Kris worked in the back room too.

Kris paid tribute to her grandmother in her autobiography *Kris Jenner ... and All Things Kardashian*. She 'taught me the value of hard work', she explained. That ethic is very much in keeping with the philosophy of Robert Kardashian and one that they passed on to their children, especially Kim.

Her childhood, however, was very different from Robert Kardashian's. His parents were married for 70 years, but Kris's parents split up when she was seven. It was a traumatic time for Kris and her four-year-old sister Karen. Mary Jo had to sell the family home and go out to work full time. Eventually, Kris's mother met a reformed alcoholic called Harry Shannon, who gave up booze for life when they married. Kris loved Harry's entrepreneurial spirit and thought he was a 'great guy'.

Mary Jo believed in bringing up her daughters to follow strict household rules, but that didn't stop her from agreeing to let her eldest go to Hawaii with Debbie to watch a golf tournament, which is where she met Cesar. Robert Kardashian didn't know at first that, while he was pursuing her, Kris had accepted her boyfriend's proposal of marriage.

Robert wasn't the least put off by her initial refusal to give him her phone number. He promptly found it via a friend who worked for the telephone company and boldly rang her up. She explained to *E!* that despite her initial hesitation and annoyance at his perseverance, they eventually realised there was a spark between them.

The path of true love didn't run smoothly. On their very first date to the movies, they went back to the house she shared with Cesar, who was away playing in a golf tournament – or so she thought. Just as they were getting down to things in the bedroom, the door burst open and in charged Cesar. He made sure that Robert didn't hang around to chat. Kris maintains they were still in their clothes. Cesar's brother verified that they were discovered in the bedroom. He alleges that his brother was suspicious of Kris and had deliberately missed the cut in the tournament so that he would be home early. If that were the case, then his suspicions were confirmed, and it marked the beginning of the end of their relationship.

As well as the problems in her love life, Kris had to deal with a family tragedy that year, 1975. Her father, with whom she had been enjoying a much better relationship in recent years, was killed in a road accident in Mexico at the age of 42. The evening before he planned to marry for the second time, he was driving his Porsche when he hit a truck head on. Kim never knew her maternal grandfather.

Two decades later, *Star* magazine in the US ran a story that Bob Houghton had been an alcoholic and had been drinking margaritas on the night of the crash. A girlfriend after his divorce, Leslie Johnson Leech, claimed, 'I broke up with him because of his drinking.'

Kris and Cesar didn't split immediately and technically remained engaged for a few more months. The end occurred with a counter allegation of cheating, which gave Kris the opportunity to leave her golfer once and for all. Cesar became a club professional in El Cajon, a suburb of San Diego, when he quit the main tour, but resumed tournament golf on the seniors' circuit when he was over 50. He never spoke about Kris while he was alive, although his brother revealed some salacious details after his death in 2011. She has never responded, preferring her first serious lover to remain enigmatically as Anthony.

She didn't waste any time and rushed into the arms of Robert, who was living the high life in his swanky new home in Deep Canyon Drive. She was trading up. He was clearly besotted with Kris and proposed within three weeks of her finally ditching Cesar. After she turned down his first proposal, Kris decided she needed her independence and wanted to see more of the world, so she trained as a flight attendant with American Airlines.

Robert responded to her rejection by dating Priscilla Presley, the ex-wife of 'The King', who was still alive and the biggest star in the world. He didn't just phone her up and ask her out. Her best friend, Joan Esposito, was dating and would eventually marry his brother Tommy, so it wasn't too surprising when Robert and Priscilla got together.

Joan was a former Miss Missouri who had been married to Joe Esposito, the larger-than-life road manager for Elvis. She forged a bond with Priscilla when they were both part of the mad Elvis world in the mid-sixties. Joanie, as she was known in those days, was a Vegas showgirl called Joan Roberts when she married Joe. As a couple, they went everywhere with Elvis and Priscilla. Joe was best man when the Presleys married at the Aladdin Hotel in Las Vegas and Joanie was matron of honour. Both women settled in Los Angeles in the early seventies after their marriages ended.

The Kardashians were very popular. Susan Stafford, the original host of the game show *Wheel of Fortune*, described her friends Tommy and Joan as 'decent and terrific people'. More interestingly, Susan had no idea that Robert Kardashian, fun and sociable, would eventually become famous in his own right. She observed, 'The longer you are in Hollywood, you find yourself rubbing shoulders with people who become headline news.' That would be particularly true of Kim Kardashian and her extraordinary family. Hollywood is indeed a very small world.

Fortunately for the history of the Kardashian clan, Robert's dalliance with Priscilla was short-lived, although he did move into her house on Summit Drive for a short time. When it ended, Robert resumed his pursuit of the woman with whom he was clearly very much in love.

After completing her training, Kris was based in New York, but flew the route to Los Angeles every week. Robert, always dapper and expensively dressed, would meet her at LAX in his

Rolls-Royce and whisk her back to the house, where they would play tennis or relax by the pool. He kept two Rollers in the garage now: one black and one white (and a convertible Mercedes for sunny days).

Robert could easily have continued living the life of the Hollywood playboy, but he was determined to marry Kris. He introduced her proudly to his close-knit family and friends, like O. J. Simpson and Al Cowlings.

Kris tells an amusing story of how she and Robert joined O. J. and the Bond actress Maud Adams on a trip to the Montreal Olympics in 1976. By now O. J. was even more famous, thanks to a blossoming movie career, with roles in *The Klansman* and the blockbuster *The Towering Inferno*. Everybody recognised him wherever he went, but nobody, including Kris, had a clue who Bruce Jenner was … until he won the decathlon gold medal.

Eventually Robert and Kris married at the Westwood United Methodist Church on Wilshire Boulevard in July 1978, five years after their encounter at the racetrack. It was a big, opulent wedding with a reception for 300 at the Bel-Air Country Club. Tommy was best man, O. J. was the principal usher and the massive Al Cowlings, known as A. C., was ring-bearer. Her younger sister Karen was the maid of honour.

Kris returned from an idyllic honeymoon in Europe, free from her job as an air hostess, happy and pregnant. She would later observe, 'The Armenian women watched and counted the weeks until I gave birth to make sure I wasn't pregnant before I got married.'

To the relief of the matrons, she wasn't, and gave birth to her first child, Kourtney Mary, on 18 April 1979. She was

23. At 24, she had her second. She had conceived again on a skiing trip to the fashionable resort of Aspen, Colorado, with O. J. and his new beautiful blonde girlfriend, Nicole Brown.

Kimberly Noel Kardashian was born in Los Angeles on 21 October 1980.

It was time for the growing family of four to move to a house of their own. With perfect timing, in 1979, Robert pulled off his biggest business deal to date, when *Radio & Records* was sold for an estimated $12.5 million. He was thought to have made about $3 million on the deal – a sum worth $10.5 million in today's money. Unsurprisingly, he stopped working as an attorney and relinquished his licence to practise law.

As a result of his windfall, he was able to buy a dream home four miles away. Tower Lane is a cul de sac that is so private it contains only three massive, luxurious mansions. 9920 Tower Lane would be the house where Kim and her siblings would enjoy an idyllic childhood. All three properties were behind massive iron gates to avoid the prying eyes of star-hungry sightseers.

Nobody knew who the Kardashians were at this point, of course, although they soon became renowned for throwing the best parties in the neighbourhood. The mansion had a large swimming pool, a tennis court, a Jacuzzi and a bar by the pool. To buy it in 2015 would cost something like $6 million. There was nothing a thousand other homes in the gilded nirvana of Beverly Hills didn't enjoy. A housekeeper took care of the shopping and the washing, allowing Kim's mother the time to go out to lunch with her friends. Uncle O. J. would stop by every week to play tennis, and there would always be a big barbecue for friends and family at weekends.

As there were so few houses in their little enclave, they decided to call theirs Tower Lane, the same name as the street, so Kim was brought up in Tower Lane, Tower Lane, which must have confused the postman. Anybody who found themselves wandering up Tower Lane would have been looking for a glimpse of either Madonna or Bruce Springsteen, who occupied the other houses during the 1980s. Bruce made it his permanent home, while Madonna was just renting for a short time. This is Los Angeles, however, so you would never walk, even to chat to a neighbour like the famous talk show host Jay Leno, who lived in the next road. The drive at the Kardashian house was almost too long to walk in any case.

It was a paradise for the little girls, and their early lives were recorded on video by a doting father keen not to miss a second of his children growing up. He called his second daughter Kimbo, or by the pet name of Joge, although she never knew why. In Armenian, the word means 'imagine'. Kim was a very sweet and pretty child, as the countless home movies show. She and her elder sister Kourtney were so close together in age that they tended to wear the same outfits and often resembled twins. Even though there was plenty of space, the two sisters shared a bedroom, which meant that they forged a special bond and became a clique of two.

There were cats and dogs, rabbits and birds, and lots of dressing up. The two cats were called Coco and Chanel, an amusing tribute to the queen of French fashion, Coco Chanel. Among the pack of dogs was Valentina, a little Bichon Frisé who, the sisters recalled in *Kardashian Konfidential*, died after eating some poison. Kourtney and Kim cried their eyes out.

Having two babies by the age of 24 didn't stop Kris from having two more by the time she was 30. Khloé Alexandra was born on 27 June 1984, and a longed-for son arrived on 17 March 1987. In the best Armenian tradition, he was called Robert Arthur, after his father and grandfather respectively. Just as Kourtney and Kim were particularly close growing up, Khloé and Robert Jr likewise played together – although the youngest daughter was regarded as a personal plaything by her two elder sisters.

If the children tired of their wonderland at home, there were always the annual vacations to look forward to: a spring break at Robert's parents' holiday home in Indian Wells, skiing in Colorado every autumn to celebrate Thanksgiving and, in between, a trip to Mexico or, if they were very lucky, to Hawaii.

One of the most important aspects of Robert Kardashian was the strength of his religious beliefs, a product of his Armenian Christian roots. He would meticulously say his prayers every morning by his bedside. He would also say grace before meals in their sumptuous dining room and often carried a Bible with him. Traditional bedtime stories for kids would be mixed with the occasional tale from his Bible. He was very keen for his family to follow his beliefs. The importance of worship, a strong spiritual bond and the belief that marriage was sacred would come to be supremely ironic in a family culture in which adultery and broken marriages became the rule rather than the exception.

The leading light in the religious community that Robert and Kris were drawn to was the famous fifties singer Pat

Boone, who would host weekly Bible studies for like-minded neighbours, including Doris Day, Priscilla Presley and the Kardashians, at his luxurious mansion. Boone was well known for baptising some 250 people in his swimming pool.

They didn't go in for any of that in the Kardashian pool, although friends were always welcome to drop in for a swimming lesson. That circle of friends widened naturally when Kourtney and Kim went to school, first to the Beverly Hills Presbyterian Preschool in Rodeo Drive, and then to the ultra exclusive Buckley School in Sherman Oaks, where today it would cost between $33,000 and $39,000 a year to send your child.

Kim would forge some long-standing friendships with schoolmates, who included Paris Hilton, Nicole Richie, fashion designer Nikki Lund, Kimberly Stewart, the daughter of Rod Stewart and Alana Hamilton, and T. J. Jackson, the nephew of Michael Jackson. Her best friend, however, is Allison Azoff, who has never sought fame outside her privileged world.

Allison is the daughter of Irving Azoff, one of the biggest names in American music. In 2012, he was named the most powerful person in the music business by *Billboard* magazine. While best known as the boss of Live Nation, Azoff has also managed the affairs of a string of famous artists, including The Eagles, Christina Aguilera, Maroon 5 and, most aptly, as far as Kim is concerned, Kanye West. Irving and Kanye were brought together by Kris, who has been best friends with Irving's wife Shelli for more than 30 years.

The Azoffs and the Kardashians lived near each other in Beverly Hills, so it seemed natural that their children would grow up together, spending time at each other's houses. Kim used to enjoy exploring Shelli's wardrobe and jewellery box, in particular, and trying on her diamond rings for size.

Kim has always been respectful of Allison's desire to keep a low profile and the pair are seldom pictured together, even though they still speak all the time. Kim often says that she and Allison 'met the day I was born' and leaves it at that. Other friendships with equally famous people may receive far more publicity, but Allison is her oldest and dearest.

This rarefied upbringing relied on Robert continuing to make plenty of money without having to go back to the meat-packing business. Not all of his investments went as well as *Radio & Records*. Irving Azoff observed, 'Some have and some haven't been successful. But he's real dependable and honest and quite an entrepreneur.'

The Kardashian family were firmly entrenched in Beverly Hills society. They were established in the pool and party circuit, with four lovely children and all the trappings that success could bring. This happiness didn't last. In 1990, the Kardashians' world fell apart.

3

A COMPLICATED
AFFAIR

———

The Kardashian family always ate dinner together, even when the children were young. After prayers, Robert would go round the table for 'The Peak and the Pit'. Everyone in turn had to declare the highlight and lowlight of their day. When Kim revealed on television that they used to do this, it was copied in homes around the country.

On one particular day in 1990, there were no peaks. That was when Robert and Kris sat them down and explained quietly that they were getting a divorce. Robert Jr was only two, so he wasn't involved, but the three girls were in floods of tears. Their parents tried hard not to reveal the true extent of their own anguish.

They wanted to cause as little disruption as possible to their children's lives, having vowed that their welfare would remain the most important consideration and they would try to act as normally as possibly. That was easier said than done: divorce papers would later make clear just how upset Kim had been by the course of events.

Robert was completely devastated. Kris had been having a tempestuous two-year affair with a younger man called Todd Waterman, a very fit and handsome footballer with a soccer team called LA Heat. She was 33 and he was 10 years her junior.

He had spotted her first in a photo at a friend's house in Beverly Hills and liked what he saw. She evidently felt the same way when they got together during a night out with friends. Their versions of events are different. She says they kissed for the first time in the hall closet of her friend's house. He says they had sex for the first time in said closet, adding, gallantly, that it was 'magical'.

They both agree that they subsequently had a lot of sex. In her memoir, Kris, who once again gives her former lover a false name – this time Ryan – recalls less coyly that they had 'wild' sex in almost every imaginable location: tennis court, pool house, garage, back seat of the car and up and down the stairs. 'Sex everywhere, all the time,' she added.

Todd confirms that the sex was adventurous, both outdoors and indoors. 'We were pretty prolific,' he remembered with understatement. His memory failed him when he was asked if they had made love in the marital bed at Tower Lane. He did say he was sure they'd had sex in the house, but he didn't recall anything specific.

They were clearly very much in love and, as sometimes happens in those circumstances, they became foolhardy and indiscreet. Todd was like a trophy boyfriend, always on Kris's arm at celebrity parties and barbecues. She was behaving like a woman obsessed. She was seeing so much of Todd, even taking a skiing holiday with him, that his mother Ilza thought Kris and

Robert were already separated: 'She wouldn't talk about her husband with me. If she did, I would have said, "What are you doing coming after my young son, with all these kids?"'

Not surprisingly, Robert became suspicious. He kept seeing Todd in the company of his wife, especially at the house, where they would play tennis together. Todd amusingly recalled that on one occasion Robert decided to umpire their game and kept calling foot faults against him.

More seriously, Robert hired a private detective to follow his wife to the modest apartment in Studio City, which she and Todd were using as a love nest. The inevitable clash with Robert is another incident that the two lovers remember differently. She recalled that it was in a restaurant in Beverly Hills, where they were having a cosy breakfast together. Todd said they were pulling out of his garage in an open-topped Jeep, when Robert dashed up in a convertible Mercedes, jumped out and started swinging a golf club at the back of the car. Todd was all in favour of stopping and confronting Robert, but Kris was worried that her distraught husband might have a gun, so the two vehicles set off on a high-speed car chase through Beverly Hills, which ended when Todd swerved into another road.

Todd, who only came forward in 2012 after he featured as Ryan in Kris's book, was concerned for his personal safety, especially after a phone call he claims he received from O. J. Simpson warning him to stay away from Kris. O. J. apparently invited Todd over to his house to discuss things further – an invitation he had no trouble turning down.

One of the cruel ironies of the affair was that Kris paid for almost everything. But she, by her own admission, had no money. She was using credit cards that were paid for by her husband. The first thing Robert did on discovering the affair and deciding on a divorce was to cancel all of Kris's credit cards. The financial implications would eventually lead to bitter and acrimonious divorce proceedings.

The whole sorry saga was shaping up like a bad episode of *Dynasty* (or a good one, depending on whether you were living it or just watching). To her credit, Kris hasn't tried to justify her behaviour other than to acknowledge how unbearably miserable she had become in her marriage. The shattering effect her affair had on her family, particularly the two eldest girls, became clear when divorce papers were revealed in *Star* magazine in the US and published in America and the UK.

The most heartbreaking incident occurred in May 1990, when Kimberly, as they called her then, found her mother crying after a 'brutal' conversation with Robert. He was so emotionally distraught by what was happening that he would call Kris some horrible names whenever they tried to speak to one another. In her statement, Kris said, 'She became so upset I had a difficult time getting her to her [school] carpool on time.' She added that Kim called twice that afternoon begging her to come home. Clearly the young girl was worried that her mother was going to leave them.

Khloé, being that much younger than her sisters, seemed fine with Todd and would happily sit in the back seat of the car if he was going out to lunch with her mother. He thought she was smart and 'just the cutest kid'.

Robert moved out of Tower Lane, leaving Kris to manage on her own. In the divorce papers, her sworn statement details what she termed was a 'luxury lifestyle'. The mortgage payment on the house alone was $15,000 a month and then there were wages for the gardener, a maid and a housekeeper, as well as $800 a month to pay for the children's clothing and $2,000 a month for herself. Credit card debts on various store cards had grown to more than $21,000.

The unhappiness that both Robert and Kris were feeling didn't end with her sailing off into the sunset with Todd – far from it. At first, they carried on in much the same way. If Robert was looking after the children at the weekend, she would drift over to the apartment in Studio City to see Todd. Reading between the lines of her account, the enormity of what she had done – giving up what was so important to her life, the privilege and luxury of what Robert provided in Beverly Hills, for sex in a tiny bachelor flat – began to affect her.

She finally realised she had made a 'ginormous' mistake when she arrived at Todd's apartment unexpectedly and discovered him in bed with a girl he had met in a bar. It was, apparently, a one-night stand. 'I think I got busted,' recalled Todd 20 years later, although he didn't remember the exact circumstances.

Though they split up soon after, there is little doubt that they genuinely cared for one another. Todd told the *Daily Mail* that he was heartbroken when their relationship ended, but he knew that it would never have worked in the long term. He observed, 'Sometimes you stop something not because you stop caring, but because it isn't practical.' At that point in his career, he couldn't give Kris anything like the life she was used to and that was before you factored in the age difference. They both ended up with nothing to show for the pain and the passion.

It wouldn't be the last time Kris enjoyed the obvious benefits of a younger male companion, but she vowed that never again would she be so vulnerable financially. It was a lesson she vigorously taught her children – Kim in particular.

Both Todd and Kris have since regretted the heartache their relationship caused Robert and the children. Todd could see how badly Kourtney, the eldest, was affected. She struggled to accept what had happened and certainly didn't want anyone to replace her dad. It may or may not have affected her attitude to marriage but, at 36, she has yet to say, 'I do'. Kim, on the other hand, appeared to deal with it more easily, but had married three times by the age of 33.

She has said that at the time she was more troubled by the size of her growing breasts, and would sit in the bathtub praying to God that they wouldn't get any bigger. For a girl in the fourth grade, who had only just turned 10, one can understand her embarrassment, especially at school, where there was always some wise guy kid happy to twang the strap of her training bra. It didn't help that her big sister would tease her mercilessly. The bath prayer didn't work. She was a C cup at the age of 13.

More serious were the health concerns of their beloved grandmothers. Both Robert and Kris's mothers faced grave problems that weren't helped by the cataclysmic events in their children's lives. Helen Kardashian had a stress-related stroke and Mary Jo Shannon was battling cancer. Fortunately, they both pulled through and the grandkids had many more happy times with them.

Just when it seemed that things couldn't get any worse for Kris or her children, she went on a blind date that changed her life. The meeting with former Olympic champion Bruce Jenner was arranged by one of her close friends, Candace Garvey. She was the wife of Steve Garvey, one of the superstar baseball players with the Los Angeles Dodgers, known during his career as 'Mr Clean'. Steve and Bruce were on the celebrity sporting circuit together. They were always bumping into each other at the various tennis, golf or fishing tournaments they were forever being invited to.

Candace obviously thought, quite rightly, that Bruce needed smartening up and that the fashion-conscious Kris Kardashian would be a perfect match. Bruce wasn't so sure, until he discovered his date had four children, just like he did.

They met for the first time at the Riviera Country Club, where Bruce was playing in a golf tournament. He was immediately smitten by his vivacious companion, who was a good listener. The casual meeting led to dinner that first night, with Bruce pouring his heart out. 'I'm 40 years old,' he told her, 'and I've never been in love.'

4

THE WORLD'S GREATEST ATHLETE

Rather like her mother in 1976, Kim had no idea who Bruce Jenner was. He was just suddenly there. She was still in the fourth grade at school and had to do a project on someone famous. She was asking Kris whom she thought she should do, when Bruce interrupted her and said, 'Why don't you do me?'

Kim replied, innocently, 'Well, who are you?' He had to explain to her that he was an Olympic decathlon champion.

Her project was a resounding success, especially when the man himself went along to the school. She pictured him taking part in all 10 events. Unsurprisingly, she got an A, which was unusual for Kim. Kourtney was acknowledged as the brighter of the two, while Kim was a steady B sort of student.

William Bruce Jenner came into the lives of the Kardashian family like a whirlwind. He was an action man who could ski, drive racing cars and power boats, play golf, water ski and, of course, run and jump. He was fearless.

It hadn't always been like that. He was shy and suffered from poor self-esteem growing up in small-town suburbia in New

York State. Nobody realised back then that he had dyslexia, and believed him to be either lazy or stupid – he was neither.

He was eight years old, a solitary child with few friends, when he started sneaking into the rooms of his mother and two elder sisters to try on their clothes. He was a boy, still in short pants, and he had no real awareness of what he was feeling or why he was fascinated by female clothing. He just knew it made him feel good. Instead of retreating more into his own private world of self-doubt, Bruce was able to find acceptance when it was discovered that he was a superb sportsman. He acknowledges simply, 'Sports saved my life.'

Bruce was the third of four children in a comfortable, middle-class household. He was born on 28 October 1949 in the town of Mount Kisco, a little over 40 miles north of New York City in Westchester County. He described his mother Esther as an 'all-American mom and housewife'. His father Bill was a tree surgeon who had competed in the US Army Olympics in Nuremberg in 1945 and won a silver medal in the 100-yard dash. Bruce was well built as a toddler and his proud dad called him Bruiser. Young William was generally known by his second name to avoid confusion with his father.

As a small boy, it was his dyslexia, rather than gender issues, which was the most obviously troubling. Not unusually for the 1950s, his learning disability wasn't diagnosed. As a result, his schooldays were 'torturous'. He even had his eyes tested, because it was feared his inability to read properly might stem from problems with his vision.

Bruce explained to *Ability* magazine, 'If you are dyslexic, your eyes work fine, your brain works fine, but there is a little short circuit that goes between the eye and the brain.' His undiagnosed problem ruined his self-confidence: 'My biggest fear was going to school. I thought everybody else was doing better than I was. I'd look around at my peers, and everyone else could do the simple process of reading. I was afraid the teacher was going to make me read in front of class. There was always the fear that everyone would find out I was a dummy.' Bruce had no enthusiasm for school and the teachers thought he was just a daydreamer.

When he was 11, in the fifth grade, a teacher set up a game in which everyone had to run around some chairs and back. The idea was to see who had the fastest time. It was Bruce. He was the swiftest in the whole school.

From that moment on, his life changed. Here was something he could excel at and receive a slap on the back from his fellow pupils at the quaintly named Sleepy Hollow Middle School. The village of the same name is famously the setting for Washington Irving's short story 'The Legend of Sleepy Hollow'. The author lived in nearby Tarrytown, as did the Jenner family. Nowadays, Sleepy Hollow is even better known for the television series that is set in the village and is, very loosely, a modern update of the original fantasy of the headless horseman.

When Bruce was a freshman at the Sleepy Hollow High School, aged 15, he asked the captain of the football team, known as the Headless Horsemen, for some help with punting the ball. Within an hour, Bruce was kicking it as far as his coach was. The young Bruce was extraordinarily gifted as a sportsman.

His family moved to Connecticut when Bruce was 16. They built a house on Lake Zoar, where they all could enjoy their passion for water skiing. Bruce was so good that he won the Eastern Regional Water Ski Championships and competed in the Nationals in 1966. At the local Newtown High School in Sandy Hook, he excelled in basketball, track and field and American football, and became all-state pole vault and high jump champion. He was unashamedly what Americans call a jock – a muscular athlete, usually good looking, whose life revolves around sports and girls and who is always one of the most popular guys in school.

Aged 18, Bruce was named the MVP (Most Valuable Player) in the track squad and the basketball team. He played both running back and quarterback in the school football team. His coach, Peter Kohut, recognised that he was an outstanding athlete: 'He was a good kid, came to practice every day, seemed like he was always in good condition.'

At this stage of his life, Bruce was a very clean-cut young man – the sort of suitor who was bound to impress your mother. Nobody knew that behind the masculine exterior beat the heart and mind of a man who was more female than male.

Bruce was never going to be a great scholar, but he did win a football scholarship to a small college called Graceland in Lamoni, Iowa. Any hopes of becoming a professional foot-baller were soon dashed by a knee injury in his first year. That turned out to be a blessing in disguise, because the athletics director, L. D. Weldon, recognised his potential and persuaded him to put all his energies into the decathlon. Bruce needed an operation to repair his damaged knee in early 1969, but when he was fully recovered, he abandoned football and became a full-time athlete, reluctantly also giving up water skiing.

Weldon was one of the most respected coaches in the country, whose CV, crucially, included training Jack Parker, who won the bronze medal in the decathlon at the Berlin Olympics in 1936. He was an acknowledged expert in the multi-event discipline and encouraged Bruce to train hard.

Success was almost immediate. Jenner broke the Graceland decathlon record at his very first try at the 10 events. At his first open meeting, he placed sixth in the prestigious Drake Relays in Des Moines, the state capital. The following year, he returned to win the competition. In 1972, he came from nowhere to place third in the Olympic Trials, earning himself selection for the US team that travelled to Munich for the summer games. He could finish only tenth, but the promise was there. He had four years to fulfil his destiny.

Bruce was still at college in 1972 when he married his girlfriend, Chrystie Crownover, a minister's daughter from Washington State. She had no idea, when they became man and wife, of the internal struggles her new husband had faced all his life. During their first year of marriage, she became the first person he confided in. She recalled, 'He told me he always wanted to be a woman. Understandably, I was speechless. It was hard to wrap your head around it because he was such a manly man.'

His confession didn't harm their marriage. In some ways, his revelation brought them closer together, as sharing a secret sometimes can. In her eyes, he remained a real guy, who was, quite simply, her hero.

After graduation, the couple moved to California, where the training facilities and the climate were better suited to an athlete with his eye on Olympic gold. Chrystie worked as an air hostess for United Airlines to support them, because in those days the Olympics were strictly for amateurs. She was entitled to free plane tickets, which were a godsend for Bruce, as it gave him the means to travel to athletics meetings all over the world. Today sport is a professional career and Bruce Jenner, an all-American hero, would have been a multi-millionaire, travelling first class around the world.

Chrystie was by his side when he flew to Montreal for the 1976 Olympics. He was the current world record holder and favourite to win. He was in second place after day one, but came charging through to claim the gold. He embraced his young wife, wrapped himself in the American flag and, for a fleeting moment, was the most famous man in the world. Now he needed to make some money.

Frank Litsky of the *New York Times* famously wrote of his triumph: 'Bruce Jenner of San Jose, California, wants to be a movie or television star. After his record-breaking victory in the Olympic decathlon, he probably can be anything he wants.' He wanted to be a woman and that was one thing he couldn't be … then. Instead, he immediately retired from athletics.

Just when it seemed nothing could interrupt a happy future, tragedy struck the Jenner family. His younger brother Burt died in a car crash. Bruce was visiting his parents' home in Connecticut and during his stay was loaned a Porsche by a local car dealer. Eighteen-year-old Burt volunteered to fill her up with petrol, but ended up crashing into a telegraph pole. He died in hospital, along with his young girlfriend, who had skipped school to go for a ride in the top-of-the-range sports car.

Bruce named his first child Burt in honour of his much-loved brother. His son was born in 1978, six years after he and Chrystie were married. Sadly, the cracks had already begun to appear in their relationship. Faced with a future that did not contain eight hours of athletics practice a day, the reality of Bruce's gender dysphoria – the technical term for his gender identity crisis – was making him unhappy and discontented with his situation.

He and Chrystie separated for the first time the following year, and he met the woman who would eventually become his second wife at a celebrity tennis tournament. It was held at the Playboy Mansion in upmarket Holmby Hills, LA, where he had been staying temporarily. Bruce won the tournament and the beautiful Linda Thompson presented him with the trophy.

She provided another bizarre link with Elvis Presley in the Kardashian family saga. His relationship with her was probably the most important Elvis had after Priscilla. She was a 5ft 9in willowy blonde, who was the reigning Miss Tennessee when she met The King. He moved her into Graceland, his famous mansion near Memphis, in 1972, and she was with him for four years.

Linda had been a speech and drama major at MSU (Memphis State University) and, by all accounts, was the brightest of Elvis's women. She was popular with the notorious Memphis Mafia – the entourage who seemed to be ever present with Elvis – and she had looked after him well. Marty Lacker, the unofficial foreman of the group, explained, 'She was like a mother, a sister, a wife, a lover, and a nurse.'

Elvis had bought an apartment for her in Santa Monica so she could pursue her acting ambitions. After he died in 1977, she became a regular member of the cast of a variety show called *Hee Haw* as a singer of country music.

Bruce was immediately struck by Linda's statuesque presence. He told her he and Chrystie were separated and they hit it off right away. He was uncertain about his future, however, and briefly reconciled with his wife. After Chrystie fell pregnant, he wanted her to have an abortion, because their marriage had failed. He told *Playboy* magazine in July 1980, one month after the birth, 'My first reaction was that I didn't want it.'

Initially, Chrystie went along with his wishes, and even paid for an abortion, but changed her mind after a conversation with a friend made her realise she didn't want to go through with the termination. She said at the time, 'I thought, "What an idiot I am." I wanted the baby very, very much. But I was conditioned to make decisions that were best for him [Bruce]. It was totally my choice to have the baby.'

Bruce now says he too rejected the idea of an abortion, but when Cassandra, his eldest daughter, was born, he was in the middle of divorce proceedings and sitting in a hotel room far away in Kansas City. In his famous ground-breaking interview with *Vanity Fair* in July 2015, he told Buzz Bissinger that he wasn't present at the birth: 'Under the circumstances I could not even see myself being there.'

Instead, he resumed his relationship with Linda. They married soon afterwards, in January 1981, in a beautiful setting overlooking the Pacific Ocean in Hawaii at the beachfront house of Allan Carr, the producer of *Can't Stop the Music*.

Bruce's son Burt was best man, even though he was only two, and spent the entire ceremony tugging at his father's sleeve, saying, 'I want up.' Linda walked down the 'aisle' to the sound of Elvis singing 'Hawaiian Wedding Song'. It was very romantic.

At the time, Linda was already three months pregnant with their first child, Brandon, who was born the following June. Fortunately, she got on well with Bruce's older children, both of whom came to the hospital to visit their new brother.

Linda and Bruce became fixtures on the celebrity circuit around Los Angeles, making friends with stars like Michael Jackson, Lionel Richie and Sugar Ray Leonard, who would later feature in the Kardashian story. They appeared on the front cover of *Playgirl* magazine in May 1982: she revealed an impressive cleavage; he showed a lot of chest hair.

The cover headline on the article read 'The Fall and Rise of an American Hero'. This bolstered the Bruce Jenner image of a man fighting against the disadvantages of life, including dyslexia. His story was one of triumph over adversity and was a considerable money-spinner during his years as a media personality and motivational speaker. It was an image he later promoted in his 1996 book *Finding the Champion Within*.

At no stage did he reveal to his audience his real struggle within. He would bounce on stage, all vigour and enthusiasm, wearing a pair of silk panties underneath his three-piece suit. Bruce, it appeared, was a master of living up to an image created for the general public. It wasn't real.

The offers flooded in after the Olympics and soon Bruce was a very wealthy young man. He appeared on all the top talk shows, including *The Tonight Show starring Johnny Carson* and *The Merv Griffin Show.* He became a well-known face on sports programmes, at one time co-presenting the popular *Wide World of Sports.*

He also revealed an entrepreneurial streak that would later fit in very well with the Kardashian flair for business. Their philosophy is all about making the most of every opportunity. Bruce bought his first plane in 1978 and started Bruce Jenner Aviation, which sells aircraft supplies.

He was marketed as a personality much more than the usual famous sportsman. He became the spokesperson and face on the packet of the iconic cereal Wheaties, the 'breakfast of champions', and a million families breakfasted with Bruce on the kitchen counter every day for years.

His acting ambitions didn't reach the hoped-for heights, however. He wasn't going to be the next James Bond any time soon. He tried out for the *Superman* movie, but the role went to Christopher Reeve.

He ended up in *Can't Stop the Music,* a musical comedy based on the New York disco group Village People. Kris Jenner refers to it as *Can't Stand the Music.* The film cost $20 million to make and returned $2 million at the box office. It was the first winner of the Golden Raspberry Award (Razzie) for Worst Picture. Bruce was nominated as Worst Actor, but the judges decided Neil Diamond deserved the award for *The Jazz Singer.*

On one level, the film could be viewed as compulsive viewing. Bruce plays a sober-suited lawyer who undergoes a transformation when he becomes involved in the world of the Village People and ends up dancing down the street in a crop top and cut-off denim shorts. If it were released today, as a snapshot of the age, *Can't Stop the Music* would probably be hailed as a must-see, glorious camp classic.

Bruce's acting career stalled at the first hurdle and didn't much improve with a guest-starring role in the popular motorcycle cop series *CHiPS*. He played Officer Steve McLeish, who took over from the lead, Frank Poncherello (Erik Estrada), for six weeks. He started off as a movie star and became 'made for TV' in the space of a year.

Bruce and Linda, meanwhile, shared an idyllic life by the ocean in Malibu, strolling along the beach together at sunset, playing sports, going to all the best parties and welcoming another son, Brody, into the world on 21 August 1983. Nothing could upset their happiness – or so Linda thought.

Just after New Year 1985, Bruce sat his beautiful wife down and told her his secret. It wasn't a confession she could ignore. The first time round with Chrystie, Bruce had been fairly light and matter of fact about things; this was far more serious and heartfelt. 'I have lived in the wrong skin, the wrong body, my whole life. It is a living hell for me, and I really feel that I would like to move forward with the process of becoming a woman, the woman I have always been inside.'

The couple tried therapy, but the counsellor confirmed that there was no cure or fix for what Bruce was going through. Linda would later write movingly that the enormity of what she had been told 'broke her heart into a million pieces'.

While Linda began the painful process of ending her marriage, Bruce began gender reassignment treatment for the first time. He had always hated his 'ski jump' nose, so a touch of plastic surgery to remove the bump and make it more feminine was a good start. He also had painful electrolysis treatment to remove his masculine beard and chest hair.

He started injecting female hormones, which led to him growing breasts. They weren't Kim Kardashian-sized or anything like that, but when his young sons saw him in the shower one day, they told their mother, 'Daddy has boobs!' She tried to explain it away, saying that his well-muscled body had turned to fat now that he wasn't training. Linda told the *Huffington Post* that she didn't reveal the truth about their father until her sons were 31 and 29 respectively. She had sought to protect them – and him.

Bruce, by his own admission, went on a downward spiral in the late eighties. He and Linda were divorced rapidly in 1985 and he found it difficult to cope on his own. He was living by himself in a one-bedroom house in Malibu, with no real close friends. His work had dried up. When he met Kris Kardashian, he had $200 in the bank and debts, he estimated, of $300,000. His clothes were old and worn, his house was a tip and he seemed to spend half his life in his grubby van. She needed to sort him out. She would give him her love and the energy to re-establish himself with the American public.

For his part, he decided to put his gender reassignment treatment on the back burner and stop taking the hormones. He couldn't go further at that point, because he feared the effect his transformation might have on his young children.

5

DOPE ON A ROPE

———

Kim wanted to be a housewife when she grew up. She was a sweet and thoughtful little girl who dreamed of being not Madonna, but a wife and mother, and maybe a grandmother one day, just like her nanas whom she adored. 'I always thought I would have lots of kids. Be getting up going to the gym every morning – super early. Coming home, making breakfast for everyone. Packing lunches and driving the kids to school.' It must have been very bewildering for a girl who wanted to play happy families to witness what was going on within her own home.

It wasn't long before Bruce was practically living at Tower Lane. The mansion was much more comfortable than his Malibu home. Robert Kardashian wasn't especially pleased by the turn of events. He blinked and his wife was having an affair with Todd. He blinked again and Bruce Jenner was sitting on his sofa.

Todd alleged that at this point he was still involved with Kris: 'I wouldn't say we were dating … she was still coming over to the apartment and we were still sleeping together when she had started dating Bruce.'

Todd found the situation troubling. It began 'messing with his head', as he puts it. Kris has never commented on his allegation, but described in her book how he arrived at Tower Lane one night and caused a scene. He subsequently moved to London to forget her and later became a successful animator.

Financially, things improved for Kris when Robert agreed to a monthly settlement, but the divorce trauma was ongoing. In the divorce papers, Robert commented on her new relationship: 'My children are exposed to another man living with their mother. I believe that is inappropriate ...'

The arguments, which were inevitably about money, and who was finally going to get Tower Lane, were apparently ended when Bruce and Robert thrashed things out over dinner. Kris gave up any claim on the house and settled in Malibu with Bruce. She observed, 'There was a period of a couple of years where it was really ugly and hard and you didn't want the kids to take sides.'

By the time the divorce was made final in March 1991, Kris and Bruce had been engaged for four months. They were married four weeks later, on 21 April 1991. Kim was 10 and a half.

Bruce had managed to persuade his own children's nanny, Pam Behan, a student from a small town in Minnesota, to leave his ex-wife Linda's house and go to live with his new family. Pam adored Bruce, her first platonic male friend. Only in Los Angeles could the attractive new nanny be enjoying a fling with Sylvester Stallone.

Linda Thompson had previously been dating the star of *Rocky* and *Rambo*, but had moved on to the multimillionaire music producer David Foster. They eventually married and formed a formidable songwriting partnership, writing, among others, 'I Have Nothing' for Whitney Houston and 'Tell Him', a hit for Barbra Streisand and Celine Dion.

Pam was responsible for making sure Kris's daughters didn't get chocolate down their pristine white dresses before the wedding ceremony. Bruce's eldest daughter Cassandra, known to everyone as Casey, was also a bridesmaid and, like the others, wore a garland of white and pink flowers in her hair. His three sons, and three-year-old Robert Jr, looked dashing in black tuxedos and pale pink bow-ties that matched the groom's. Only Kourtney, still missing her dad, looked slightly uncomfortable about the happy family day out, She did, however, manage a weak smile for the wedding pictures.

Kris and Bruce were married in the garden of the Bel Air home of Terry and Jane Semel. He was the boss of Warner Bros, and subsequently chairman of Yahoo! This was the orbit of extreme wealth and influence the Kardashians already inhabited. In the world of the Kardashians and Jenners, everyone is a 'dear friend', but the generosity of the Semels was obvious.

After the divorce, relations between Robert and Kris settled down for the sake of the children. Kourtney still had a problem with Bruce taking her father's place, but they saw plenty of Robert. He had moved back into Tower Lane and was in charge every other weekend, a time when he played the devoted dad.

Robert tried to keep everything as normal as possible. As always, he took the children to church at weekends and, if they were with him during the week, he made sure he drove them to school. He was very popular with Kim's friends and would entertain them with a variety of spoonerisms – if he was going to take a shower, he would tell them he needed to 'shake a tower' – the sort of harmless sense of humour he had always had.

Nikki Lund, whom he insisted on calling Dicky, recalled that Robert was always stricter than Kris: 'He was a fun kind of guy, but he had a responsibility as a man to daughters as beautiful as these. He would take us to church. He prayed and read the Bible. He was a really good dad. Kim was a sensitive girl and definitely spiritual.'

Robert gave Kim a Bible, which he signed, and it became her most treasured possession. The word Bible is one of her favourite expressions, said at the end of a sentence to indicate that she swears it's true. She, Nikki and her other friends were young Christian girls, although they possibly liked church more because they could wear jeans there on a Sunday.

Kim was one of those girls who could fit into any group. She had her circle of friends, like Kimberly Stewart and Nikki Lund, but she was equally as happy mixing with Kourtney's group – the nerds, as she called them. With her closest pals, she devised a special sign language that they all learned so they could 'talk' about people who were in the room or class with them. Nikki recalled, 'It was a way of being in a group. It was our little thing. We were obsessed with it.'

Kim was becoming fascinated by clothes. She and Kourtney barely had time for breakfast in the mornings, because it took them so long to get ready. They would grab a vanilla sandwich cookie on the way to Pam's car for the morning school run from Malibu to Beverly Hills. Pam, who wrote a book called *Malibu Nanny*, was thrilled to discover the house they were then living in used to be home to Sean Penn when he was courting Madonna.

Kourtney was definitely the boss, perhaps because she was older and a little brighter; certainly, she was the fastest reader in the household. The two sisters used to play fashion games together. One favourite, at least with Kourtney, was when she pretended to be the leading fashion designer Donna Karan, creator of the DKNY label, and poor Kim was her beleaguered assistant. Kourtney used it as a means to make fun of her. Kim recalled, 'She would just make me do anything she said. She would do it on purpose and embarrass me in front of her friends.' Despite the natural sibling rivalry, the two girls were very close.

At their new home, they had use of the obligatory pool and Jacuzzi, as well as a magnificent view of the ocean from the patio. Kim preferred to spend a lot of her free time in her room, however, indulging her passion for making things, particularly jewellery. She had every conceivable size, shape and colour of bead and would carefully sort and select them to make the right necklace, earrings or bracelet.

One of the jobs of the nanny was to make sure the children were tucked up comfortably in bed at night. Kim would often talk in her sleep. Sometimes she would even have a conversation with Pam, even though she was in a deep slumber. On one occasion, she shouted out, 'There's an elephant on my desk.' Pam told her to get it off the desk, whereupon Kim, still fast asleep, replied, 'Help me. Help me. Get it off.' Pam had to leave the room before her laughter woke up her young charge.

Kim may have been a quiet girl when she was 10, but she had blossomed into a much livelier teenager by the time of her eighth-grade graduation from her junior school El Rodeo in Whittier Drive, Beverly Hills, in 1994. She was filmed at the party afterwards by another student eager to make a movie of the night. There's always one home-movie maker who wants to be the next Spielberg.

The already curvy 13-year-old Kim is excited and enjoying herself, dancing madly, in a white blouse, perfect make-up and a shorter than usual bob haircut. She is talking straight to the camera, 'Is anyone getting a tape of this? I hope you do, because when you see me when I'm famous and old, you're gonna remember me as this beautiful little girl.'

She continues to lark about as the cameraman starts to walk away: 'Excuse me, are you leaving? My name's Kim Kardashian. I'm the dopest of the ropest person in this class. I'm dope on a rope.' When someone off camera interrupts, 'Define "dope", Kim', she answers, 'Dope is Kim.' She seems to be displaying a confidence she says she never had as a girl. She ends the clip by comparing herself to a classmate: 'I'm more popular than she is … everyone loves me. I'm so popular and everyone loves me …'

She's just a schoolgirl having fun on a big night out, but it's interesting that she should be using 'dope' as hip-hop slang for excellent or wonderful. Perhaps she picked it up from her first serious boyfriend, Michael Jackson's nephew T. J.

From a young age, Kim preferred black men. She wasn't brought up in the Deep South like Britney Spears, where racism was still rife. This was Beverly Hills, where black families had just as much money and prestige. Lionel Richie and Sugar

Ray Leonard were good friends and neighbours of the family. Lionel was the father of Nicole Richie, whom Kim was at school with. Sugar Ray was so close to the Kardashians that he was Khloé's godfather. Most of the Jackson clan lived in the area. And there was Uncle O. J., too, of course. He lived on North Rockingham Avenue, in exclusive Brentwood, with his wife Nicole, whom he had married in 1985. The sociable Nicole had become very much part of Kris's wide circle.

By 1994, the Kardashian family had undergone much change. Kourtney had started high school at an all-girl Catholic school called Marymount, on Sunset Boulevard, and Kim would be joining her at the start of the next academic year. Kris and Bruce had decided that travelling to and from Malibu was becoming too much of a logistical challenge and had rented a house in Benedict Canyon.

The most dramatic change was that Kim's father had a new woman in his life. He had sold Tower Lane and leased an enormous 15-room house 10 miles away, in the pretty suburb of Encino. He was making a fresh start with his fiancée, Denice Shakarian Halicki, a graceful blonde, who wore very short skirts and was generally described as a 'knockout'. She also happened to drive a Rolls-Royce, which had been left to her by her late husband. She was Armenian on her father's side, but didn't have the exotic features of the Kardashians. Instead, she had inherited her Norwegian mother's looks. When she was 16, there had been talk of an arranged marriage, but that had come to nothing and she was able to pursue a career as a model and actress.

In 1983, she met Toby Halicki, who had become a multi-millionaire thanks to his stunningly successful cult film *Gone in 60 Seconds*. He was a larger-than-life character, one of 13 children, who, in a great Hollywood story, came to Los Angeles, aged 15, with nothing but an extensive knowledge of automobiles and the salvage business that his family ran in New York.

His hit movie cost under $100,000 to make, but grossed more than $40 million at the box office. There was little in the way of a script, but there were lots of cars. For the film's finale, Toby performed an amazing 39-metre jump, which resulted in him compacting 10 vertebrae and walking with a permanent limp.

He married Denice in May 1989, just before starting work on the sequel *Gone in 60 Seconds 2*. She was to be one of the stars, while he would again write, direct and perform most of the stunts. He had already bought 400 cars to be sacrificed in an orgy of vehicle destruction. He was preparing for a stunt during filming near Buffalo, New York, when a telegraph pole snapped and fell on him, killing him instantly. They had been married for three months.

Denice met Robert Kardashian through mutual Armenian connections, and they helped each other at a difficult time in their personal lives. Her late husband's considerable fortune was tied up in probate for many years and she went to Robert for legal advice. She wasn't the super-rich widow many might have assumed she was – at least not then. She had a traditional Christian upbringing and the couple shared a strong religious connection.

While relations had improved a little with his ex-wife, it wasn't a case of coffee mornings and trips to the beach together. It was awkward, especially if Bruce was around.

When Robert went to their house to pick up the children, the two youngest, Khloé and Robert Jr, would be waiting outside. He would then honk the horn, which was the signal for Kourtney and Kim to run out of the house to join them.

The journey back to Encino took no more than 30 minutes. The new house was on Mandalay Drive, in a very quiet neighbourhood with manicured lawns and his and her luxury limousines in the driveway. While it didn't have the extreme privacy of a gated community, the residents kept to themselves and tended to live in the same house for many years. It was very comfortable, but you were only likely to speak to your neighbours if you met them while you were collecting your letters from the mailbox.

Robert suggested that Kourtney and Kim might like to spend more time at his house, as the peaceful surroundings might be better suited to the serious study he wanted for his daughters. Kourtney was particularly keen, as she was still reluctant to accept Bruce. Kim wanted to stay close to her sister, and both girls enjoyed Denice's company.

The new house was just a short 10-minute drive from Uncle O. J.'s mansion in Brentwood, but Robert had seen his old friend only twice in two years. O. J. put in an appearance at a surprise fiftieth birthday that Denice had thrown for Robert in February 1994, and gave him an autographed football jersey. They also bumped into each other by accident in Palisades Park in Santa Monica in May, when they were both playing with their children. Robert was throwing a baseball with his son, while O. J. was helping his daughter Sydney practice her basketball skills. The two children knew each other well and were happy to pass the time together while the two men chatted on the grass about their troubles with women.

Their mutual business interests had dwindled, mainly through lack of success. In the 1980s, O. J. had joined Robert in a venture called Concert Cinema, which screened music videos in cinemas before the main feature. It was early days for MTV, but demonstrated how Robert thought ahead. In this case, what was clearly a good idea proved too expensive to run, and after a year they closed the business without making a profit.

The blossoming friendship between Kris and Nicole had made it difficult for the two men to remain buddies. O. J. and Nicole had struggled with marital problems, which culminated in their divorce in 1992, after seven years of marriage and two children together. Nobody knew that their strife included domestic violence.

Since his divorce from Kris, Robert's social circle had inevitably changed. O. J. was more likely to bump into Bruce Jenner on the celebrity circuit, although, as a football hero and movie star, O. J. was still far more famous than the former Olympic champion. Surprisingly, Robert didn't even know that Nicole was living in a condo in Bundy Drive, Brentwood.

The morning of 13 June 1994 started like any other for Robert Kardashian. As he always did, he said his prayers and then worked out for 30 minutes before starting work in his large office in the house. He no longer kept any business premises. Just after 10 a.m., the phone rang. It was Shelli Azoff, buzzing with the story that Nicole had been killed. She had just found out about it at the hairdresser's, so the whole world, except Robert, had heard the bombshell news. He phoned

Kris and discovered it was true. His ex-wife had been due to lunch with her friend that very day.

Without being asked, Robert rallied round his friend of 23 years. He invited O. J. to stay in his home to escape the media storm that inevitably exploded around the murder. It transpired that Nicole had suffered horrendous stabbing injuries, including one violent open wound that exposed the larynx and spinal chord. A local waiter and aspiring actor called Ron Goldman was also found dead outside the home on Bundy.

Four days after the murders, Robert had to stop his friend from killing himself, when he found O. J. in the bedroom with a gun. He told him, 'You can't. This is my daughter's bedroom.' Both Kourtney and Kim were staying in the house, but neither registered the magnitude of what was going on.

A warrant was issued for O. J.'s arrest and his chief lawyer, Robert Shapiro, was told his client needed to turn himself in at a police station. Shapiro had co-opted Robert on to the team, realising that Bobby, as O. J. still called him, had a special relationship with Simpson and would be useful to him. It also meant that they would now be protected by attorney–client privilege. Robert would need to reactivate his law licence, which he had allowed to lapse.

He was still concerned that his friend was going to end his life after O. J. disappeared from his house when he was supposed to be leaving for the station. He had apparently made a run for it in a white Ford Bronco driven by his buddy Al Cowlings. It became the most famous and bizarre slow-speed car chase in history, as a flotilla of police vehicles, with more than 20 helicopters soaring overheard, followed them down Interstate 405 at 35 miles an hour. The police didn't want to intercept the 4 X 4 because O. J., who was lying low on the back seat, reportedly had a gun and they wanted to avoid a violent end. Thousands lined the route and stood on overpasses to cheer him. Eventually, after 90 minutes, he gave himself up outside his Rockingham home. Millions watched on television, mesmerized by what they were seeing. It was described by one lawyer as 'the day Los Angeles stopped'.

Meanwhile, Robert was in front of the TV cameras for the very first time, reading a handwritten document that O. J. had left at the house. It was his suicide note to the world. Robert, in his steady deep voice, read the letter in front of more than 100 members of the media: '… Don't feel sorry for me. I've had a great life, made great friends. Please think of the real O. J. and not this lost person. Thank you for making my life special …'

This was the exact moment when life changed for the Kardashians. Now the media were shouting out and asking Robert how he spelled his surname. They mostly got it wrong. Kim and her siblings became the children of the famous lawyer Robert Kardashian. He would sit beside O. J. Simpson throughout the 'trial of the century'. O. J.'s confidante and erstwhile manager, Norman Pardo, observed drily, 'The Kardashians would be nothing without O. J. Simpson.'

6

NEVERLAND

———

Incredibly, 10 weeks after the grisly killing of Nicole Brown Simpson, Kim's life was rocked by another violent murder, which affected her just as deeply at the time.

All the Kardashian children grew up with the music of Michael Jackson blaring out from the sound system at the parties and barbecues their parents had. Robert Kardashian liked doo-wop, but this failed to impress his offspring. Kim enjoyed the music of all the Jacksons, but Janet Jackson was definitely her favourite in her youth. It was the next generation of the famous family with whom she came into contact, however, simply by moving in the same circles in Beverly Hills.

Kim was 13 when she started dating T. J. Jackson, the youngest son of Tito Jackson. The initials stand for Tito Joe, after his father and grandfather. They had met first of all at the Buckley School, but kept bumping into each other at parties. He was two years older than Kim, but she was a precocious young teenager.

T. J.'s father was the third oldest of the 10 Jackson children. When he was 18, he married Delores 'Dee Dee' Martes. She had been born in New York City to Dominican parents, but as a girl moved to LA, where she met Tito at Fairfax High School in West Hollywood. They married at the height of the Jackson 5 success in 1972 and had three sons, Taj, Taryll and T. J.

Despite the family's enormous wealth and fame, Dee Dee was determined that her three sons would have a normal childhood. Tito observed, 'She saw what the Jacksons had to endure to be successful.' All three boys attended the Buckley School, where they excelled more in sports than music. They were good looking and well liked. Their mother adored her sons, whom she called the three Ts. Even after their parents divorced in 1993, the family remained close. Despite their regular upbringing, the boys couldn't wait to follow in their famous family's footsteps.

Their Uncle Michael doted on his three nephews and was a frequent visitor, acting almost as a third parent and giving them advice about enjoying the best years of their lives. They witnessed him being besieged by fans after one concert. He turned to the boys and said, 'Are you sure you want to do this?' Of course they were. They called themselves, naturally enough, 3T and set about recording their debut album with their father as their manager. T. J. had just turned 16. It was very exciting for Kim to have a boyfriend who was going to be a pop star.

On 27 August 1994, the brothers received an early morning call from the daughter of their mother's new boyfriend, telling them she had been in an accident. They were about to head off to the studio, but instead they rushed to the hospital in Inglewood, where she had been taken, to discover that she was already dead. Dee Dee was 39.

Initially, it was assumed the death was accidental. The boyfriend, a businessman called Donald Bohana, told police that they had been swimming that night at his house in Ladera Heights. He had popped inside briefly and when he returned Dee Dee was at the bottom of the pool. Her sons were suspicious of this explanation, as they were well aware that their mother couldn't swim and would never go near water.

Their misgivings proved entirely correct, when a coroner's report found that the numerous cuts, scratches and bruises on her body suggested 'blunt force traumatic injuries' and a non-accidental 'assisted drowning'. The Jackson family, unhappy with the lack of action from the district attorney's office, filed a wrongful death lawsuit against Bohana a year after the dreadful news.

The suit detailed 58 injuries Dee Dee had suffered, including fingernail gouges to her breasts. Tito explained, 'It's plain to see that it was more than a simple drowning. My sons came to me and said, "Dad, don't let him get away with this."' The action speculated that there had been a row over money, in which Dee Dee had refused to help Bohana, who had massive debts and had filed for bankruptcy.

The lawsuit alleged that Bohana assaulted Jackson over a four-hour period and killed her by holding her head under water in the swimming pool. He then dialled 911 and told an emergency operator that someone had fallen into his pool.

The Jacksons would have to wait until 1997 for the case to come to criminal trial in the Los Angeles Superior Court. Bohana was found guilty of second-degree murder and sentenced to 15 years to life in prison. Tito added, 'She was just a well-caring mother, and these kids were actually robbed of something that nothing can bring back.'

For her part, Kim was a 13-year-old trying to cope with a grieving boyfriend and a father desperately trying to help Uncle O. J., who would soon be standing trial for the murder of one of her mother's best friends, Auntie Nicole. It was a grim welcome to an adult world.

Dee Dee's tragedy brought T. J. and Kim closer together. He was polite, respectful and softly spoken. Her parents liked him very much, although her father warned her about the perils of interracial dating, even in a place as broad-minded as Beverly Hills: 'He explained to me that he's had a lot of interracial friends, and it might not be the easiest relationship. He said I should prepare myself for people to say things to me.'

One of the perks of dating a member of the Jackson clan came when Kim celebrated her fourteenth birthday in October 1994. The party was held at Neverland, Michael Jackson's famous 3,000-acre ranch near Santa Barbara, about 100 miles north of Los Angeles. Even though she was growing up as a privileged youngster in Beverly Hills, where birthdays and holidays were celebrated with no expense spared, this was something entirely different and totally thrilling. Michael Jackson's indulgent folly was a children's paradise – no wonder her friends were keen to join her. T. J. and his brothers were also there, while Kris and Bruce drove everyone and joined in the fun.

The amusement park was accessed from the main house by the Neverland Express, the ranch's own bright red train. Michael called the steam engine Katherine after his mother.

Kim and her friends rode on the Ferris wheel, a carousel, a wave-swinger, a super-slide and a host of roller-coasters. The private zoo contained giraffes and parrots, alpacas and elephants. It was Michael Jackson's fantasy world made real. He had missed out on a proper childhood because of the demands of recording and touring when he was a small boy. He never enjoyed Christmas or birthdays the way ordinary children might. He explained, 'I wanted to have a place that I could create everything I never had as a child.'

Kim loved it. She recalled, 'When you drove up, there were baby elephants and chimpanzees in overalls, and there were all the rides. It was everything you can possibly imagine. The memories I have from that place will last for the rest of my life.'

Although she would meet Michael many times, he wasn't at the party. He had spent a year dealing with an accusation of sexually abusing a 13-year-old boy, so perhaps it might not have been the most tactful move to have played host at a fourteenth birthday party full of excited children.

He had married Lisa Marie Presley the previous June in what would prove to be a short-lived marriage. Ironically, they had been in negotiations to be the stars of the reality show *Newlyweds*, which was eventually made by Nick Lachey and Jessica Simpson.

Neverland provided a perfect birthday party for Kim and one she still talks about: 'It was just me and my friends. It was something I'll never forget.' Disappointingly, her father wasn't there to enjoy it with her. Instead, he bought her a course of make-up lessons, which probably proved more worthwhile in the long run.

Great days like the Neverland excursion strengthened her blossoming relationship with T. J. Kim enjoyed being in a settled relationship, despite being so young. T. J. even moved in with Kris and Bruce for a short time, while he was coming to terms with what had happened.

After they had been going out for a year or so, she approached her mother to discuss birth control. She told Oprah Winfrey, 'When I did want to have sex for the first time, I was almost 15.' Kris, who was heavily pregnant with her fifth child, was supportive and understanding when Kim told her she was going to sleep with her boyfriend. Kim continued, 'She was like, "This is what we're going to do, we're gonna put you on birth control" and she was really open and honest with me.'

T. J. has remained gallant about what happened between him and his girlfriend, thus ensuring he remains welcome in the Kardashian household. All he has said is: 'We became extra close when my mom passed away. She dropped everything to be with me.'

3T eventually finished recording their first album, entitled *Brotherhood*, which proved to be a much bigger hit in Europe than in the US. It reached number 11 in the UK charts and a single from it, 'Anything', only just missed out on the top spot. They may not have been superstars, but Kim Kardashian, a high school teenager, was dating a member of a boy band. Her classmates were hugely envious.

From being a popular, if rather anonymous, girl at school, Kim was becoming far better known. Not only was she going out with one of the Jacksons, but her father was on television every single day when the trial of the century began on

24 January 1995. It transfixed a nation and caused a huge division within her family.

On the one hand, her mother was convinced of O. J.'s guilt and was happy to voice that opinion. Her father, meanwhile, was standing by his old friend. Kris observed how confused her children were because their parents were on different sides of 'a crazy situation'.

The scale of public interest was enormous. While he was remanded in jail, O. J. was getting an estimated 3,500 letters of support a day. An estimated 95 million people had watched the notorious slow-motion car chase. The *Washington Post* reported, 'No one as well known and celebrated as Simpson has ever been charged with such a crime in the history of this country.'

Centre stage was Robert Kardashian, described by the newspapers as O. J.'s 'personal attorney', who sat by his side in court every day. Even before the trial began, the news programmes would feature his regular visits to O. J. in jail. When Robert went to eat out at a fashionable Beverly Hills restaurant like Spago, the room went silent and everyone turned round to stare, as if Tom Cruise had just walked in. He was happy to chat to well-wishers and the curious. One night someone asked him what O. J.'s jail cell was like. 'It's a seven-by nine-foot cage,' he replied.

Before the ordeal of the trial took hold, Kim's father seemed in good spirits about the case. At one of his parties in Encino, he asked guests if they wanted to see how O. J. slipped out of the house for the now famous drive. He nodded at Al Cowlings, who ambled out of the party, got into his white Ford Bronco and drove off.

Explaining to his children what was happening to Uncle O. J. was more problematic, especially as both Kris and Bruce openly discussed his guilt. He had to fall back on the old 'innocent until proven guilty' line. He was at least encouraged by his daughters wanting to write to the man with whom they had spent many happy days and holidays. Kim supported her father. She confirmed, 'I definitely took my dad's side. We just always thought my dad was the smartest person in the world, and he really believed in his friend.'

Robert, by all accounts, was aware of the business opportunities that might accrue from the notoriety of the case. He helped to secure a £1 million advance for O. J.'s book, *I Want to Tell You*, which was published three days after the trial began. O. J. ostensibly wrote the book for two reasons – financial benefit and a desire to respond to the 300,000 letters he had received since his arrest. He wrote, 'I want to state unequivocally that I did not commit these horrible crimes. I loved Nicole. I could never do such a thing.'

He certainly needed the money. When he and Nicole divorced in 1992, he was earning $1 million a year. Now he faced ruin, whatever the trial verdict, and still had to pay $15,000 a day to his defence team. Only Robert was giving his services for free.

At least Kim's father never had to give evidence at the trial, protected by attorney–client privilege. The prosecution had been desperate to question him about O. J.'s garment bag, which he was seen carrying on the day of the murders.

The Kardashians were as divided inside the courtroom as they were outside. Kim and Kourtney were caught in the middle of a difficult situation: 'Kourtney and I would go to the trial with my dad and we'd sit on his side and I remember looking over and my mom was on the other side sitting next to Nicole's parents, and it was so much tension.' The girls were worried that their mom would be mad at them for sitting with their dad.

Any good humour Robert may have brought to the saga soon left him as the days turned into months. One of the first casualties was his wedding plans with Denice. They were put on hold because of the demands of the case. Eventually, they split up. She has never spoken of the exact reasons, although she may well have been uneasy at the depth of his involvement in the trial and just wanted to get on with her life.

Instead, while Robert was at the Los Angeles courtroom every day of 1995, she set about reviving her late husband's last project, the sequel to *Gone in 60 Seconds*. The new film, which had the hugely successful producer Jerry Bruckheimer and Disney on board, eventually came to screens in 2000 and starred Nicholas Cage, with Angelina Jolie in the role that Denice would have played. It turned into more of a remake than a sequel, but still it returned over £237 million at the box office.

The evening before the trial began, Robert drove over to his ex-wife's house to give her a letter he had written to her and his children, in which he explained why he had made such an enormous commitment to Uncle O.J. She quoted the letter in full in her memoir.

Robert, clearly under enormous strain, recognised how the tragedy had invaded their privacy and that the division in the family was very sad. He said he valued his family above all else and that their lives were far more important than this one case. 'My life will never be the same,' he wrote emotionally.

Kris was expecting to give evidence about the domestic violence she knew about in the Simpson household. In the end, she wasn't called, as the prosecution decided, probably wrongly, that it would have an adverse influence on the jury. She did talk to reporters, however, revealing that Nicole knew she was in danger long before she died.

Kris spent her entire pregnancy absorbed in the case, either watching it on television or attending in person with Bruce. Some of the aspects of the case will never be forgotten, including the bloody glove the prosecution made O. J. try on, only to discover it didn't fit. 'If it doesn't fit, you must acquit,' said his lead defender, the renowned black attorney Johnny Cochran, who introduced the alleged racism of the LAPD so skilfully into the defence arguments.

The world awaited the verdict on 3 October 1995. Robert and Johnny had been to visit O. J. in jail and they had prayed together. The jury spent less than four hours reaching its conclusion and, genuinely, nobody knew what might happen. They ruled 'not guilty' on both counts of murder.

Robert looked stunned and bewildered, as if he couldn't believe what he was hearing; he didn't even smile. O. J. slapped him on the back. Johnny Cochran was elated and slapped O. J. on the back. While the formalities were being concluded, Robert took off his glasses and wiped his eyes.

His children were at school. He had seen little of them during the last few months, as he was concerned for their safety at his house, which was receiving a great deal of public attention. He was incensed when someone scrawled 'nigger-lover' on his car. They had spent the time at Kris and Bruce's house and Robert did his best to get there at weekends. Robert and Bruce would discuss the situation, keen for the family not to be torn apart.

When Kim, Kourtney and Khloé got home on the day of the verdict, Bruce, who had always believed O. J. to be guilty, was still watching it unfold on TV. He recalled, 'They came in and said, "Ah, I told you he didn't do it!"' Bruce asked them to sit down while he explained something to them: 'Look, just because he got a not guilty verdict doesn't mean he didn't do it and I just don't want to hear his name any more.'

Robert never expressed any opinion about O. J.'s innocence until he was interviewed by Barbara Walters a year later and admitted he did have doubts: 'The blood evidence is the biggest thorn in my side that causes me the greatest problems. So I struggle with the blood evidence.'

Robert helped the renowned writer Lawrence Schiller with his classic book *American Tragedy*, co-written by *Time* magazine reporter James Willwerth, which provided the inside story of the defence team during the trial. According to Dominick Dunne of *Vanity Fair*, he received a 'substantial proportion' of Schiller's fee. There were also rumours that Robert was the source of many post-trial stories about O. J.

He had to piece his life back together. When Denice left, she had taken all the furniture and the television sets. They were hers to begin with, but the house was literally empty without her. She had only kind words to say about her former fiancé, however. 'O. J. used Robert,' she said. 'Robert went over to the house on Rockingham as soon as he heard about the murders, like any friend would, and O. J. used him from then on. It's been terrible for Robert. His friends have left him.'

Robert's relationship with O. J. was never the same again. A friendship that could have lasted a lifetime vanished in 10 months inside a crowded courtroom. Schiller and Willwerth wrote, presumably with Robert's blessing, that the doubts would never leave him. He also realised that for years his friend had kept his troubled life with Nicole from him. He had seen them have only one argument the whole time he had known them. He went to the victory party at Rockingham, but barely saw O. J. again after that.

The epic case wasn't finished. A civil action was launched by the families of both victims against O. J. for the unlawful killing of Nicole and Ron Goldman. They won the case and were awarded $33.5 million in compensation and damages. This time, the events that took place over five months in a Santa Monica courthouse weren't televised. Robert was required to give a deposition for the court, although what he was able to say was still heavily governed by attorney–client privilege. He was able to comment on Nicole for the first time: 'She was kind. She was sweet. I loved Nicole. She was a fun person … She was a good wife and an excellent mother.'

The house on North Rockingham Drive, where O. J. had lived for 20 years, was sold for close to $4 million and was promptly demolished by the new owner, an investment banker. The former sports star moved to Miami to start a new life. In December 2008, he was found guilty of 12 felonies as a result of an armed robbery and kidnapping at a Las Vegas hotel-casino. He received a minimum sentence of nine years and a maximum of 27. Robert Kardashian wouldn't live to see his friend sent down.

The murder trial never goes away. It is part of American history, a modern legend. Kim is asked about it at some point during most interviews. She has become adept at avoiding it, like a politician swerving an awkward question. She simply acknowledges that it was the 'biggest struggle' within her family apart from her parents' divorce: 'It's the biggest separation my family's had, so why even bring it up.' She was asked about it yet again by *Rolling Stone* magazine in July 2015. 'It's weird,' she said. 'I try not to think about it.'

7

THE REAL WORLD

Having a steady boyfriend meant that Kim wasn't prone to sneaking into unsuitable nightclubs as a teenager. While her more spirited friends may have been up for an adventure, Kimmy, as she was generally known, wasn't a party girl during high school. She had a large social circle and they could usually be found hanging out at each other's extremely nice houses.

She was happy with T. J., although she could have had her pick of the boys. She always had great sex appeal and was a very pretty girl – almost innocently so. The nanny, Pam Behan, remarked that she didn't let the many compliments she received go to her head. She was never conceited about her looks. Pam observed, 'She knows she is beautiful because everyone tells her she is beautiful. Yet she maintains her sweetness.'

Although unpleasant adult troubles intruded, in the form of her parents' ugly divorce, the O. J. Simpson furore and the murder of her boyfriend's mother, she was able to enjoy being a teenage girl without going off the rails. Her great friend

Nikki Lund recalled, 'We made little coffee cakes and painted our nails and talked about our next diet.'

The girls tried every diet going. They sampled the popular Atkins and South Beach Diets. They also took over the kitchen to cook up vast quantities of cabbage soup when that was the latest weight-loss fad.

After Kim started dating, she became aware that all the popular girls around her seemed to be skinny and blonde. She was the anti-blonde – petite, buxom, bottom-heavy and bothered by the female Armenian characteristic of too much dark body hair. From the age of 13, Kim was a regular visitor to the beauty salon for her bikini wax.

Her schoolgirl hero wasn't a string-bean runway model, but J.Lo, the shapely Hispanic actress and singer. From the mid-nineties onwards, Jennifer Lopez was in possession of the most photographed and appreciated bum in the world.

Like all teenagers, Kim had many favourites. As well as Jennifer Lopez and Janet Jackson, she followed leading R & B artists, including Babyface, Mary J. Blige and the vocal group Jodeci. She had a special affection for the Spice Girls, who brought 'girl power' to Marymount. She was 16 when they burst onto the music scene in the US with their breakthrough number one, 'Wannabe', in February 1997. That year, their debut album, *Spice*, was the world's biggest seller.

Kim was an admirer of Victoria Beckham and her image as Posh Spice. One friend confided, 'She liked the idea of being posh and she thought Victoria was the prettiest Spice Girl.' Kim wore her hair then in a shortish bob like Posh and tried to do her make-up to imitate the well-known sultry pout.

Occasionally, her school would have an 'off day', when you could ditch the school uniform for a day and dress as you please. Kim and her friends would go as the Spice Girls. She had a short-sleeved leather dress with a slit up the side that mirrored the sort of outfit that the chic and fashionable Posh would wear. The girls would each be a different character and spend hours getting ready. They enjoyed dressing up and playing their parts more than the music, although it was good fun to practise 'Wannabe' or 'Spice Up Your Life' in front of the mirror. They were never brave enough to give a *Stars in Their Eyes* type of performance in public.

For her sixteenth birthday, Kim was given a new white BMW 318 saloon. It was a rite of passage for each of the sisters to be given a car on reaching the age when they could start driving. Their father would often produce contracts for his children to sign to ensure they understood the meaning of responsibility. While it was his way of having fun with his kids, it did have a serious purpose. The car contract was no exception.

Four days after her birthday, Robert produced the document. In it, he calls himself her 'wonderful and kind' father. Kimberly, as she was referred to, had to agree to drive her younger sister and brother to their activities, run errands for her dad, not talk back to her mother or father, ensure that she maintained a good grade average at Marymount, not take drugs, smoke cigarettes or marijuana or get drunk.

She was one of the few girls at her school who didn't have a credit card for her personal use. For her car, however, her father provided her with a gas-only one for Standard Oil, so she could fill up with petrol whenever she needed it. It was in the contract that she had to keep up the payments on the card. She also had to agree to wash the car once a week. Last, but by no means least, she was responsible for all repairs. She explained, 'If I crashed it, I had to be responsible for paying for it.'

The contract was more an indication of her father's affection than anything else. He even states in paragraph seven of the agreement that 'your dad loves you very much'. It was something lovely and precious between a father and his daughter. Kim, who pranged the car almost immediately, didn't see it that way.

She was crawling along in bumper-to-bumper traffic, when she dropped her lipstick, reached down to pick it up and rear-ended the car in front. She recalled, 'I tapped someone. It was so not a big deal, but I had to pay for it.' It didn't help that the driver of the other vehicle saw the name Kardashian on her documents and realised she must be the daughter of O. J. Simpson's lawyer. 'They sued me for a lot of money.'

As a result of the mishap, Kim needed to find a Saturday job to help pay for things. She was strolling through the centre of Encino on a day off from school, when she saw that a local boutique called Body was looking for a part-time shop assist-ant. 'It was the coolest clothing store in the Valley,' recalled Kim proudly. She loved being around the latest fashions and would often go to the store after school to work for an extra hour or two before heading back to her father's house.

In pre-mobile phone days, all the schoolchildren had beep-ers with different coloured cases that would clip onto a belt or a bag. A beeper was a pager that they would carry to keep in touch with their parents or, more usually, their friends. Kim would change her colour every weekend. She was keen to make small fashion statements even then, and would disappear to her room to devise different coloured headbands. She used fish wire to sew on flowers and made sure they matched her eyeliner and the colour of the top she was wearing. Her parent's entrepreneurial character rubbed off on her, because, as well as wearing the accessories herself, she would hawk them round little boutiques in Hollywood, trying to sell some for a few dollars. Her job meant she was in retail; her little sideline was her start in business.

Kourtney had moved into her dad's full time, because the quiet atmosphere there was much more conducive to studying, which she needed to do to realise her ambition of going to university. Kim didn't harbour such aspirations, preferring to spend her evenings talking for hours on the phone to her friends rather than with her nose in a schoolbook. She was happy to stay over at her dad's to keep her sister company, especially as life at Kris and Bruce's house had become chaotic with the arrival of their baby half-sisters.

Kris had given birth to their first child, Kendall, on 3 November 1995. They gave her the second name of Nicole to honour the memory of Nicole Brown Simpson. Yet another daughter, Kylie Kristen Jenner, was born on 10 August 1997. It was all a bit much for the two older girls.

Staying at Robert's became even more practical when Kris and Bruce decided they needed to move from the house in Benedict Canyon, because it was too small for their growing family. They were still renting, and Kris was determined that they should have a place of own. They found their next house purely by chance. She had been invited to lunch by a friend who lived in Hidden Hills in Calabasas, which, in Beverly Hills terms, was the sticks. Kris didn't even know how to get there, other than it was a long drive out on the Ventura Freeway. Once there, of course, she fell in love with its tranquillity and privacy. She talked Bruce round with the promise that he would still be able to play golf. Together they found a house that required a lot of work, but it was the start of her family's love affair with the little-known community.

Thanks to the impetus Kris gave him, Bruce's career was again moving forward. To a large extent, Robert Kardashian hadn't needed Kris in his working life. He had been content for her to raise his children in a traditional family unit. Bruce and Kris worked as a team. As well as overseeing the proper marketing of his motivational speech, 'Finding the Champion Within', they produced an infomercial for a line of stair-climbers and a keep-fit video, which showed Bruce coaching Kris. Their business prospects hadn't been harmed by her involvement in the O. J. Simpson trial, although that was the last thing on their minds at the time.

Kim wasn't half-hearted about working out. For her, any pain was always worth it. She enthusiastically joined in the craze for Tae-Bo that swept through her circle of friends. They all had the video on how best to perform the aerobic exercise and would work out at each other's spacious homes. The name Tae-Bo is a blend of taekwondo and boxing. It's a sort of martial arts dancing and great fun to do, as well as good exercise.

Kim, like many teenagers, was swayed by what was 'in' and popular at school. They all watched *Melrose Place* so they could talk about it the next day. The popular prime-time soap followed the lives of young men and women living in an apartment complex in West Hollywood. It was the follow-on series from the hugely popular *Beverly Hills, 90210*, another Aaron Spelling-produced programme. Coincidentally, Kim was actually at El Rodeo School, which has a 90210 postcode, when that show aired.

Even though she was only 11 when it finished, she also liked *The Golden Girls*, which she watched as reruns. Another favourite sitcom was *Growing Pains*, which featured a teenage Leonardo DiCaprio in an early role. It was the story of a family of two parents and four children and followed the dramas of their everyday lives.

The most inspiring film for Kim was the cult success *Clueless*, because she loved the fashions and decided she was going to be the main character, Cher Horowitz, played by Alicia Silverstone. 'I literally had at least 10 of the outfits Cher had,' she confessed. In the film, the heroine is a rich and privileged girl living in a Beverly Hills mansion, like Kim was, and her father is a lawyer.

The show that had by far the most significant influence on Kim began broadcasting on MTV in 1992. It was called *The Real World* and is widely acknowledged to be the model for the modern reality shows that followed, including *Keeping Up with the Kardashians*. It is no surprise to learn that the production company Bunim/Murray is responsible for both programmes. They also produced *The Simple Life*, with Paris Hilton and Nicole Richie.

In the show, a group of seven or eight young adults are selected to share a house and interact – or, more precisely, fall out – with each other. It's a simple formula that has worked well over the years, from *Big Brother* to the Kardashian block-buster. It has always been hugely popular with a teenage audience in the US. Its themes include plenty of dysfunctional behaviour, addiction, drunkenness, eating disorders, sexuality, racism, politics, religion and, of course, an on-screen wedding or two – all the ingredients of classic reality television are here. Kim loved it.

Jonathan Murray explained the thinking behind the ground-breaking show: 'We've always been interested in what the people across the street were doing. We're gossips. So, at the very beginning of *Real World*, it was like being a fly on the wall watching these people lead their lives.'

He is most proud of the storyline in the third series that featured a gay man, Pedro Zamora, who was dying from AIDS. His inclusion brought the subject of HIV into millions of living rooms around the country. Even President Clinton told Jonathan that Pedro's story made more of a difference than anything he could do from the Oval Office. The producer recalled proudly, 'We got to deliver to our viewers entertaining television but also television that actually changed their lives.' When Pedro died, the audience felt they had lost someone they knew. It demonstrated the positive effect reality TV could have. During its first season, an article in the *New York Times* said: 'The series has been steadily evolving into the year's most riveting series, a compelling portrait of twenty-somethings grappling with the nineties.'

It's easy to see how *The Real World* came to represent the standard to which other reality shows aspire. Kim Kardashian, watching in her father's house in Encino, was so hooked on the show that she abandoned her ambition to be a housewife with a large family. Instead, she wanted to be on *The Real World*.

A more pressing concern was the realisation that her elder sister was going away to college. Kourtney was accepted by Southern Methodist University in Dallas, Texas, to study communications and journalism. It was not a happy time. She was homesick, and her family back in Los Angeles, particularly Kim, missed her terribly. After sticking with it for two years, she transferred to the University of Arizona, where she had many friends. Her new course of theatre studies suited her creative side much more. Part of the major involved acting classes and being filmed – skills that would serve her well in the future.

Kourtney persuaded Kim to live full time with their father, who would have been on his own when his eldest daughter left. Kim enjoyed the settled nature of being in Encino. As well as working at Body, she started helping out at her father's business, which was called Movie Tunes, Inc. It was proving to be another success story.

The company provided music for cinemas, fulfilling a need for both movie theatres and record companies wishing to increase exposure for their performers. Originally, artists used Movie Tunes, Inc. as an outlet when they were unable to secure the radio airplay they wanted, usually because they were considered past their sell-by date. By the time Kim came on board, however, bigger stars, including the Spice Girls and Janet Jackson, were involved. Her job was principally to answer the telephones, do the filing and help burn the CDs.

Each month, Movie Tunes, Inc. produced a 14-song, hour-long music show for cinemas, which, according to Robert, reached more than 75 million theatregoers. The captive audience that had come out to watch a film was encouraged to buy a disc of the music from a concession stand. Robert had identified another essential marketing tool for the music business, just as he had done 20 years earlier with *Radio & Records*.

Her work experience was preparing Kim for life after Marymount. Before she left high school, when she was 17, her parents had to write a letter with advice about her future. They both said very similar things about demanding respect and being respectful in return, treating others how you would want to be treated, having a strong head and not succumbing to peer pressure. Robert's phrase was the most memorable: 'Know your self-worth.' It could have come from one of Bruce's motivational speeches. Always the doting father, Robert couldn't resist adding that she should know what a pretty girl she was.

She looked forward to her senior prom. She managed to persuade her father that she needed a dress by her then favourite designer, Mark Wong Nark. She still loves his dresses. This one was white and floor length, with a square neckline and a slit up the front. T. J. was on hand to accompany her, looking immaculate and suave in a black tuxedo. Kim wore her hair up and the two of them looked like a very glamorous young Hollywood couple, which, of course, they were. They even managed two of the cheesiest grins for the official photographer, revealing pearly smiles that even the most expensive Beverly Hills dentist would have been proud of. They looked very happy together.

Sadly, however, they broke up soon afterwards. The relationship had been winding down, as the demands of touring with

3T took T. J. away more and more. He remained popular with Kim's family, though. In the very small world they inhabited, the Kardashians didn't sever links with the Jackson clan. In fact, Kourtney started dating T. J.'s elder brother, Taryll.

Kim, meanwhile, was soon to make a dramatic life choice. She would leave the safe cocoon of her Beverly Hills upbringing in favour of the real world.

PART TWO

KIM KARDASHIAN

8

MRS THOMAS

———

Kim looked at pictures of interracial couples in the teen magazines she bought as a schoolgirl and thought they looked cute together. Very occasionally she has gone out with white guys. When she was 19, for instance, she went on one date with the actor and former child star Joey Lawrence, but it was nothing. She knew from an early age the type she liked and has never made a secret of her attraction to black men.

Damon Thomas wasn't cute. He was flash and edgy and came into her life like a whirlwind the moment he walked into Body one Saturday afternoon. He was much cooler than the safe celebrities of Beverly Hills with whom she had grown up. He was 10 years older than her, for a start, and that was flattering.

In 1999, Damon was a record producer going places. He told Kim that he had just started a production team called The Underdogs and that he personally worked with Babyface. That got her attention, because Kenneth 'Babyface' Edmonds was one of her favourite artists and wrote some of the most memorable songs of her teenage years, including the Boyz II Men classics 'End of the Road' and 'I'll Make Love to You'.

He helped Damon learn about production, while they worked together on a number of songs, including co-writing and producing 'These Are the Times', which was a top five *Billboard* R & B chart hit for the vocal group Dru Hill in the autumn of 1998, and 'Never Gonna Let You Go', which made number one in the same chart for the singer Faith Evans in 1999.

Less auspiciously, Damon had a run-in with the rapper Dr Dre (Andre Young). The two had apparently got into a fight at an apartment in Woodland Hills, just up from Calabasas. Dr Dre faced assault charges after Damon suffered a broken jaw in the row. A spokesman for the city attorney said 'the incident stems from an inappropriate remark that Mr Thomas had made to Mr Young's girlfriend.' Dr Dre subsequently was fined $10,000 and sentenced to 90 days' house arrest.

For The Underdogs project, Damon teamed up with former college basketball player Harvey Mason, Jr, who had spent a lifetime among the musical elite of Los Angeles. His father, Harvey Sr, was a jazz drummer who played with outstanding performers, including Herbie Hancock and Quincy Jones. He used to take his son along to recordings.

While Damon was a protégé of Babyface, Harvey Jr was working with another leading producer, Rodney Jerkins, and his Darkchild crew on projects involving Whitney Houston, Michael Jackson and Toni Braxton.

When Damon and Harvey decided to work together, they were a dream team. They joined forces initially to write a track called 'I Like Them Girls', which they went on to produce for the album *2000 Watts* for the male model-turned-singer Tyrese.

There's no doubt that Kim found Damon exciting, especially as she had lived a comparatively sheltered life and was, after all, a Catholic schoolgirl. She had been a big fan of 'N Sync at school, and this new man in her life was actually friends with Justin Timberlake. He was also writing a song for Pink, one of the hottest new acts. T. J. was lovely, but Damon was different. He was a man making his way in the world purely on the basis of his talent.

She was swept away by it all and decided to leave the comfort of her father's house and move in with Damon. He had an apartment in Romar Street, Northridge – a Valley neighbourhood that wasn't the least bit fashionable and was even more remote than Calabasas. Neither of her parents knew she was sharing her new home with a boyfriend, although Kris was suspicious when Kim arrived in Hidden Hills one day behind the wheel of a top-of-the-range Jaguar sports car. How on earth could she afford that while she was still working at Body? Kris even phoned up Robert to find out if he had anything to do with it. She didn't know that her daughter was involved with a music high-flyer.

Damon took Kim to Justin's twentieth birthday party in Las Vegas in January 2000. While they were there, it seemed like the perfect time to get married. She became Kimberly Thomas on 22 January 2000. It wasn't the fairy-tale Beverly Hills wedding Robert Kardashian or Kris Jenner had wanted for their beautiful daughter. Their own big day had been perfect and, naturally, they hoped for something similar for Kim. As it turned out, Robert Kardashian would never have the opportunity to walk any of his daughters down the aisle.

Kim didn't know how to tell her family, so she didn't. Instead, Mrs Thomas returned to Northridge and kept her secret for three months. She did tell her friends, however, and swore them to secrecy. That didn't work, because one of them rang Kourtney to tell her the news. She went online and found her younger sister's marriage certificate from Vegas. Kourtney did what any big sister would do in these circumstances – she told her mother.

Kris rallied round. She may not have been happy about the situation, but she wasn't a hypocrite. After all, she had been younger than Kim when she became engaged for the first time, and she was only 22 when she got married.

Kim's father wasn't as philosophical about the situation. He refused to speak to his daughter, perhaps more through disappointment than anger. When he finally met Damon, he didn't like him and he didn't care for the relationship. He would have preferred her to have waited and, according to friends, was happy to tell her what he thought. He didn't want her to be with Damon. He wasn't as understanding as her mother.

Kris reveals in her memoir how, when she first met him, she tore into Damon for taking advantage of her teenage daughter, but she accepted they were married and did her best to include Damon in family gatherings. He remained a bit of an outsider, however. In her book, he isn't even afforded the privilege of a pseudonym. He isn't named at all. He is just 'the husband'.

Kim gave up her job at Body less than two months after her marriage. She would later state, in an astonishing court declaration, that she did so because Damon told her to. 'He said that he did not want me to have contact with my old boyfriends, who would be able to reach me at the clothing store. He said that he wanted to know where I was at all times.'

If all the allegations in the divorce papers are to be believed, this was the start of an unhappy period in Kim's life. She claimed that Damon preferred her to stay at home and wanted her to prepare meals for him, even if he arrived home at 4.30 in the morning after a long session in the studio.

Damon, she alleged in August 2003, wouldn't allow her to leave the house unless he knew exactly when and where she was going. She claimed that she couldn't go to the mall by herself, or dine with friends she had known since she was a child and that he even tried to poison her mind against her family, calling her mother and sisters 'evil'. She said, 'Damon decided what we would do and when we would do it. He was very much the "King of the Castle".'

Now that she no longer had her wage from Body, she needed to find other ways of supplementing the income she had from helping her father at Movie Tunes, Inc. Working in the boutique had given her the opportunity to meet clients whom she could advise on their wardrobe choices. It was an upmarket store, so customers invariably had some money to spend and were happy to pay Kim extra for her help. That revenue was now lost as well.

She needed to find something she could do at home or a sideline she could work on during the quieter moments at her father's office. It was while there that she started taking an interest in eBay. The ubiquitous online auction site seems to have been around for many years, but it only launched in September 1995. Kim spotted its potential. Arguably, the most useful attribute she inherited from her mother and father was their entrepreneurial spirit — the ability to identify a way to earn money and to exploit the opportunity fully.

She was a huge fan of Manolo Blahnik shoes. They were the must-have fashion footwear for celebrities and well-off women. Their appeal greatly increased when they featured heavily in *Sex and the City*. In the third series, broadcast in the autumn of 2000, the lead character Carrie Bradshaw, played by Sarah Jessica Parker, is mugged for her pair of Manolos, as they are popularly known.

Kim became aware of them when J.Lo wore them. She still absolutely adored J.Lo and couldn't stop singing her break-through hit 'If You Had My Love' around the house and in the car. She checked with a store and they had five pairs simi-lar to the ones J.Lo sported, but they were $700 each.

She did what any young entrepreneur would do under these circumstances. She borrowed the money from her father, who, as usual, demanded that she sign a contract agreeing to repay the money with interest. She bought all five pairs and then put them up for sale on eBay. It was her first real business success. Each pair sold for $2,500; altogether, she made a profit of $9,000. From that moment on, if there was anything in her wardrobe that she wasn't wearing, she would sell it on eBay. She was very unsentimental about it.

Meanwhile, her husband's fortunes were also on the up. The new millennium began the golden years for Damon and The Underdogs. They produced many tracks for Tyrese and old friends, such as Babyface and Brian McKnight, but also branched out to a more mainstream audience, by working with Lionel Richie and with Victoria Beckham on her solo album. Most of their recordings for Kim's teenage favourite ended up as B-sides to singles, but one track, 'Girlfriend', made the final cut. The album wasn't the success everyone had hoped for, though.

Much more successful was a collaboration with Justin Timberlake. The singer was passionate about basketball and had idolised Michael Jordan growing up in Tennessee, so he formed an easy friendship with Harvey Mason, who had played practically at professional level. Brian McKnight, one of the smoothest R & B vocalists, was also mad about basketball, so recording often took a back seat while the four friends went outside to shoot hoops.

The Underdogs wrote and produced 'Still on My Brain' for Justin's debut album, *Justified*. It was a slow and soulful number about lost love. Beautifully sung, it is a stand-out track and one that hasn't dated. While, as fans thought, the song might be about Justin's break with Britney Spears, it could just as easily reflect any painful split.

In her divorce papers, Kim claimed that an appalling incident occurred on a day when she and Damon were going skydiving with Justin. She alleged: 'Before we left our home, Damon hit me in the face and cut my lip open. I fell onto the bed frame and banged my knee hard. I was limping when we went skydiving.'

Her declaration states that Damon started hitting her a few months into their marriage. She points out that she is 5ft 3in tall and weighs 107 pounds. Damon, she says, is 5ft 10in and 175 pounds. In one incident at her mother's house, she claimed that he became angry after learning she had paged someone on her beeper: 'I told him the name of the friend. He became enraged and punched me in the face. My face was bruised and swollen as a result. I thought about calling the police, but was afraid and decided not to do so.'

It was a relief for everyone when they separated in early 2003. After she was no longer living with Damon, she claimed she experienced the worst of his violence against her. She recalled in the papers how she went back to the house to collect some personal items on the night before the rest of her belongings were due to be moved. She described what alleg- edly happened when she went into the bathroom to collect some toiletries: 'Damon screamed that I should get out of his bathroom immediately. He came at me and slammed me against the closet wall. He held me up against the wall with his hands around my neck and threatened to choke me. He then took one hand and punched the wall right next to my head.

'He then grabbed me by my hair and told me to get out. He put one hand against my back and pushed me up the stairs (the front door is on the ground level and the bedroom is one level below ground). At the top of the stairs, he threw me across the room and I hit my head against the front door. I got up and ran out of the house. I was frightened.'

Kim has never repeated these allegations in public or in interviews. They weren't included in Kris Jenner's book or in *Kardashian Konfidential*. For his part, Damon emphatically and vehemently denied these incidents ever took place. He told *In Touch* magazine, 'It's just absolutely not true.' He pointed out that she had never filed a restraining order or a protective order against him throughout their marriage, and accused her of using the alleged abuse as a bargaining chip in their divorce battle.

Damon actually sued Kim for divorce. He did so, he said, because she was unfaithful to him with 'multiple guys'. She, in turn, denied this allegation. Clearly, there were many areas of dispute as the divorce took its course. One of them was the story of her liposuction.

Kim said she had lipo, which cost $3,650, because Damon wanted her to be 'perfect'. He countered that she wanted him to pay for that and for additional work. Damon said he bought her clothes to fit her new shapelier outline. He said he was happy to pay for them – until he saw a picture on the cover of a magazine of her with another man, which showed her wearing the very clothes he had paid for. Damon observed, 'It was not, as a husband, anything you wanted to see.'

The date in question was the dancer and choreographer Cris Judd, who, in a curious twist, used to be married to Kim's idol, Jennifer Lopez. They had wed in Calabasas in 2001 and divorced after less than a year.

For the most part, Damon has remained silent about his marriage to Kim and what he thought of his ex-wife, even though he has had some very negative press coverage. Some years later, however, in 2010, he gave an interview to *In Touch* in response to the divorce papers being made public. He was very outspoken, claiming she was jealous and competitive with her sisters and desperate to be famous. He called her, unflatteringly, a 'fame-whore'.

It really is a case of whom to believe in an acrimonious split. When the divorce was made final, Damon was ordered to pay Kim $56,000, which was by no means a large sum. There wasn't much left after she settled the debt she had run up on her credit cards of $40,000. Fortunately, he agreed to cover her legal fees, totalling $20,000. Of more importance to her than money at this point, however, were the precious possessions which she had left behind at Damon's house: an inscribed Bible from her father, a signed Manolo Blahnik book, her high school yearbooks and about a hundred other books that made up her library.

Her financial concerns were insignificant next to Damon's, which included a tax liability of more than $700,000. His career continued its upward path, though. In 2003, when his private life was in turmoil, The Underdogs signed a deal with the legendary Clive Davis at J Records to start a new label, Underdog Entertainment. This was big news in the music business. Damon gushed, 'Clive has a true love for artists and their music, and that is exciting to us.'

The rise of The Underdogs culminated in 2006, when Damon and Harvey produced the soundtrack for the Oscar-winning film *Dreamgirls*, loosely based on the early days of The Supremes. Two of the big ballad tracks became modern classics: 'Listen' by Beyoncé and Jennifer Hudson's powerful 'And I'm Telling You I'm Not Going'. Damon and Harvey won a Black Reel Award for the soundtrack and derived enormous kudos from their work.

Only Harvey seemed to kick on after this triumph, however. He formed Harvey Mason Media in 2008, has won six Grammys and is a major success story. His website's online biography of his career and achievements doesn't mention Thomas's contribution.

Damon hasn't done as well financially in recent years, filing for bankruptcy in 2012. The documents revealed he owed more than $3.5 million, mainly in back taxes. His principal asset was a Lamborghini worth $170,000. Damon still works at Harvey Mason's studios on Vineland Avenue, North Hollywood, but has been living more modestly in Northridge.

One thing is sure about Kim's first marriage: it wasn't a happy one for either of them. Perhaps Kim was indulging in some teenage rebellion a little later than most young people. She demonstrated for the first, but not the last, time that she possessed a strong will and that if she wanted to do something, then she would press ahead and do it.

In 2015, blissfully married to Kanye West, she looked back on her first attempt and told the TV host Matt Lauer, 'You think you know so much about love when you're young and you look back later and probably realise it is not what you thought it was.'

9

THE DEATH OF ROBERT KARDASHIAN

While Kim was involved in her bitter divorce, she received some awful news. Her father, Robert Kardashian, was dying. It came as a terrible shock to all the family when, in July 2003, he told them that he had oesophageal cancer. The oesophagus, or food pipe, is the tube that carries food from your mouth to your stomach. He had suffered badly over the years with severe acid indigestion and was forever taking antacids to relieve his discomfort. His cancer had already advanced to Stage IV, which meant that it had spread to other organs in his body, leaving little room for hope.

Grimly, his illness wasn't the only one casting a shadow over the family that summer. Kim's maternal grandfather, Harry Shannon, was in hospital in San Diego and sinking fast. Kris Jenner's 78-year-old stepfather, whom she affectionately called Dad, was admitted after a car accident. Tragically, he caught a staph infection and never made it home. Robert managed to travel to San Diego for the funeral, but it would be his last trip.

Robert's private life since the O. J. Simpson trial had been interesting, to say the least. Out of the blue, he had married a woman called Jan Ashley in November 1998. Jan, who lived nearby in Encino, had no children and they got married so they could have a child together. Robert wasn't the sort of man who would contemplate such a thing outside marriage.

According to divorce papers he filed the following May, he couldn't go through with it: 'Approximately two months after our marriage, I changed my mind. I decided that since I already had four biological children, I did not wish to have any more. The respondent [Ashley] and I both entered into this marriage with the expectation of having a child together. I am the one who changed my mind.'

It was a most curious episode in Robert Kardashian's life. Much later, Jan would put the blame for the demise of her short-lived marriage firmly on the shoulders of his children, who she claimed were after him for 'money, money, money'. She didn't look back on her time as Mrs Kardashian with great joy. 'It took me about one day to get over it,' she said.

Robert moved to Lake Encino Drive, another smart street in Encino. The house, on a corner and with no view, was nothing like the best in the neighbourhood. It was still a desirable property, just not in the same league as Tower Lane. He began dating an elegant blonde woman called Ellen Pearson, who was involved in real estate. They had started seeing each other in 1998, but had split up before he became involved with Jan. After meeting again at a party in December 1999, they resumed their relationship. Robert bought a second house near his parents in Indian Wells and the couple divided their time between the two homes.

They became engaged in 2002, and planned their wedding for the following year. They decided to have a honeymoon before getting married and enjoyed an idyllic holiday in Italy in May and June 2003. On their return, they thought they had plenty of time to finish the preparations for the big day at Hotel Bel-Air on 5 August 2003. On a weekend visit to Indian Wells in early June, however, Robert complained of stomach pains and decided he needed to see a doctor. A few weeks later, on 11 July, he was given the bleak diagnosis and told his family. Ellen recalled, 'He was a religious man. He was not at all concerned about passing, because he believed in God. He just hadn't wanted to go so soon.'

His deterioration was rapid and the wedding had to be cancelled. He could eat very little and was losing a lot of weight. Kim did her best by going to the house and making him his favourite Cream of Wheat, a type of porridge that is popular in the US. Robert liked his served especially sweet, so Kim would always sprinkle a layer of sugar in the bowl before she stirred in the cereal. It was something she had enjoyed preparing for her father when she was a little girl and here she was, a 22-year-old woman, trying to do something nice for her dad before he died.

Robert was well enough to marry Ellen at the house in Encino on 27 July. His four children were there, as were his brother Tommy, sister Barbara and Ellen's daughter April. Understandably, it was a very small affair, with a subdued celebration in the garden afterwards.

The circumstances of Robert's demise set off a decade and more of feuding between stepmother and children, with allegations and counterclaims flying all over the place concerning the access the children had to their father in his dying days. They now seem to have settled their legal issues.

Ellen became the second person Kris Jenner couldn't bring herself to name in her autobiography, calling her 'a woman he had only been dating a short time'.

Robert Kardashian passed away on 30 September 2003. He was 59. The funeral at the Inglewood Park Cemetery was standing room only, as his many friends gathered to pay their respects. Kim gave an address, which, unused to public speaking, she found very hard. Afterwards, everyone went back to the Bel-Air Country Club, which, by grim coincidence, had been the venue for the reception when he had married Kris. Al Cowlings was there, but O. J. Simpson didn't attend, which was probably a good thing. He would have been the focus of attention rather than the celebration of Robert's life.

O. J. had tried to reach Robert on the phone before he died, despite the two not having spoken for years. He was gracious about his former friend after his death: 'It's shocking when a friend close to you passes. I loved Bobby. We had one disagreement over the years, about a book he did for money. He explained it to me. I understood it, and we put it aside. Bob was there when I needed him most.'

The newspaper obituaries, unsurprisingly, focused on Robert's involvement in the O. J. Simpson trial. The *New York Times* spelled it out in its headline: 'Robert Kardashian, a lawyer for O. J. Simpson, dies at 59'. His family barely received a mention in the article. The *Guardian* pointed out that few would have heard of Robert if he had not sat beside O. J. throughout the trial. Until she found fame in her own right, Kim was frequently described as the daughter of O. J. Simpson's lawyer.

One of the issues that has caused much subsequent speculation is how much money Robert had and what his children actually inherited. He had made a considerable amount from the sale of *Radio & Records*, but that had been nearly 25 years before and since then he had provided an extravagant lifestyle for his family.

There is no doubt that Kim and her siblings were indulged and spoiled as children. They admit it themselves. By Beverly Hills standards, they were comfortably off, but not particularly wealthy. According to Jan Ashley, they weren't rich. She maintained, 'He didn't have any money. He always pretended he had money.'

Ellen maintained that he had large mortgages on the two properties in Encino and Indian Wells. She became president of Movie Tunes, Inc., which was now based on Ventura Boulevard in Studio City. Financial difficulties, however, led to her filing for Chapter 7 bankruptcy in 2010. The house in Indian Wells was repossessed by the bank and sold. The Encino house was also sold. She began working for a real estate company called Western Resources Title as part of their sales force based in San Diego. She hasn't remarried and still calls herself Mrs Ellen Kardashian. She remembers Robert fondly: 'He had a lot of dignity, a great outlook on life and a fantastic sense of humour. We were very much in love.'

Details of Robert's will weren't made public, although apparently there was an insurance policy that would benefit his children in due course. They were also left 'his personal tangible and intangible property', a clause that would be contentious in a future vicious legal action between Ellen and the Kardashian children.

Robert's daughters reacted in different ways to the shock of his death. Kourtney joined her mother in a new venture. For years they had talked of running their own store and now was the perfect time to focus on something new and take their minds off a miserable year. They opened a children's boutique called Smooch in the centre of Calabasas. Kris had been helping to run a similar shop, which had been the family business for 30 years, while Harry was ill and that had inspired her to open her own.

Kourtney relished the opportunity and threw herself into running everything. Her life revolved around it: 'I used to work in the store all day, every day, stay hours after closing and was obsessed with it. Smooch was my baby … in a weird way, the store really helped me deal with my father's death … I put my feelings into the store!'

Khloé, aged 19, wasn't as fortunate. She was so upset that she had found it too difficult to visit her ailing father. The emotional stress caused her hair to fall out and she had to wear wigs, extensions and hats until it grew back. She started drinking too much and spent most nights going to clubs with an unsuitable crowd. She was very unhappy.

Kim planned a holiday in Mexico for her twenty-third birthday in October 2003. She needed to relax and get away from her troubles. The night before she flew, she made a sex tape with her boyfriend that would have an extraordinary effect on her future.

All three of his daughters saw Robert Kardashian as the greatest influence on their lives. They try hard to keep his memory alive by marking special occasions throughout the year, including the anniversary of his birthday or his passing, or Father's Day. On his birthday, they return to his favourite Armenian restaurant in Hollywood, called Carousel. He used to take his family there for special celebrations so they could sample the authentic, unpretentious food. Kim usually ate chicken, although she was also partial to the feta cheese appetiser.

Sadly, Robert Kardashian didn't live to see the birth of his grandchildren, nor did he witness what would have been one of his proudest days – when his only son, Robert Jr, graduated from USC, his old alma mater, with a degree in business in 2009. His ex-wife Kris Jenner observed, 'The one regret, if I had to do it over, was divorcing Robert Kardashian.'

To mark the fifth anniversary of her father's death, Kim posted a touching eulogy on her website. His absence has somehow made his presence in their lives greater. She said he was watching over and protecting them: 'There isn't a day that goes by when I don't think about him or wish he were here.' She concluded simply, 'I love you, Dad.'

10

QUEEN OF THE CLOSET SCENE

———

Kim's new boyfriend was a handsome young rapper and actor called William Ray Norwood, Jr, known as Ray J. They were introduced by his sister, Brandy, a very popular singer and TV actress, at a party in early 2003. As far as he was concerned, Kim was a married woman and off limits, but there was an instant attraction between the two. It wasn't long before they couldn't keep their hands off one another.

Ray J would later reveal that Kim left Damon for him as soon as they started having sex and said their passion for each other was intense. Wild and extreme sexual chemistry, according to the indiscreet Ray J, was a big part of their relationship: 'We were like animals, sexually free to try anything.'

Ray J and his sister were from McComb, Mississippi, the Southern town where Britney Spears was born and went to school. They were unlikely ever to have bumped into her though, because the area was notoriously racist and, historically, a stronghold for the Ku Klux Klan.

They escaped that prejudice when their parents moved to Carson, California, 13 miles south of downtown Los Angeles.

Their father was the gospel singer Willie Norwood, and both children learned much of their vocal technique from listening to their father sing in church. He wasn't the only musical one in the family – the rap superstar Snoop Dogg is a first cousin (his mother Beverly is also from McComb). From a young age, the Norwood children were involved in the performing arts.

Brandy, who is two years older than her brother, made her television debut, aged 14, in 1993 and signed with Atlantic Records the same year. Kim's husband, Damon, featured on her first, eponymously titled album, playing piano and keyboards. He also co-wrote and produced two tracks, 'I'm Yours' and 'Love Is on My Side', which he composed with Robin Thicke, who would become a household name 20 years later, thanks to the song 'Blurred Lines'. Harvey Mason, Jr worked on her second album, *Never Say Never*, so both Underdogs knew her well. She was very much part of the new wave of young black talent sweeping the music business.

Ray J always seemed to be hanging on to his sister's coat-tails, a pace behind. He had a record deal at 14, but was dropped by Elektra Records after just one album. His sister's career continued to prosper, however, with the success of 'The Boy Is Mine', her 1998 duet with Monica. It was the bestselling single of the year, with sales of 2.6 million.

Kim worked for Brandy after meeting her through Damon. She had realised that she couldn't make a living buying and selling her own possessions on eBay, and had displayed early business acumen by expanding into closet organising and personal styling. Progress was slow. At first, she would take every opportunity to go through the things her friends no longer had a use for, advising them which items they could sell and then splitting the profits with them.

She took her business a step further one day when she was visiting the Pacific Palisades home of Sugar Ray Leonard and his second wife, Bernadette. Sugar Ray had been a family friend of her father since before she was born and was also a long-standing friend of Bruce Jenner. They had both won gold medals at the Montreal Olympics and Ray, too, had subsequently carved out a career as a motivational speaker.

Bernadette had a massive closet, as big as a bedroom, which was seriously disorganised. Kim explained, 'I said to her, "You really need to clean out your closet." Well, we spent the whole night doing that.' She persuaded Bernadette that it would be far better to sell the thousands of dollars of designer clothing on eBay than to throw away the expensive dresses and accessories. It was the start of the next stage of her career.

She became 'Queen of the Closet Scene' when Bernadette started recommending Kim's skill to her friends. Kim used her own seller's account, and photographed every article so that it looked its best. She would write little paragraphs describing the items, so she had the best chance of selling every single thing. This wasn't an idle pursuit; it was work and it was supplying her with an income. Kim was very methodical and precise. She had never been a teenage girl whose bedroom was a mess of clothes. She liked everything to be clean and tidy, labelled and folded.

Although she was incredibly well organised, she could still be endearingly dippy. She was thrilled when she could afford to buy her own Range Rover. She had a new mobile to put into the middle console in the car as well, and she bedazzled the cell so it would stand out. Unfortunately, she put so much decoration on the phone that, when she came to slot it into the console, it didn't fit.

She had discovered a niche market. Soon, big names, like Cindy Crawford and Serena Williams, Rob Lowe and the acclaimed saxophone player Kenny G, were taking advantage of her services. Kim was learning very quickly that it was all about connections in Los Angeles. If you didn't make enough of them at school, then it helped to be with someone who had them. Her mother was an accomplished networker from the moment she moved to LA, and Kim was keen to follow her example.

Working for Brandy as a personal stylist was another step forward, although it wasn't entirely glamorous. She still had to go and pick up the dry cleaning if there was a specific outfit she was recommending her client to wear. Brandy had seen her name on a worst-dressed list, which wasn't the best news for someone in demand on the red carpet, and had asked Kim for fashion advice.

The singer had branched out into the world of reality television in a way that Kim hadn't seen before. The great majority of reality shows seemed to be about putting real people – usually celebrities – into unreal situations. That was not the premise of *Brandy: Special Delivery*, which ran on MTV for four episodes in June and July 2002. Brandy was expecting her first child with her then husband and producer Robert 'Big Bert' Smith – although he later revealed they were never officially married. The show linked things that were going on during the pregnancy with events in her professional life. She shops, she goes to parenting classes, she appears on TV, she discusses pregnancy with her mum, she is in the recording studio, she has an ultrasound of the baby, she enjoys a baby shower and she has a photography session. Ray J wasn't forgotten, and appeared in a couple of episodes. After Brandy gave birth to a daughter, Sy'rai, there was nowhere for the series to go.

For Kim Kardashian, it was an eye-opener. Here was someone she knew turning her life into entertainment. Throughout her career, Kim has done very little that could be described as original, but she is unsurpassed at absorbing influences and making sure she does it bigger and better.

Kim was warmly accepted into Paris Hilton's entourage when she was hired to sort out the dressing room and closet in her Spanish-style townhouse in North Kings Road, just below Sunset Strip in West Hollywood. Kim had a growing reputation as the best person for this kind of job. Organising Paris's wardrobe was quite a task, because it was so big. It was rather like refitting and restocking a boutique.

Paris Hilton was a phenomenon. She was by no means the first person to be famous for being famous, but she maximised the celebrity of her name and turned it into a huge money-spinner for herself. Kim had known her first in preschool. When the two became friends again after Kim's marriage split, she was able to watch and learn from a master.

Superficially, at least, the two women couldn't have been more different. The tall, willowy, blonde Paris Whitney Hilton was born into a level of American high society that was a division above the relatively new money of the Kardashians. The surname Hilton was one of the most famous in the US, mentioned in the same breath as Getty or Rockefeller. Her great-grandfather, Conrad Hilton, who founded the Hilton hotel chain, was married to Zsa Zsa Gabor; her great-uncle, Conrad 'Nicky' Hilton, Jr, was one of the husbands of Elizabeth Taylor.

She is the eldest child of real-estate developer Richard Hilton and actress-socialite Kathy Richards. She was always introduced back then as the heir to a $360-million fortune, but, in fact, she was one of multiple heirs. She spent her childhood moving between the couple's many five-star luxury homes, which included mansions in The Hamptons and Bel Air, as well as a suite in the Waldorf Astoria hotel in Manhattan. Her family was huge. She is the eldest of four children, with a younger sister and two brothers. She had 10 cousins on her mother's side, and her father had seven siblings. Christmas, Halloween and Easter were big family events, with her father on hand to record everything lovingly on video – just as in the Kardashian household.

Paris began modelling as a child and was given the nickname 'Star' by her mother. In 2000, while Kim was settling down to domestic life as a married woman, Paris signed a contract with Trump Model Management in New York. Donald Trump is a friend of her father. She had already become a fixture in the gossip columns, thanks to a romance with Leonardo DiCaprio. The renowned 'Page Six' of the *New York Post* seemed to have a Paris story every day. A controversial feature in *Vanity Fair*, with eye-catching pictures by David LaChapelle of her in hot pants, with younger sister Nicky, enhanced the impression that everyone was talking about her. It was an early example for Kim of how a photograph was the most effective way of obtaining publicity.

The voracious daily coverage of the glamorous life of Paris Hilton was an example of how publicity, both good and bad, would lead to more publicity and thereby increase one's fame. In many ways, it was a template for turning oneself into a brand that Kim would have been foolish not to try to emulate, Paris was so successful at it.

In 2003, she signed with the Fox television network to star in a new reality show with her sister Nicky called *The Simple Life*. The idea was to inject humour into the reality television genre by taking the two socialites out of their comfort zone of designer dresses and credit cards and putting them to work on a farm in Arkansas, a state in the Deep South. Paris had, of course, never worked a day in her life. The idea was inspired by an old sixties sitcom called *Green Acres*, which starred Eddie Albert and Eva Gabor.

The head of casting at Fox, Sharon Klein, explained, 'They wanted to see stilettos in shit.' Sharon was impressed with Paris, whom she found funny, genuine and not at all stupid: 'She was in her own reality and not embarrassed to talk about it. There was a sweetness about her.'

The show was scheduled to begin in December 2003. On 5 November, the 'Page Six' column revealed that there was an explicit sex tape involving Paris in circulation. She had made it in May 2001 with her then boyfriend Rick Salomon. He, apparently, was in the habit of filming himself having sex with his girlfriends, and Paris was no exception. This one wasn't going to win any Oscars, although it was shot in a realistic, grainy black–and–white mode, or night vision.

Salomon, it transpired, was a handsome character, who made his living as a professional poker player after giving up a career as a teenage drug dealer. He admitted, 'In my teens, I dealt in drugs big time.' After Paris, he married Shannen Doherty, one of the stars of *Beverly Hills, 90210*. They had apparently been dating for just two days before becoming husband and wife. The marriage was annulled after nine months, and Shannen reflected, 'I haven't made the best choices in men.' He also enjoyed hot-tub parties with Pamela Anderson, whom he married in 2007 and again in 2014. Salomon is one of the bad boys women love.

There is no doubt that the video, though rampantly exhibitionist, was originally made for personal consumption. The dialogue, such as it is, was too embarrassing to have been planned. Paris told Rick to say he loved her and wanted to kiss her; he just wanted to take off her pants.

Salomon offered the tape for sale on his personal website for $50 a time and then negotiated a distribution deal with Red Light District Video. He is said to have made millions from it. After many legal proceedings and lawsuits from both of them, Paris was reported to have settled for $400,000, plus a share of the profits, and to have given most of the money to charity. She had no further contact with him. He continued to prosper, however. When he played in the 2014 World Series of Poker, he won $2.8 million.

Her then media consultant, the much-respected Elliot Mintz, observed that it was a terrible experience for Paris. 'It's something that will always be a footnote to her life. She was wounded and then took a deep breath and then moved forward. She did not allow it to stop her, which is saying more than most of us could say if a personal video tape that we recorded with somebody of that nature suddenly was available around the country. So nothing to be proud of, but the true measure of a woman or a man is how well they can adapt to something that occurs in their life and move forward, which I think she did with grace.'

Paris handled the situation with good humour in public. Three days after the premiere of her reality show, she appeared on the fabled *Saturday Night Live* in a sketch of double entendres with the comedian and presenter Jimmy Fallon. He asked her, 'Is the Paris Hilton roomy?' She replied, 'It might be for you, but most people find it very comfortable.'

The press storm surrounding the sex tape was very welcome publicity for *The Simple Life*. Her sister Nicky had dropped out, apparently not relishing the prospect of the full glare of public attention, so her place was taken by Nicole Richie, the adopted daughter of Lionel Richie.

The interesting aspect of *The Simple Life* as a reality show is that there was nothing real about it. Paris and Nicole were placed in a situation that they would never have come across in their lives. It was completely fabricated. It was, in effect, a situation comedy with them playing themselves or, more precisely, a version of themselves. In these programmes, the participants are creating on-screen personas. Paris Hilton is a far more sophisticated woman than the clueless heroine of this series.

She was certainly smart enough to understand that she could use its popularity to increase the profile of her brand as Paris Hilton. She signed a music contract with Warner Bros and started recording an album in 2004. She produced a best-selling book, *Confessions of an Heiress: A Tongue-in-Chic Peek*

Behind the Pose, which featured countless photographs of Paris fashions, recollections of childhood and helpful hints on how to behave.

She appeared in acting roles in several popular television series, including *The O.C.*, *Veronica Mars* and *Las Vegas*. She also made some forgettable films, such as *The Hillz*. The publicity poster for the film naturally featured Paris, as she was by far the most famous person in it. She even won an award for the horror movie *House of Wax* – the Teen Choice Award for best scream scene.

She launched her own fragrance and line of jewellery, and was earning hundreds of thousands of dollars in personal appearances. As an example of how to maximise a brand, Kim couldn't have had a better one. Elliot Mintz observed, 'There is no question that she was influenced by Paris. Her eyes were open, her ears were open, but that is a lot different from saying she made a conscious effort to imitate Paris. I don't think there was an agenda. She observed the phenomena happening to Paris at the time.' In the future, it would certainly be extraordinary how many aspects of the Kim Kardashian story would mirror the celebrity branding of Paris Hilton, whether consciously or unconsciously.

Paris adopted Kim as her companion for nights out to the fashionable clubs of Los Angeles. Nobody knew who Kim was – she was just referred to by Paris as 'my friend' and that is how everyone regarded her. She even appeared fleetingly in *The Simple Life*.

They have a boring conversation inside Paris's closet about an outfit that she might wear to visit India – her 'if-I-ever-go-to-India outfit'.

LEFT & BELOW: The young Kim Kardashian grew up happily in the rich and privileged world of Beverly Hills. Here she is sharing carefree moments with close friend Nikki Lund.

BOTTOM: Her family remained close after her mother remarried. From left to right: younger sister Khloé, older sister Kourtney, stepfather Bruce Jenner, mother Kris, Robert Jr and Kim.

Bruce already had four children of his own, so there were now eight youngsters and two adults to fit into family portraits. Kim is far right.

Salad days ... Newly married in 1991, Kris and Bruce were keen to promote keeping fit and eating healthily.

ABOVE: An Easter-egg hunt in Mexico, 1994. It was the last vacation with 'Uncle O. J.' Simpson and his wife Nicole (pictured together in the back row). She was murdered two months later. Kim is front right.

RIGHT: Kim's father, Robert Kardashian, became famous defending O. J. at his murder trial. At O. J.'s house after the 'not guilty' verdict, they still had plenty to talk about.

LEFT: Now a celebrity, Robert arrives for the Grammy Awards with his then fiancée, Denice Halicki.

LEFT: Kim's first husband, Damon Thomas (pictured in shades with business partner Harvey Mason, Jr), was a cool record producer, but their Vegas marriage didn't prove to be happy ever after.

BELOW: Kim made *that* sex tape with hip-hop artist Ray J in 2003, and they were still together when they went to a fashion launch in March 2006.

ABOVE: Multi-talented TV host Nick Cannon was good fun for a couple of months. They strike a pose at a party for Kanye West at a New York restaurant in September 2006.

ABOVE: American football star Reggie Bush looked like he might be husband number two when they watched a basketball game in New Orleans in January 2010 ... But the couple split after dating for two and a half years.

LEFT: Paris Hilton was an old school friend whom Kim went to work for when she was a celebrity stylist. They both loved shopping and made sure their handbags were large enough.

ABOVE: Three of these celebrities took part in notorious sex tapes – Kim, her boyfriend at the time, Ray J, and Paris Hilton. Tennis great Serena Williams, a close friend of Kim's, is the odd one out.

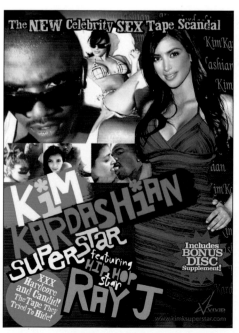

LEFT: The sex tape that launched a multi-million-dollar fortune. 'Kim Kardashian Superstar' was a premature description back in 2007, but not today.

Kim poses with her little sisters, Kylie (left) and Kendall Jenner, at a launch in October 2007 for *Keeping Up with the Kardashians* at the Chapter 8 restaurant in Agoura Hills, California.

My, how you've grown! Kendall and Kylie tower over Kim when they watch the MTV Awards together at The Forum in Inglewood, August 2014.

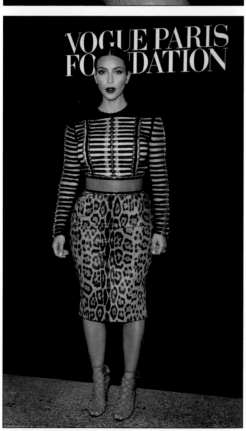

TOP LEFT: Kim is happy to be asked to the annual *Teen Vogue* Young Hollywood party at the Sunset Tower Hotel, Los Angeles in September 2006. She loved the grown-up magazine and this was the next best thing to being at one of its big fashion events.

TOP RIGHT: Kim looks gorgeous and almost demure in front of her first *Playboy* cover at a celebration party at the Retreat Club, New York, in November 2007. Not quite *Vogue* though ...

LEFT: Kim is serious and seriously chic at the inaugural Vogue Paris Foundation Gala at the Palais Galliera in July 2015 ... well it is *Vogue!*

The essential Kim Kardashian ...

Kim: You're not allowed to show any of your hair.

Paris: Are you allowed to have blonde hair? If you travel there, do you really have to do this?

Kim: I think so or you'll get shot.

An urban myth grew up that Paris Hilton ordered Kim Kardashian to 'clean out my closet'. Paris probably did ask Kim to clean out her closet at some point – after all, that was what she was originally paying her for – just not on film.

Elliot met Kim in the closet one day when Paris was trying on clothes to decide what to wear. He saw Kim at the house frequently and then she started to go out with them in the evenings. The old school friends were clearly pals, but Kim was always careful to get in the car after Paris and enter buildings a step behind her.

Elliot was very impressed by Kim, who was completely different to many of the entourage. 'She was low maintenance and undemanding. She was gracious. She was extremely polite. She was somewhat reserved. She would never create an embarrassment. She was not a drinker or substance abuser. She never got into arguments or quarrels with other people.

'She was also very punctual. If we were all going to some location at 10 p.m., then she would be at that spot at 10 p.m. If I told everyone that we were leaving in 10 minutes to avoid our car being followed by the press – perhaps at a service entrance – then Kim would be there 9 minutes and 50 seconds later.'

It's easy to understand why Kim was so well liked. She was the nice best friend in a movie, who was never going to embarrass the star – in this case, Paris Hilton. She wasn't the person handing out business cards or collecting them. This was her first exposure to a bona fide celebrity world and all its accompanying madness. She didn't reach into her handbag on evenings out, take out a Filofax and write notes.

If you look at many of the things she later attempted, they were tried first by Paris, with varying degrees of success. Elliot maintained, 'Paris is the mother of reality television. She created it.' It would be fair to say that *The Simple Life* brought the reality genre into the mainstream. It ran for five series, three with Fox and then two with E! before it was cancelled in July 2007.

The producer, Jonathan Murray, who would later be the man silently pulling the strings on *Keeping Up with the Kardashians*, wasn't entirely happy about his former show. 'With Paris and Nicole, we never reached the point where they would just trust us to shoot. It often felt like they were doing the light, fluffy story on our show, and then there would be this whole other story about them in the tabloids. For viewers, it began to feel like they got the truth from the tabloids rather than from the show.' Reading between the lines, it would seem that Murray was looking for a show that the public thought was more genuine.

11

VIVID IMAGINATION

With Smooch proving to be a success, Kourtney decided she wanted to expand and open another store – this time for grown-up women. She asked Khloé if she would like to be involved and her sister jumped at the opportunity. At first, they decided not to include Kim, who seemed busy with her own life and would have little time to help. Her work with Brandy and Paris was going well and she was trying to enhance her reputation as a personal stylist. She was also having her fair share of problems with Ray J.

Kim was offended that her sisters didn't appear to want her in their new venture and told them so. For the sake of family harmony, they invited her to join them. Her first priority, however, was making a name for herself. She opened a Myspace profile, using the sobriquet Princess Kimberly. She acquired 856 friends on the now outdated social networking site. Her mini bio read: 'I'm a Princess and you're not, so there.' She listed 'My Daddy' as her hero. It was an early, if underdeveloped, recognition that social networking was a vital ingredient in self-promotion.

Kourtney and Khloé basically ran the shop without her. When they found the premises around the corner from Smooch, they dragooned Bruce to do the shop-fitting and transform the place into the chic boutique they had in mind. They decided to call it DASH.

All the girls helped with choosing stock, but it was Khloé who took on the day-to-day running of the store, while Kourtney continued to look after Smooch. Kim would bring her friends and those employing her as a stylist to DASH and encourage them to buy clothes. It was an astute move, because she earned something from both ends of the deal.

Indirectly, the store led to her final breakup with Ray J. After nearly three years together, their relationship was going through a particularly rocky patch towards the end of 2005 and into 2006. Ray described what happened in a book called *Death of the Cheating Man: What Every Woman Must Know About Men Who Stray*, a collaboration with lifestyle guru Maxwell Billieon. Ray related how he suspected her of playing away, but was so caught up in his own straying that he didn't care. He said there had been a breakdown in trust and she seemed to be checking up on him at every opportunity: 'She literally thought I was cheating with every girl I ran across.'

He complained that 'KK' – as he referred to her in the book – seemed to know every time a girl called for him or left a voicemail message. It later dawned on him that she must have been checking his phone. He confessed, 'I used sex with other women to dull the pain and ease my conscience.'

The most dramatic incident came when he flew in from New York on Kim's twenty-fifth birthday. He'd planned to meet up with another woman before he went home to his girlfriend. When he landed, he discovered there was a message on his phone from Kim, who was far from happy: 'I know you're back in LA, you piece of shit!' she shouted, before telling him she never wanted to see or talk to him ever again. Ray went off to have 'fantastic' sex with the other woman before trotting home, where he patched things up, at least temporarily.

Then Kim fell out with Brandy over money. Ray didn't go into any details – it wasn't relevant to a discussion on cheating – but later Brandy's mother, Sonja Norwood, filed a lawsuit against Kim and her siblings for running up credit card charges without permission. Sonja alleged that in 2004 Kim had been authorised to make one purchase only on the Norwood American Express card in her capacity as Brandy's stylist. She claimed that Kim made unauthorised purchases and passed the card number on to her brother and sisters, who then also made unauthorised purchases, including items from their two stores, DASH and Smooch. The suit alleged the total amount charged was $120,636. Sonja was asking for the return of the money plus 10 per cent interest.

The Kardashians issued a statement: 'The charges against the Kardashians are meritless. Both Kim and Khloé were employed by the Norwoods and never used their credit cards without express authorisation. The Kardashian family looks forward to proving the absurdity of these claims in court.' Mrs Norwood, who told *People* magazine that the Kardashians had reneged on a promise to repay the debt, was also looking forward to her day in court.

In the event, neither party got their wish and the case was dismissed with prejudice, which meant that it couldn't be appealed or filed again. It was over permanently. Media reports described it as an 'apparent settlement', but the details remained confidential. Neither the Norwoods nor the Kardashians have subsequently commented on the lawsuit. Brandy and Kim are no longer friends and the singer was stony-faced when asked about Kim in a television interview in 2014.

Once she and Ray J were no longer an item, Kim was free to date whomever she chose. She couldn't help but notice that anyone Paris went out with was snapped by the paparazzi and appeared all over the magazines as a result. Such publicity would be gold dust for both her and, just as importantly, DASH.

In May 2006, she went to the movie *The Da Vinci Code* in Calabasas one afternoon with Nick Lachey at a time when his divorce from Jessica Simpson was going through. When they came out, there was a mass of photographers waiting to record the event. Nick was very unimpressed and would later imply that it was Kim who tipped them off. When he was asked if those shots sparked the start of her rise to stardom, he replied, 'That's one way to interpret it.'

He continued, 'Let's just say this. We went to a movie. No one followed us there. Somehow, mysteriously, when we left, there were 30 photographers waiting outside.' He added, 'There are certain ways to play this game, and some people play it well.'

The *New York Daily News* quoted a friend saying, 'She wanted to get her photo in the magazines and knew being seen next to Nick would be big news, since he had just ended his marriage. She was in communication with editors at the celebrity weeklies and provided them with details of the date to guarantee her spot in the limelight.'

Kim herself admitted that the date with Nick was her first taste of being the centre of attention. She said that people were curious about who he was with. The liaison with Nick Lachey, who wasn't really Kim's type, amounted to exactly nothing, but did get her name into the media. By itself, it wouldn't be enough to change things. It was just a brick in the wall at this stage.

The following night, Kim was with Paris as usual. The two of them went to their crowd's usual hangout, the Hyde nightclub on Sunset. In *Kardashian Konfidential*, she recalled that for the first time, as they arrived, the paparazzi shouted her name instead of her celebrity friend's. Paris may not have been best pleased at her companion stealing the show. Certainly, their friendship began to cool as Kim became better known.

Paris was already a paparazzi favourite before her sex tape was released, but there is little doubt that *1 Night in Paris* greatly enhanced her fame. Kim, too, had a sex tape, which, as Nick Lachey would say later, 'was already in the can'.

The pornography grapevine was aware that there was a new sex tape being offered around in the winter of 2006. Kim heard about it as well, but didn't believe the rumours. She even gave an interview to *Complex* magazine – her first front cover – in which she denied the existence of any tape. On her way back from a trip to New York, she took a call from Kourtney, who told her that the sex tape she had made with Ray J was now in the public domain.

The first thing she did was to go round to her mother's house and tell her everything. She broke down in floods of tears as she came clean about the existence of the tape – a startling confession from a young woman who neither drank nor did drugs, but tended to be impetuous where men were concerned. Kim was devastated that her most intimate moments with the boyfriend she loved might be seen by the whole world.

Kris Jenner was mortified when she realised the graphic nature of the tape: 'I cried myself to sleep. I don't think anything can prepare you for something like that when it comes to your daughter. I had to go into a room and cry for a couple of days and say, "OK, pull yourself to-fucking-gether!"'

They decided they needed to handle the situation – to try and gain some control over what was happening. It was the only sensible thing to do. They learned the tape was now in the hands of a company called Vivid Entertainment, one of the leading distributors of pornography in the US. Steve Hirsch, the Vivid chairman, announced the forthcoming release of the tape in February 2007. He said, 'We are comfortable we have the legal right to distribute this video no matter what others may say.'

Kim countered by telling the media of her intention to sue Vivid. She said, 'Everyone is pretty disappointed and very confused as to what's going on and who's behind this. We're just going to get to the bottom of this and do whatever we have to do to stop it.'

When the story appeared in *E! News*, Kim was described as one of Paris Hilton's closest friends, a socialite and the daughter of O. J. Simpson's defence attorney, Robert Kardashian, a stylist and fashion designer, and the stepdaughter of Bruce Jenner. It mentioned that she co-owned the boutique DASH in Calabasas. She was also going to be in an advertising campaign for the high-end clothing line Christopher Brian Apparel, it said. The 'actor-rapper' Ray J only merited a sentence, in which we learned he was the brother of Brandy and co-starred with her in the sitcom *Moesha*. In the media coverage, he was being left far behind, even though he was rumoured to be in a relationship with Whitney Houston. The article was a useful barometer for judging where Kim stood in terms of public recognition at the time.

The piece also mentioned Damon Thomas and said Kim had been linked to Nick Lachey, the rapper known as The Game (Jayceon Terrell Taylor) and Nick Cannon, the actor, rapper and TV presenter who went on to marry Mariah Carey. Cannon dated Kim between September 2006 and January 2007.

He described their breakup on *The Howard Stern Show*. He recalled that the sex tape was to blame: 'This was my issue. We talked about this tape … and she told me there was no tape. If she had been honest with me, I might have tried to hold her down and be like, "That was before me", because she is a great girl.

'She's actually one of the nicest people you'll ever meet. But the fact that she lied …'

That had been Kim's knee-jerk reaction when she first heard the rumours about her tape. If she denied it, the whole nightmare might go away. Now she was taking action. She filed a right to privacy lawsuit to try to stop the release of the DVD. Her complaint accused Vivid of 'egregious commercial exploitation and violation of Plaintiff's most personal and intimate sexual relations with her former boyfriend of three years.' She described the tape as being 'extremely hurtful not only to me, but to my family as well.'

Ray J seemed strangely on the sidelines while all this was going on, but he and Kim remained on good terms. She said she didn't suspect him of handing the tape over to the 'porn pedlars'.

Kim realized that she needed to talk to Vivid if she wanted to have any kind of control of the situation. This was common practice and made good sense for both sides, then at least there would be a fixed outcome and it would call a halt to paying expensive legal fees. Kim's lawyers must have told her that there was no guarantee of success when pursuing a legal claim, and, what's more, even if she were successful, a sex tape might take on a life of its own once it was leaked and couldn't be removed from the Internet. An agreement needed to be reached.

Kim was a novice in such matters, as was her mother, despite her astute handling of Bruce's affairs. The larger-than-life character Joe Francis, so claims a source, had a hand in helping Kim. He was the boss of the mild soft porn franchise Girls Gone Wild and a great friend of the Kardashian family. He had launched the brand in 1997 and it soon became a byword for young, attractive women, often tipsy, flashing their breasts and bottoms for the camera and generally whooping and hollering as they did so. It was a brilliant concept from a smart and savvy 24-year-old entrepreneur. His cameramen would go to all parts of the country, trawling bars and college parties for girls willing to participate. There was never a shortage of volunteers. The girls might well be taking their tops off at the end of a fun night in any case, so he was just tapping into what was already happening and giving it a nudge. The favourite hunting ground was the Easter vacation time in the US known as spring break, which is traditionally a chance for college students to let their hair down.

The franchise produced a variety of videos, all with *Gone Wild* in the title. One of the most popular was *Girls Gone Wild: Doggy Style*, hosted by none other than Ray's first cousin, Snoop Dogg. The brand was incredibly popular, because it was perceived as inoffensive high spirits and not pornography. There were no penises in *Girls Gone Wild*.

Joe was very much part of the Paris Hilton set that included Kim and would descend on the clubs of Hollywood for a good time in the evening. Invariably, Joe would be accompanied by a number of beautiful blondes. His parties at his Bel Air mansion were legendary and rivalled the *Playboy* ones for popularity. He was said to be earning $29 million a year from his business and had two private planes, which he was happy to lend to his friends.

Back in 2003, it was widely reported that he'd had a fling with Paris herself. He was, however, prone to be indiscreet. He was once asked on *The Howard Stern Show* who gave the best oral sex among his many celebrity conquests. He didn't hesitate: 'Paris is the best ... Paris is amazing in bed ... better than anyone.'

He also reportedly dated Kourtney, and did introduce her to the father of her three children, Scott Disick, in 2005. He was good friends with Kris Jenner, who found him entertaining and great company. He often flew the Kardashians around – to Las Vegas or Mexico.

He was involved in a long, drawn-out legal saga of his own that had begun in 2003 in Panama City, Florida. He had fallen foul of the authorities there, who took exception to him using the town as a venue for a spring break pay-per-view filming for Girls Gone Wild. Both his Ferrari and his Gulfstream jet were confiscated. The chain of events would end up costing him many millions, as well as his liberty. From March 2007, he would spend nearly a year in jail.

Before he was jailed, however, he was able to help and reassure Kim. Joe was already a friend of Steve Hirsch and would be able to bring all the parties to the table. A meeting was arranged at the Girls Gone Wild offices between Steve, Kim and Ray J to discuss a way forward.

Vivid is a much more hardcore company than Girls Gone Wild and there was certainly no shortage of penises in their productions. Steve is a very different character to the larger-than-life Joe, despite their friendship. A separate source who worked for Vivid observed, 'He was the antithesis of Joe Francis. He was very clean and sober. Steve was a businessman who understood financial opportunity. He was calculating and very smart.'

Girls Gone Wild already had a connection to Vivid through its website. They had a marketing agreement that if you were buying or browsing for something on the former's site, there was a link to buy something more hardcore from the latter. In the trade, it was known as an up-sale.

The source at Vivid explained, 'We used to describe the pornographic world in terms of narcotics. *Girls Gone Wild* and *Playboy* were cigarettes. Pretty soon, though, you would want a glass of whisky to go with that and that's when you came to Vivid. Pretty soon after that, you want to move on from whisky to marijuana and that's when you started getting into crazy Evil Angel hardcore and then, finally, you end up on heroin – watching the most disgusting things you can find.'

Kim's sex tape was definitely whisky, maybe taken with a little water, and much more suitable for distribution by a company like Vivid rather than Girls Gone Wild. Steve could see great possibilities for his company and was hugely keen to agree terms. According to a source at Girls Gone Wild who had sight of the agreement, Kim and Ray J received $300,000 each in respect of the tape. They would also receive a residual on videos sold or downloaded.

The lawsuit was duly dropped. Steve Hirsch said, 'We are pleased that Kim has dropped her legal action against us. We met with her several times and reached a financial arrangement that we both feel is fair … we've always wanted to work something out with Kim so she could share the profits.' Reports that she was paid $5 million to give up the suit were wildly inaccurate, although once again such inflated figures increased the value of the product in the public's mind. The source from Girls Gone Wild claimed, 'That was all a nonsense figure.'

Ironically, the media interest in the sex tape created by Kim's legal action was just the sort of publicity that would guarantee its success. The source said, 'The appeal has to be that you are watching some footage that was supposed to have been shot in the privacy of somebody's bedroom that's never been seen before. That is the whole allure – you are seeing something that you are not supposed to see.

'Filing a lawsuit created sensationalism and media frenzy. That's the only reason why anybody cared about this tape, quite frankly – because it was forbidden fruit. You know back then if Kim Kardashian had been hired by a pornographic company to do a video, nobody would have given it a second thought.

'The implication in the legal action was that the sex tape was so scandalous and risqué that she would go to any length to prevent you from seeing it. Unintentionally, it was really brilliant marketing.'

Vivid needed to prepare quickly for the release of the tape. A series of top-level meetings was held at the offices on Cahuenga Boulevard in Studio City. The company started buying up every single domain name that its staff could think of involving Kim K, Kim Kardashian sex tape and so on. This was essential so that any related online searches would be directed back to Vivid and the sale of the tape. It was a laborious, if inexpensive, exercise, but it still needed to be done for a successful launch. When you have a property like this particular sex tape, you don't just register one site and you have to include all the possible misspellings. They made sure they registered Kim Kardashian Superstar, which would be the eventual title of the tape. One did slip through the net, however. They failed to claim Kim K Sex Tape and this one had to be bought separately; it cost as much to capture and re-register as all the other 200 or so put together. Even then, it was more about time spent than the cost, which was no more than $2,500.

Meanwhile, one editor, working alone, started assembling the footage that Ray J had shot into a marketable form. This was somewhat problematic, as the tape was an old-style pre-digital VHS one; the images they put on the website the company had created for the tape were basically poor-quality screen grabs.

Steve Hirsch, a greatly admired figure in the world of pornography, had a knack for spotting something that might be big. When he got a sense of who Kim Kardashian was, he decided this was something the company should get behind with all its resources. Ostensibly, Ray J was still a bigger name, but it's always better from the marketing point of view to concentrate on the woman involved, the more vulnerable victim of circumstance. The interracial aspect of the film would add a certain frisson for the tape's buyers.

Steve's staff initially thought they were dealing with a hip-hop artist having sex with one of his dancers. It only dawned on them during the marketing process that Kim Kardashian was actually the star and not Ray J. He was able to keep a low profile, although he was spotted driving a swanky new Lamborghini around Hollywood, thanks to his windfall.

One of the benefits to Vivid of having secured an agreement with Kim was that it would have made it easy to deal with the legal requirements of Statute 2257. It's basically a law based around the minimum age requirement for participation in porn. Kim's age at the time of making the tape wasn't a problem – nor was there now any question of privacy violation. They had set up an agreement for adult programming with CinemaNow, an online movie site that allows filmmakers to distribute their films through streaming and downloads. They had the right to pre-sell the tape online so people could buy a digital copy in advance.

Everything went smoothly. A company source observed, 'It was one of the easiest, most successful roll-outs that Vivid ever did. It was one of those things where you always expect about four or five things to go wrong and almost nothing did.'

'It just caught fire,' observed the source at Girls Gone Wild. It was a money-printing machine. From the very beginning, Vivid was making $1.2 million a month from *Kim Kardashian Superstar* in online sales alone. Thanks to her royalty arrangement, Kim was on her way to becoming a very rich woman – a millionaire in her own right.

The media stories suggested that as part of the agreement with Kim, Vivid was going to stop distributing the tape at the end of May, which naturally signalled to potential buyers that they had better order it soon or miss out altogether. Eight years later, it is still the star attraction of the Vivid catalogue.

The tag line on the video case read '*Kim Kardashian Superstar* … she's 9½" from stardom'. It became clear within a couple of minutes that the number referred to Ray J's impressive credentials.

The film itself was a curious combination of pornography and inoffensive holiday footage. It began on the night before they set off for LAX to fly to Cabo San Lucas for her birthday. There are about five minutes of very energetic sex, with some bizarre dialogue that seems to come from a very bad porno film. Kim, face down on the pillow, comes out with such gems as: 'Baby, you are fucking me so good' and 'I want you to cum all over my face.' It's not the least romantic or loving.

Both Ray J and Kim spend the whole movie talking to the camera, which is evidently set up on a tripod. At the airport, Ray asks, 'Anything you want to tell your fans, Kim?' It's as if he is shooting a showreel of Kim, which might even have been the original point.

On the plane, he is in boisterous mood, speaking to the lens: 'Check it out. We are about to do *Girls Gone Wild in Cabo*, *Kimberly Gone Wild in Cabo*.'

Kim is unimpressed. 'Don't talk about *Girls Gone Wild in Cabo*.'

Ray J continues to lark about and taunt Kim: 'I'm saying that is what you said; you wanted to do *Girls Gone Wild* … Oh, I'm bad, we record. I'm sorry.'

Kim tells him to shut up.

During the interminable middle section in Cabo, she does her make-up, wears a bikini, sips a piña colada, swims in an infinity pool, in which she and Ray J embrace, worries that she is looking chunky in her swimsuit, goes to a fun restaurant and hangs out in a club. It's all absolutely harmless.

All the time, Ray J provides a running commentary in quite a likeable fashion, and Kim looks stunning. He specifically says that it's a 'personal private video for only our eyes to see'. The film ends a year later with some graphic sex scenes in a hotel bedroom in Santa Barbara. She complains that her boobs are saggy, but she 'puts them up real nice'. They give each other plenty of oral sex, with Kim literally having to grab Ray J with both hands. There is one priceless moment when Ray J tries to film between Kim's legs. She hides her private parts with her hand and says, 'I'm shy.'

All in all, Kim earned a great deal of money for 15 minutes of sex on film. In any case, Ray J did all the work. The Kardashians have had to face many allegations over the years that they were complicit in the sale of the tape, but they have never wavered from their version of events. Despite issuing legal proceedings against Vivid, Kim had to deny the rumours she was actively involved. She told the *New York Daily News*, 'I'm not poor; I'm not desperate. I would never attempt to sell a tape. It would humiliate me and ruin my family. I have two successful businesses, and I don't need the money.'

Some have suggested that she was just copying Paris Hilton or even that Paris herself encouraged her. Kim's former boyfriend Nick Cannon told Howard Stern that he suspected Kim of having something to do with the release of the tape, 'I still think she might have even had a part to play ...' He wasn't alone in thinking that.

Kim continues to be asked about the sex tape, year after year. She admitted to Oprah Winfrey that *Kim Kardashian Superstar* introduced her to the world, but she regretted it was in a 'negative way'.

The public interest will never go away, but the circumstances of its release into the world revealed that behind her obvious beauty and physical attributes, Kim was a powerful and strong-willed woman capable of taking control of her destiny. She spoke of it yet again in *Rolling Stone* magazine in July 2015: 'I thought about it for a long time. But when I get over something, I get over it.'

12

KEEPING UP WITH KIM

———

Kim was not the first Kardashian to follow in the footsteps of Paris Hilton. Her elder sister Kourtney was one of the stars of the 2005 E! reality show *Filthy Rich: Cattle Drive*, which was a blatant rip-off of *The Simple Life*, with a large helping of the hit film *City Slickers* thrown in. Intriguingly, it was Kim who appeared in the original trailer for the show, worried about what she was going to do without a hairdryer in the rugged Colorado landscape. In the short clip, she also asks, 'Are there showers there?'

In the end, though, Kim didn't do the show and it was Kourtney who set off with nine other offspring of wealthy parents to sample the delights of Steamboat Springs. At least she had a familiar face with her. Her best friend from school, Courtenay Semel, was also making her TV debut. She was the daughter of Terry and Jane Semel, who had hosted Kris and Bruce's marriage in 1991. She was very keen for the eldest Kardashian to join her when she was cast in the show.

One of the other young women was Brittny Gastineau, the daughter of the New York Jets footballer Mark Gastineau, whom she hadn't seen for many years. Brittny had already starred in another short-lived reality show for E! called *The Gastineau Girls*. Kourtney thought that Brittny would get on well with Kim and introduced them after the show had finished. She was right, because they became best friends.

During the eight-week series, the five boys and five girls were divided into two teams and made to compete against each other for rewards. The losers got nothing – a basic reality show tactic. Among the more interesting tasks was munching on bull's testicles and giving a cow a rectal examination, which basically meant sticking your entire arm up a cow's backside – perhaps that's what put Kim off.

The show ran from August until October 2005, but wasn't picked up for another season. That may well have been because E! had acquired *The Simple Life* after it had been dropped by Fox. There seemed little point in continuing both shows: they were too similar and Paris Hilton was a better prospect. None of the show's cast did particular well afterwards. Brittny became best known for her friendship with Kim, while Courtenay ended up in rehab and was a target for Hollywood gossips because of her many alleged gay affairs. She said stories of flings with both her friend Lindsay Lohan and Paris were false. In an interview with *Curve*, the bestselling US lesbian magazine, however, she said, 'I'd like to say that I'm kind of the Don Juan of the lesbian world.'

Kourtney hadn't seemed the most natural performer in front of the cameras, but the relative failure of *Filthy Rich: Cattle Drive* didn't put off the rest of the clan. Bruce Jenner was often on television as himself, popping up in an Olympians edition of *Weakest Link* and as a judge on *Pet Star*, the search for America's most talented pet. Most notably, he was a contestant in the US version of *I'm a Celebrity … Get Me Out of Here!* In the 2003 season, set in New South Wales, Bruce just missed being in the final three and was the seventh celebrity to be voted out of the jungle. The winner was Cris Judd, who would inadvertently cause some difficulties for Kim in her marriage that year. *I'm a Celeb* didn't fare well in the US, not helped by problems with the live link, caused by the time difference with Australia.

Brody and Brandon Jenner, the sons from Bruce's marriage to Linda Thompson, had starred in their own reality show on Fox called *The Princes of Malibu* in 2005. It wasn't a success, although the premise was quite fun. Their mother spoiled them and thought they could do no wrong, while their step-father, David Foster, wanted them to get proper jobs and behave responsibly.

Fox cancelled the show after screening only two of the six episodes that had been filmed. Linda had filed for divorce from Foster the day after the show premiered, which wasn't the best timing. Brody moved on to a coming-of-age reality series called *The Hills*. It was a follow-up to the popular *Laguna Beach: the Real Orange County* and followed a group of rich young people making their way in Los Angeles. *The Hills* did well, although it received some criticism for appearing too scripted. Perhaps what was needed in the overcrowded reality marketplace was a combination of the two shows – the drama of a family and the chaos of young (rich) lives.

E! was just one of the networks desperate to find a winning formula. They didn't realise that exactly what they were looking for was on their doorstep – well, almost – in Hidden Hills,

Calabasas. Kris Jenner has always credited the casting director Deena Katz for realising that the mad family life of the Kardashians would make great TV after she was at the house for dinner one night. Deena had worked on *Big Brother* and *Pet Star*. She arranged a professional introduction to Ryan Seacrest, the host of *American Idol*, and the president of his production company, Eliot Goldberg. They successfully pitched the idea to E! Importantly, the company brought in to oversee everything and handle the daily production of the programme was Bunim/Murray, which was responsible for two of the biggest reality successes, *The Real World* and *The Simple Life*.

One of the recurring illusions surrounding the Kardashian family is the way they never seem to have to go to the lengths most wannabes have to in order to succeed. The endless phone calls, being placed on hold, waiting in reception and rejection emails seem to pass them by.

Conspiracy theorists believe that E! commissioned the show based on Kim's new sex tape fame. The timing is very tight in terms of which came first – a true chicken or egg situation. Television experts believe that E! wouldn't have placed a bet on an untried television programme when nobody knew what the public reaction to the tape might be. What E! did successfully was harness the media interest in Kim and use it to their advantage.

Filming for the first episode began with Kris and Bruce's sixteenth wedding anniversary on 21 April 2007. The news that she was dropping legal proceedings against Vivid Entertainment was reported nine days later, on 30 April. By then, the sex tape was already a huge success. A few weeks later, television media started reporting that the star of the graphic sex tape was to feature in a new reality show.

The sex tape alone wasn't enough of a hook to promote Kim and she was still referred to as Paris Hilton's best pal and Bruce's stepdaughter. However, the press material did say that the new series would focus on her family life and pointed out that she had nine brothers and sisters in total.

This didn't give entirely the right impression, as the older Jenner children had very little to do with their father during his marriage to Kris. His eldest son, Burt, for instance, told *Vanity Fair* that he didn't remember seeing his father more than twice a year for roughly a decade. Brandon went through periods of two or three years of not hearing from his dad. When the Northridge earthquake hit the Los Angeles area in January 1994, Brandon, then 12, told his mother that Bruce had called to check they were all right. She was delighted that he had rung, until Brandon confessed, 'Mom, I'm just kidding.' While he was undoubtedly a caring father to Kendall and Kylie, he didn't attend the high school graduations of his older children. He said he wasn't invited, while they maintain that he was.

There was a chasm in the family no matter whose recollection is correct. A reality show about all things Kardashian was hardly likely to improve that. The split between the two branches of Bruce's family wouldn't sit well in a show that was all about 'family' and the bond that existed between them whatever was going on in their crazy world.

The family theme would develop as the series progressed. For the moment, they needed Kim's new-found notoriety to perk up interest in the show. In the months leading up to the autumn premiere, it was important to keep Kim in the public eye. She made it onto a list of the top ten bottoms in Hollywood, but at position number eight was well behind the winner, Jennifer Lopez, and the runner-up, Beyoncé.

She also had to refute a rumour that among the out-takes of her tape with Ray J was one in which she received what is known in the sex trade as a golden shower. 'I'm not knocking anyone else,' she said, 'but I've never personally participated in that. I think it's degrading.'

The publicity leading up to the launch seemed to involve either sex or Kim's bottom. She had to counter allegations that hers had been surgically enhanced since the sex tape days. Finally, if you had missed the sex tape and the bountiful back-side, there was still time for it to be announced that Kim was going to be on the cover of the December issue of *Playboy* in a 12-page picture spread personally chosen by Hugh Hefner.

Unsurprisingly, the first-ever episode of *Keeping Up with the Kardashians*, which was broadcast on 14 October 2007, focused heavily on Kim and her rear in particular. The opening scene is a picture of her from behind, leaning over to get something out of the fridge. Her ass looks enormous, certainly several sizes bigger than when she was filmed with Ray J.

Kris says in an aside to the family, 'I think she has a little junk in the trunk.' That gives rise to some banter and a half-hearted 'I hate you all' from Kim. It is Kim who addresses the audience, 'Welcome to my family. I am Kim Kardashian ...' Kris introduces herself as Kim's manager, not everyone's.

For the opening credits, Kim is late for the family shot and then arrives wearing a knockout red dress that completely overshadows the others. In the episode, Kim has been asked to appear on *The Tyra Banks Show* in New York and her mother tells her she will be asked about the sex tape. Kris, speaking directly to the camera, says, 'As her mother I wanted to kill her, but as her manager I knew I had a job to do and I really wanted her to move past it.'

Kim explains, 'That was with my boyfriend of three years and whatever we did in our private time was our private time and never once did we think it was going to get out.'

In an amusing scene, Kourtney pretends to be Tyra and asks her why she did it. Kim replies, 'Because I was horny and I felt like it.' She goes off to record the show in New York, taking her friend Brittny Gastineau along for moral support. Disappointingly, we never see any footage of Kim's first TV interview.

We are introduced to the other members of the family, although only fleetingly to the son, Robert. Much more airtime is given to Kourtney's handsome and tanned boyfriend, Scott Disick, whom Kris doesn't trust.

The critical response to the show tended to be more negative than positive. The reviewer in the *New York Times* said, '*Keeping Up with the Kardashians* is, as the title suggests, a window into a family – a family that seems to understand itself only in terms of its collective opportunism.' She added that the show was about 'some desperate women climbing to the margins of fame.' *Daily Variety* online observed, 'Once you get past Kim's prominently displayed assets, there's not much of a show here, and no discernible premise.'

The rest of the series relied heavily on the physical attributes of the female cast. In the second episode, Kris hires a nanny to help at the house and look after Kendall, 11, and

Kylie, aged 10. She turns out to be a stunning blonde and completely inappropriate. The gag of the episode is that Kris hasn't met her and doesn't know how unsuitable she is. Bruce, settling into his role as the long-suffering dad, quickly realises that when he sees her sunbathing topless. When Kris does finally meet her, she quickly shows her the door in a plot involving some stolen jewellery. The nanny was quite obviously an actress hired for the occasion and not, as Kris said in the show, hired from a 'reputable agency'.

She was, in fact, Bree Olson, then an up-and-coming porn star, who would later become one of the best known and most applauded in the business. In 2006 alone, she had made 16 films, including *Young As They Cum 21* and *Cock Craving Cuties*. In 2007, she made 75, and *Keeping Up with the Kardashians*.

Casting directors often turn to actresses in the porn world when they want to find someone to play a super-sexy vixen completely at ease with taking off her clothes. In this episode, Bree, more a cute blonde than a siren figure, unselfconsciously removes her top at the pool.

Bree was hired for one day and spent 15 hours being filmed at the house. In the end, her footage amounted to little more than five minutes. This is the reality of the reality. The cameras are on the Kardashians all the time to see how they react to a situation that is often manufactured. Khloé was particularly outspoken in this instance, declaring on the phone to Kris, 'Mom, there is a whore watching your children.'

Bree, who is an intelligent and articulate young woman, didn't mind. She laughed, 'I'm surprised it wasn't worse.' It was the reaction she was hired to generate. The producers told

Bree exactly what to do, but the family was unscripted and allowed to roam free. She was instructed to help the youngsters with their homework, but to do a really bad job at it. She was also told to go into Kris's closet and try on her jewellery.

The youngest members of the cast, Kendall and Kylie, seemed the most unaffected by what was going on around them and shrugged off the cameras. When filming stopped, they went on their computer to show Bree a puppy they were excited about getting. When the producers sent Bree down to the pool to sunbathe, the girls followed and made her play poolball for an hour.

Bree enjoyed her day and was happy to be part of it. Each of the cast gave her a hug goodbye. 'They were super nice,' she said. In 2011, Bree, who has given up the porn business, achieved headlines as one of actor Charlie Sheen's girlfriends, or 'goddesses' as he liked to call them.

The third episode indirectly involved more porn, when the girls were hired for a photo shoot to model a new swimsuit range for Girls Gone Wild – not traditionally what the franchise was known for. Joe Francis had apparently phoned Kris to hire the girls and fly them down to his luxurious private estate, Casa Aramita, in Punta Mita, Mexico. He couldn't appear himself, because he was in jail in Florida. A company insider recalled, 'We decided it would be great publicity for both sides if the Kardashians were involved. We were going to fly a designer, Ashley Paige, to Mexico and the girls were going to try on the bathing suits and contribute, as if they had helped create them, and the E! cameras would follow along. It would all culminate with a billboard on Sunset Boulevard of the Kardashians in bathing suits. It was completely contrived.'

The billboard did appear, but the swimwear line was very short-lived. Buyers began to cancel orders when it became common knowledge that Joe was in jail. It did provide some lovely television moments, as Bruce had to pretend to be outraged and follow them to the location. Again, the plot line was an excuse to put Kim and her sisters in skimpy clothing. Kris and her daughters all agreed that it was 'classy'.

In the fourth episode, *Playboy* rang up to ask Kim to appear on the cover. The sex tape was forgotten as Kim hesitated about whether to do it or not, although there wouldn't have been much of a plot if she hadn't. Again, it was deemed 'classy'. Kim explained, 'It was something that I felt really nervous about doing at first … It's not a nude photo shoot by any stretch. It is not as revealing as some people might want. I keep it classy and covered up. I do bare my whole butt. And a little bit of my chest. But that's it.'

Kim looked sensational for the shoot. Her modesty was protected by a strategically placed large string of beads. When the issue came out, she was wearing a lovely red swimsuit on the cover. The headline wasn't at all subtle, though, and declared: 'Hollywood's New Sex Star Kim Kardashian Takes It All Off'.

The strategy of promoting Kim in these first few episodes worked. E! said the programme had already reached 13 million viewers. Young women, aged 18 to 34, were hooked on the show. The vice-president of the television company who was in charge of series development, Lisa Berger, enthused, 'The buzz around the series is huge.' After just a month on air, *Keeping Up with the Kardashians* was renewed for a second season.

Kim did well in another poll in 2007. In December, the *New York Daily News* published a list of the 'Top 50 Dumbest People in Hollywood'. Lindsay Lohan placed first and Kim was second. She would soon be proving everybody completely wrong.

13

DANCING PRINCESS

For a man who could sprint 50 metres up a football field in little more than 5 seconds, Reggie Bush was slow out of the blocks with Kim. She couldn't believe that the star running back with the New Orleans Saints didn't ask for her number when they met at the 2006 ESPY sports awards.

In July, she accompanied Bruce Jenner for the evening at the Kodak Theatre in Hollywood. She was definitely interested when she saw the handsome, well-muscled young man sitting with Matt Leinart. Kim knew Matt well, because he was dating Paris Hilton, and he was happy to introduce her to Reggie, who had been his college teammate at her father's old alma mater, USC. Kim recalled that first meeting: 'My first impression of Reggie was "This guy is so quiet. Why is he not taking my number?" Matt tried to set us up, but it took a while.'

It took months. Reggie was only 21, whereas Kim was a 25-year-old divorcee. Despite already being a millionaire, he might have been overawed by her. Eventually they agreed to a date, but it wasn't the romantic experience she was hoping for. They arranged to meet at a car wash, before heading off for a meal at Chipotle Mexican Grill on Wilshire Boulevard.

After their relationship eventually went public in the spring of 2007, they quickly became one of the top celebrity couples in Los Angeles. Reggie maintained a bachelor apartment in Beverly Hills, where Kim was now living. She had bought a condo in South Clark Drive. So when *Keeping Up with the Kardashians* began, Kim was no longer in Calabasas, preferring to be nearer her friends, even though it meant a dull drive along the freeway to get to work.

Reggie had had a modest upbringing in the San Diego area. His mother was a deputy sheriff at a correctional centre and his stepfather was a security guard at a local high school. His biological father, Reginald Alfred Bush, Sr, had split from his mother before Reggie was born and had very little to do with him growing up.

Reggie was arguably the USC Trojans' best-known player since O. J. Simpson. In 2005, he too won the Heisman Trophy and a host of other awards, but became a controversial figure following allegations that he and his family received improper benefits while he was an amateur player at the university. He returned the Heisman voluntarily in 2012 and sanctions were imposed on USC by the NCAA, the National Collegiate Athletic Association. Robert Kardashian would have been horrified.

Those off-field problems didn't stop Reggie from becoming one of the richest young sportsmen in the country after he signed with the New Orleans Saints as a top NFL draft pick. He was a good role model for Kim in that he signed endorsement deals with Pepsi, Adidas, Pizza Hut, Subway and

General Motors – making an estimated $5 million. In a three-year period with the Saints, 2007–2010, he earned a reported $27.5 million for starting 27 games. That was close to $1 million every time he put his helmet on. *Forbes* magazine didn't consider him value for money and included him in their list of the NFL's biggest salary flops.

The problem for Kim and Reggie as their relationship developed was the most common one faced by celebrity couples: how to survive long absences brought about by conflicting schedules. Kim was tied to *Keeping Up with the Kardashians* and he was living in New Orleans for six months of the year.

She did her best to fly in regularly, and particularly enjoyed their domestic time together, when they played board games or lay in bed watching television. Kim isn't a woman who wants to dress up and look fabulous all the time. She was content just to relax with her boyfriend. She would have been quite happy to have stayed at home and raised a family with her first husband and that remained an aspiration.

Kim, it seemed, has a nurturing spirit. Even with Ray J, when they weren't having sex, she kept a clean and tidy house and made sure his clothes were immaculate. She was impressed with Reggie's fashion sense, but that didn't stop her from taking him shopping and picking out what he should wear. Being a stylist was what she did best.

Kim once made the plaintive observation that she had too often been cheated on and had her heart broken. She wasn't including Reggie in that list and was looking forward to settling down with him. When Tyra Banks asked her, in a 2008 interview, if she would marry Reggie if he asked her tomorrow, she replied without hesitation, 'Of course I would … We have such a good relationship. He gets along with everyone in my family.' She was in love.

She did her best to be the dutiful WAG to her high-profile boyfriend, but admitted, 'I'm not really a sports girl. But I sit with all the wives and they know everything and I don't, so they are teaching me … I don't really watch if he's not playing. I'm not that big of a football fan yet.'

The trade-off for Kim taking an interest in football was that Reggie had to appear in her reality show. He wasn't especially keen on having the cameras follow him around, but he did it because it was important to Kim. He had been on television before, playing himself in the series *The Reggie Bush Project*, in which his biggest fan sets off on a mission to meet his idol.

Inevitably, Reggie was asked about the sex tape. He was philosophical: 'We don't talk about it, and we don't think about it. With Kim, and with anybody in life, it's not my place to judge, no matter what they've done – good, bad or indifferent.'

The couple seemed like the perfect fit when they were out together, usually smiling and holding hands. The media decided that only the Beckhams generated more star power as a sporting/celebrity couple. This interest meant that Kim had to counter the usual pregnancy and wedding rumours: 'I am not pregnant. I am definitely going to wait until I am married before I get pregnant. Marriage is soon, but I would say five years away. I have to get engaged first. I would say in about a year. You know, we are taking our time and he's young and I don't want to rush into anything.'

* * *

Kim was keen to embrace every new opportunity that came about because of her television exposure. It is a tried and trusted route for reality stars – one season they are on *The X Factor* and the next on *I'm a Celebrity*; they appear in *Celebrity Big Brother* and then try *Celebrity MasterChef*; a good run in *Strictly Come Dancing* leads to a part in a West End musical. One opportunity provides a window for another.

Kim, encouraged by her mother, was determined to exploit her status as the star of *Keeping Up with the Kardashians*. The first thing she wanted to try was acting. As she made clear, it wasn't a prospect she relished: 'I promised myself that this year I would do things that are kind of outside of my comfort zone.'

She was true to her word when she appeared in a bizarre video for the Fall Out Boy single 'Thnks fr th Mmrs', taken from their number one US album *Infinity on High*. Understandably, after the sex tape, she had received plenty of offers to play the hot girl riding in a car with a cool singer. She turned them all down, but her interest was piqued by the rock band's storyline: it was about the making of a video in which every character other than Kim and the band was played by a chimpanzee.

She was very nervous about performing her scenes. The closest she had got to an ape previously was at Neverland and now she had to act with a whole gang of them. It didn't help when their trainer told her not to look them in the eye or call them by name. She sat alongside them and was told not to move, which was 'basically freaking her out'. 'It was really scary because they are so strong and you don't know what they are going to do.'

In the video, Kim was the love interest of the band's resident heart-throb, bassist and songwriter, Pete Wentz. She already knew Pete, which made filming a little easier, but she had never met the chimpanzee who was playing the director. She explained, 'We had to have a make-out scene and the director, played by the chimp, kept on saying that Pete was doing it wrong. He tried to step in and show him how to kiss me. He touches me and Pete gets angry and runs off.' Kim, looking ravishing in a Marilyn Monroe-style frock, follows him to the dressing room, where they have a proper kiss, which she found almost as nerve-racking as the chimp's.

The video was different and refreshing, though it was hardly likely to further her ambition of starring in a James Bond movie. Kim wanted to film a love scene with Daniel Craig. As she pictured it: 'I would be drowning, wearing a bikini with a gun in a sachet, and he would dive in and get me.' She evidently saw herself as a mixture of Ursula Andress and Halle Berry.

Kim didn't get Bond, but she did make her first film, which, with supreme irony, was called *Disaster Movie*. It came fourteenth in an *Empire* online poll of the 50 worst films ever. Kim auditioned and was cast as Lisa Taylor, one of the main female roles, by the writer/director partnership of Jason Friedberg and Aaron Seltzer, who were responsible for other parodies, including *Date Movie* and *Meet the Spartans*.

The basic plot was that a number of reality television stars, including Kim, play characters who, while trying to deal with an end-of-the-world meteor strike, keep bumping into characters from other films, as in 'Look, it's Indiana Jones'. The highlight for male Kim fans was a spurious wrestling match with Carmen Electra, the former star of *Baywatch*, who was also a cover girl for *Playboy*. Kim's character survived the busty bout, but is subsequently killed when she is hit by an asteroid, which looked suspiciously like an enormous cheese boulder, falling unexpectedly out of the sky. The scene is actually very funny.

The reviews were poor. Nobody seemed to get the joke. The *Observer* reviewer said: 'it would be the Worst Movie Ever Made were it actually a movie at all.' He thought there wasn't a single laugh in it. The *Independent* commented, '*Disaster Movie* isn't so much a film as an insult to moviegoers everywhere.' The *New York Times* said the film had a shelf-life of five minutes, 'which may be longer than it took with most of its gags.' The film, which cost $20 million to make, grossed an estimated $31.7 million worldwide, so it wasn't a complete box-office flop, though obviously a disappointment.

Kim received her first award nomination – not for an Oscar but a Razzie for Worst Supporting Actress in 2008. She took it with good humour: 'There is steep competition in my "worst supporting actress" category, I have to admit, including my fantastic co-star Carmen Electra (you go, girl!).' In the end, the award went to Paris Hilton for *Repo! The Genetic Opera*.

Undaunted by the failure of her acting debut, Kim moved on to dancing. Family friend Deena Katz was now the senior talent producer on *Dancing with the Stars* and she picked Kim for the new series. Initially she wasn't too keen, but it seemed a great opportunity to be showcased on one of the big networks. At the time, the ABC blockbuster was the top-rated show on American television, pulling in more than 15 million viewers. *Keeping Up with the Kardashians* was the most popular on E! with just 1.6 million.

Kim and her reality series were set to receive many weeks of extra publicity. The challenge confronting her was that she had never really danced before and wasn't a natural. She wasn't one of those stage school graduates who found remembering their dance steps easy. Kim had never had lessons and had to practise day and night so she wouldn't embarrass herself. On the very first show, she revealed her problem was that she had terrible balance. It couldn't have helped wearing such high heels. She observed, 'Elegance and clumsiness don't mix. It isn't easy for me.'

She did gain some advantage, however, by being paired with the reigning professional champion, Mark Ballas. Their opening dance was a foxtrot to the *Pink Panther* theme. It was perhaps not the best choice of number, as it is normally associated with the bumbling Inspector Clouseau rather than anything smooth and sexy. She looked surprisingly slim in an elegant purple dress, with her hair in a 1920s Coco Chanel bob. She had worn it in a similar style at her eighth-grade graduation, when she was 13. The leading fashion commentator Alison Jane Reid said, 'I really like Kim in retro mode. Her hair in a bob accentuates her cheekbones and amazing doe eyes. The dress is classic showgirl – very elegant, with a liberal sprinkling of sequins and side splits, so she can show off her fabulous pins.'

To Kim's relief, she kept her feet and made few errors. The audience was cheering afterwards, especially Bruce and Kris. The judges were not so enthusiastic. Len Goodman thought the dance cold and said there was no chemistry between her and Mark. Bruno Tonioli told her, 'You have to make it more available', and that she needed to bring the audience with her. The more charitable Carrie Ann Inaba said she needed to move her neck more, because keeping it so still was preventing eye contact. She scored 19 points out of 30, which was enough to keep her in for another night.

The next evening, she and Mark were the last couple to dance the mambo. She admitted that everyone was going to expect her to be sexy, but that wasn't really her, particularly where her shapely rear was concerned. 'Everyone thinks I know how to shake my butt and I really don't!' Kim looked to be concentrating so hard that she forgot to feel the music. She found it difficult to find a rhythm to 'Baby Got Back' by Sir Mix-a-Lot. Mark danced frenetically to compensate for Kim's uneasiness, but the judges liked it even less than the foxtrot.

She needed to improve the following week for the rumba. Her friend Robin Antin, the choreographer of Pussycat Dolls, was brought in to try and cajole her to move more sexily. Once more, she looked fabulous in a white dress that highlighted her curves, but the judges were unimpressed. Bruno unkindly said she was colder and more distant than Siberia. Both *Dancing with the Stars* and the UK equivalent, *Strictly Come Dancing*, are more about forging a connection with the audience than the ability to look sensational in a frock. It's not just about trying hard, but showing improvement. Kim wasn't doing that, and the viewers voted her out.

She was the third contestant to be eliminated, but in real terms had lasted only one week on the show – a huge disappointment. It was still a surprise, because she came across as genuinely nice and modest. She had the natural charm of a girl enjoying her prom night. The producers must have been seething, because she brought so much glamour and interest to the show. Afterwards, she was gracious: 'Every dance was a huge accomplishment for me, and I did the best I could.'

One of the show's hosts, Samantha Harris, said, 'Everyone told me that getting to know her outside of the tabloids and the reality show has been so refreshing, since Kim is such a sweetheart. I feel the same way.' Mark also said she was a great girl, while observing that 'dancing was not her thing'. Her family obviously rallied round, but the best comment came from Bruce: 'She had a lot of guts to say yes to do this show with no dance background at all. Success is not measured by heights attained, but by obstacles overcome.'

After her disappointing debuts as an actor and a dancer, it seemed inevitable that Kim would try her hand at singing. Her first husband, Damon Thomas, had frequently told his beautiful wife that she should give it a go, and he wasn't the only record producer keen for her to make a disc. She didn't rush into anything, but waited for what she hoped would be the right project.

One way for the Kardashians to release information is for certain websites to carry a rumour. In this case, TMZ, one of the preferred outlets, started the whisper in the autumn of 2010 that she was in the studio working with the superstar producer known as The-Dream (Terius Youngdell Nash). He had co-written two of the biggest hits of recent years, 'Umbrella' by Rihanna and the Grammy-winning Beyoncé track 'Single Ladies (Put a Ring on It)'. An anonymous insider helpfully said that Kim had a really good voice.

At first, the stories suggested that she was recording an album. They gained credibility when Kanye West was seen entering the building in Culver City, where they were shooting the video for the first single. Nobody knew the title yet, but apparently it was written by The-Dream. The acclaimed director Hype Williams was brought in to oversee the filming.

Hype had worked closely with Kim before. He had shot the photograph for her 2007 *Playboy* cover and had made her look sensational. He also worked closely with Kanye West, winning a BET (Black Entertainment Television) Video Director of the Year Award for 'Gold Digger'. He made so many of the rap artist's videos, they were practically a team. He was also responsible for the videos of a who's who of modern pop culture, including Jay Z, Babyface, Nicki Minaj, Beyoncé and John Legend.

Kim couldn't have had three bigger hitters on her team than The-Dream, Kanye West and Hype Williams. As a bonus, the recording adventure was filmed for her spin-off reality series *Kourtney and Kim Take New York*. Kim had trouble with her vocals and at one point had to leave the studio to compose herself. The resulting single 'Jam (Turn It Up)' was played on the radio for the first time during Ryan Seacrest's morning show on KIIS FM, which was practically keeping it in the family.

The reviews were uninspiring. The *Liverpool Echo* critic wrote, 'I'm her biggest fan, but her new song is so cheesy! I think she should stick to what she knows best.' The *New York Daily News* was the most unpleasant, saying that Kim was the worst singer ever to come out of a reality series. The reviewer called 'Jam (Turn It Up)' a 'dead-brained piece of generic dance music, without a single distinguishing feature.' He wasn't any kinder about her singing, which he thought 'a bit of breathing that's been auto-tuned into something vaguely approximating a vocal.'

The track was nothing like as bad as that. The overall sound came across as retro, harking back to the catchy Scandinavian sounds of the late nineties chart band Aqua. Sales weren't strong enough for the song to reach even the lower echelons of the charts in the US, with only 14,000 downloads in its first week on iTunes.

For some reason, the video was never released. Kim posted some stills. Six months later, some footage did show up of Kim in a white top and hot pink shorts, writhing around suggestively. The implication was that the video was completed with a view to being released only if the song performed well.

Kim quickly distanced herself from the project, maintaining that there was no record deal and there would be no album. Both Kourtney and Khloé said the video was for their sister's eyes only, which made it sound like it was a sex tape. The celebrity gossip columnist Perez Hilton pointed out sarcastically that she had hired Hype Williams, practically the biggest name in the business, to produce a video just for private use.

For once, Kim's sense of humour failed her. Several years later, in 2014, she called the song a fun experience, but something she shouldn't have done. She confessed, 'What gave me the right to think I could be a singer? Like, I don't have a good voice.'

Despite her hopes for the future, her relationship with Reggie Bush had foundered. She had been so positive about it. They first admitted to problems in the summer of 2009, and put them down to spending too much time apart. Kim couldn't give up her life and career in Los Angeles, where *Keeping Up with the Kardashians* was filmed: 'It's not going to be much of a show if I'm in New Orleans separated from my family.' For his part, Reggie seemed unable to make the commitment to the future that Kim was looking for.

They managed to rekindle the romance later that year, and Kim was thrilled when the Saints won the Super Bowl in February 2010. The E! cameras filmed her running on to the pitch to give her man a kiss of congratulations. That made it seem a little staged, especially as her mother was in attendance.

By the end of March, it was all over for the second time. She had been genuinely fond of Reggie, but he was no longer a priority in her life. She was determined to work even harder and make the most of her chance of lasting fame.

14

DATING HER WORK

Kim was getting a reputation for being a workaholic. She was completely driven to make her business a success. She observed, 'You have to stay committed. Some people start and stop, or get a bit lazy. Every year my mom and I write out a goal sheet.' Her elder sister Kourtney commented, 'She's dating her work.'

When *Keeping Up with the Kardashians* began, only Kris took it as seriously as Kim did. Kim was desperate for it to do well, while her sisters viewed themselves as store owners dabbling in television. They would fool around when the 'boss', as they called Kim, wasn't in the room. They would be jumping on the sofas and pushing each other about like a pair of playful puppies.

Kim and her mother were busy forging a formidable partnership. They were both proving to be smart businesswomen. It would have been lovely for Kim to have been nominated for an Oscar instead of a Golden Raspberry, or to have won *Dancing with the Stars*, but neither was meant to be. The consolation was that she was keeping herself in the conversation.

She was being talked about at water coolers, even when she failed at something.

It was as if Kim stood in front of a mirror and decided how best to utilise every bit of herself from top to bottom and head to toe. She would take every opportunity that came her way and make sure she was personally involved and not just a celebrity robot. An endorsement for ShoeDazzle, another for Famous Cupcakes and a fitness DVD were just the start of her empire building.

As her fame grew, so did her confidence and, more and more, she became her own woman. She embraced social media and was rumoured to be paid as much as $10,000 for announcing on Twitter that she liked a particular salad. She told her then 2.7 million followers at the start of 2010: 'The Carl's Jr. grilled chicken salads came out yesterday! I'm on my way to Carl's Jr. for lunch now … Have you tried them yet?'

The parent company behind the campaign, CKE Restaurants, said, 'Kim is an absolute Internet sensation and she has a vast audience that is already following her online. Her site is heavily trafficked as well.' They wanted to target 'young, hungry guys and gals' – exactly the people who followed her online and on the show. She even hosted 'The Ultimate Salad Lunch Date', in which she interacted with fans, while nibbling on a cranberry, apple and walnut grilled chicken salad in 2009.

This was one minor example of Kim's thoroughness. This was treating business responsibly – a lesson first learned from her father and then from her energetic, driven mother. It wasn't rocket science, but it worked. Kim's campaign was deemed more successful than all the company's previous celebrity campaigns put together, including 1.8 million views for a 30-second commercial on YouTube and a further 2.1 million views for all the other Kim-related salad videos. The number following her on Twitter almost doubled that year to more than 5 million – a magnet for endorsement deals.

Brad Haley, an executive vice-president with Carl's Jr, was impressed: 'Kim Kardashian has been an absolute joy to work with and her genuine charm, charisma, beauty and brains have endeared her to a huge base of fans.' The food chain initially wanted her to front a campaign for a burger, but found that she really wasn't good at eating burgers. She was, in any case, on a low-carb diet. It was lucky that they had a new salad option on the menu at the right time.

While the ink was drying on one contract, another was being prepared for signature. Kim became the face of FusionBeauty, the international skincare brand. All three sisters signed a retail deal for their own fashion line with the bebe chain. They did the same for a range of outfits for Beach Bunny Swimwear and began a beauty line with a self-tanning gel called Glamour Tan.

In February 2010, Kim brought out her own perfume called Kim Kardashian, the 'voluptuous new fragrance'. It had always been an ambition to have her name on a fragrance. Her dad would always bring her a bottle of perfume when he returned from a trip away. He gave her the first-ever scent she used, Tribu by Benetton, after a visit to New York. They don't make it any more, but she kept the distinctive yellow bottle, with the garish red top, safe in her dressing room because it reminded her of him.

She moved on from Tribu to Angel by Thierry Mugler. The only problem with that was her father would invariably buy a bottle for whichever girlfriend he had at the time. When he broke up with any of them, Kim, being loyal to her dad, would hate the women and the scent would remind her of them. She had to give up wearing it. Her own fragrance had a hint of gardenia in it, her father's favourite smell. No sooner had the first Kim Kardashian fragrance hit the shops than she was working with her team to produce a second, called Gold.

In August, she teamed up with Loren Ridinger to design a luxury range of earrings for a new jewellery line, the Kim Kollection. Then she released a line of signature watches. It was relentless. She was paid huge sums just for turning up at a club – a $20,000 fee soon grew to $100,000, a reflection of the power of television and her growing popularity.

The branding philosophy of the Kardashians was simple: first, extend your brand as far as you can and always react to situations – if you put on weight, land a deal to promote diet supplement pills; secondly, be as visible and share as much as possible – the public are as interested in the bad times as the good; thirdly, use Facebook, Twitter, Instagram and any other online method you can think of to connect with the public.

In 2010, there were more online searches for Kim Kardashian than for Barack Obama or Justin Bieber. At the end of the year, she topped a list of the highest-earning reality TV stars, with an estimated $6 million. Khloé and Kourtney were seventh and eighth with $2.5 million. Kris Jenner didn't make the list but, if her 20 per cent fee for being their manager were taken into account, it would have earned her nearly $3.7 million.

Kim's earnings had grown so fast that it was time to look for a new home. She wanted to stay in Beverly Hills to be close to her friends and favourite haunts. She found a Tuscan-style villa for $4.8 million in a quiet cul de sac off Mulholland Drive. Her new mansion had five bedrooms, four bathrooms, a Regal pool and Jacuzzi, media room and fireplaces outside for cool winter evenings. The garden boasted an immaculate lawn and a waterfall.

The original idea was that she would move into it with Reggie, but that didn't work out, so she was a single girl in a luxurious mansion. It was more private than her lovely condominium in South Clark Drive, which she put on the market for a little over $1 million. She liked the high walls and security gates that kept the paparazzi at bay until she was ready to greet them with a smile and pose for a picture.

She was working so hard, there seemed to be little time for her to enjoy her new home. Certainly, since *Keeping Up with the Kardashians* began, she appeared to have the least exciting private life of the four Kardashian siblings.

She wasn't the first to have a child. That honour belonged to her elder sister Kourtney. At 5ft 0in, Kourtney is the smallest Kardashian and, by reputation, the most intelligent – at least academically. In the first episode of *Keeping Up with the Kardashians*, we were introduced to the relationship between her and boyfriend Scott Disick, which has been a constant in the programme ever since.

Scott, who is three years younger than Kourtney, proved to be an asset to the show, because he was always antagonising Kris or Khloé and seemed to be on the verge of splitting with Kourtney or marrying her. He is a man of mystery in that nobody seems to know what he actually does for a living.

He didn't grow up as one of the Beverly Hills set, although his parents, Jeff and Bonnie, were well-off residents of Eastport, Long Island. The family money came from the real estate business of attorney David Disick, who was Jeff's father. Scott's only claim to fame as a teenager was as a young male model for the covers of a series of adolescent romance novels. He is pictured as a handsome young man gazing meaningfully into the distance in poses designed to make teen girls swoon. The grown-up Scott was a bit of a bad boy – perfect for a show dominated by women.

The relationship between Kourtney and Scott, who has a reputation as a man who enjoys a party, has never been one of cosy, happy families. They split up for the first time in 2009, during which time he allegedly saw other people, but they got back together when she discovered she was pregnant.

Scott and Kourtney had their first child, Mason Dash Disick, on 14 December 2009. His arrival at the Cedars-Sinai Medical Center on Beverly Boulevard – hospital to the stars – was shown on an episode of *Keeping Up with the Kardashians*. At the end of the delivery, Kourtney leaned forward, carefully pulled the baby out and laid him on her stomach. The birth was actually filmed by Scott, using a video camera, and the footage was handed over to the technicians at E! to make it suitable for broadcast.

Scott appeared to have anger issues during the filming of one of the show's spin-offs, *Kourtney and Khloé Take Miami*, in which he punched a wall mirror during a drunken argument. Once more, they split amid rumours that Scott had an alcohol

ABOVE: Kim's lifelong best friend Allison Azoff, pictured on her left, is not often photographed and ignores the celebrity world. She made a rare outing to support Kim at her bachelorette dinner at TAO in Las Vegas.

ABOVE: Kim turned out to be badly matched with second husband Kris Humphries, who had a height advantage of 18 inches. Even with six-inch heels she still had another foot to go.

RIGHT: Kim and Kris's wedding in Montecito, California, was a dazzling affair. Guests could wear white or black. Her Mother chose white while her stepfather opted for an elegant black tuxedo.

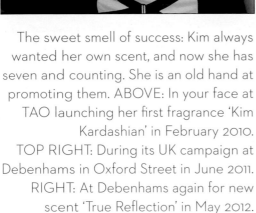

The sweet smell of success: Kim always wanted her own scent, and now she has seven and counting. She is an old hand at promoting them. ABOVE: In your face at TAO launching her first fragrance 'Kim Kardashian' in February 2010. TOP RIGHT: During its UK campaign at Debenhams in Oxford Street in June 2011. RIGHT: At Debenhams again for new scent 'True Reflection' in May 2012.

Most of the cast of *Keeping Up with the Kardashians* were on hand to launch the suitably named Kardashian Khaos at the Mirage Hotel in Las Vegas in 2011. The boutique was not a success and closed after three years.

Keeping up with the Jenners: A pregnant Kim joins her other family – Brandon, Brody, Bruce and Brandon's wife Leah – at the 2013 release party for *Cronies*, the first EP from indie group Brandon & Leah.

TOP LEFT: Kanye West is a huge influence on Kim's fashion choices. Her dress for the Met Ball in 2013 was described as a 'pair of curtains'.

TOP RIGHT: Kim and Kanye reworked her designer outfit at home for the GQ Men of the Year Awards. Kanye suggested the latex top.

LEFT: The monochrome look they both love was a dazzling success when Kim wore gold, including a new hair colour, to the *Hollywood Reporter* Women in Entertainment breakfast.

Sometimes being a celebrity can be great: Laughing in the front row at the
BET Awards in Los Angeles with Kanye, Jay Z and his wife Beyoncé
(although she doesn't seem to be in on the joke).

But sometimes it can be horrid: Surrounded and almost crushed by the paparazzi,
selfie-seekers with their smartphones, security personnel or just people who want
to gawp at the star in Paris.

LEFT: Kanye called Kim a natural mother. Here she shares a tender moment with baby daughter North at the Givenchy Show, Paris, in September 2014.

BELOW: In a relaxed mood after leaving the Valentino Haute Couture Show at the Hôtel Salomon de Rothschild in July 2012.

Kim and Kanye love Paris and, in particular, the Fashion Weeks, which they always attend if they can. Here, unselfconsciously, they share a private moment at the Balmain Show in March 2015.

Caitlyn Jenner said Kim had been 'by far the most accepting' about his gender transition. They take a walk in October 2014 before her stepfather told the world.

Kim was in the audience when Caitlyn made an inspirational speech as she accepted the Arthur Ashe Award for Courage at the ESPY Awards in Los Angeles in July 2015.

Kim showed her serious side when she paid her first visit to Armenia in April 2015 and laid red tulips at the Genocide Memorial in the capital, Yerevan.

The following month, more frivolously, she turned heads at the 2015 Met Ball in New York in a Roberto Cavalli gown – truly, a bird of paradise.

problem. He attended therapy, and they were reunited. He told Ryan Seacrest in an interview, 'I had to take a look at where my life is going – or where it was going to go if I kept acting the way I was.'

Kourtney turned out to be a natural mother, which surprised her family, who had always cast Kim in that role. Kourtney had seemed the sister least bothered about having children. Instead, she doted on her son, who was soon crawling around happily while the cameras kept running in the reality house. She became very protective of her boy, politely but firmly refusing all requests from fans who wanted to take a selfie with the newest member of the Kardashian clan.

She returned to work, helping to run DASH, which had now expanded with branches in Miami and New York. It gave the producers at E! the excuse to devise the spin-off series featuring Kourtney.

Kim also wasn't the first of the sisters to say 'I do' on the show. Khloé married NBA basketball player Lamar Odom, after knowing him for just a month.

Khloé had always seemed the most volatile and unpredictable of the three sisters. She had gone her own way as a teenager; she was home schooled and never had a steady boyfriend. Disappointed to receive a used car for her sixteenth birthday, she decided her mother wouldn't miss her Range Rover if she took it for a joyride with some friends. She dropped it off at a valet stand while she went to a party and returned to find it in flames: 'My friends and I saw this car on fire and we were like, "Whoa, that person is screwed!" And then I was like, "Fuck, that's my car!"'

Khloé was hurt in a serious car accident when she was 16. Apparently, she was thrown through the windscreen. As a result of her injuries, she suffers from short-term memory loss. She was knocked unconscious and suffered damage to her knees that required three operations to correct.

She was unimpressed when she met 6ft 10in Lamar, a star player with the LA Lakers, at a welcoming party for the team's new signing, Ron Artest, one of the most famous players of the era. Khloé was there with her younger brother Rob and was irritated by a man she didn't know staring at her.

In a loud voice, she declared, 'You're so rude. You're staring at me.'

Rob tried to keep her quiet. 'Please be nice,' he said. 'That's Lamar Odom. He's like the best basketball player.'

She recalled, 'I did not like Lamar. I hated him.' She thought him a typical and annoying basketball player.

A week later, she had clearly changed her mind. The pair were spotted laughing and joking over dinner at STK Los Angeles. Khloé invited him to meet Kris and Bruce at their home in Calabasas. They became engaged 26 days after they met.

Lamar's upbringing couldn't have been more different than the Kardashian children's. His father, Joe Odom, was a heroin addict. His mother, Cathy Mercer, a prison officer at the Rikers Island Correctional Facility, was left to bring him up as a single parent. They lived in the notorious South Jamaica area of Queens, New York. The neighbourhood, which was also home to the rapper 50 Cent, was wrecked by the crack cocaine epidemic of the 1980s and 1990s when Lamar was a boy. He observed, 'Any time you see these inner city kids in the NBA [National Basketball Association] … you've got to understand their background wasn't all peaches and cream.'

Lamar was left devastated when his mother died from colon cancer when he was 12. He recalled, 'She got sick in January and by July she was gone. It was tough to see somebody you love so much hurting like that.'

Instead of disappearing into an uncompromising urban world, Lamar was taken in by his grandmother, Mildred Mercer, and, because of his height, made rapid progress in high school basketball. He was so good, *Parade* magazine named him Player of the Year in 1997, when he was 18.

He joined the Los Angeles Clippers at the age of 20. He moved from there to Miami Heat on a six-year contract worth a reported $65 million. He was selected for the US team for the 2004 Olympic Games in Athens; they won the bronze medal.

He stayed in Miami for only a year, however, before going back to LA – this time with the Lakers. He said, 'This is a dream come true. This is the Yankees of basketball. The big stage.' His team, which also included Kobe Bryant, won back-to-back NBA championships in 2009 and 2010.

Lamar was by now one of the richest young sportsmen in the country, and he had a steady girlfriend. Liza Morales was his high school sweetheart and the mother of his three children. He was 18 when they had their first child, a daughter called Destiny. Two sons followed: Lamar Jr in 2005 and Jayden in 2006. Tragically, their youngest son died from Sudden Infant Death Syndrome (cot death) before he was seven months old.

Lamar and Liza eventually separated and he met Khloé not long afterwards. Liza couldn't believe it when she suddenly got a text saying he was getting married. She admitted, 'There aren't words to explain how I felt that day.'

Kris Jenner had just nine days to organise the wedding. Fortunately, a wedding planner was called in to help. The E! cameras followed the whirlwind arrangements: registering for gifts, fittings for the Vera Wang wedding dress, bachelorette party, rehearsal dinner and, of course, the wedding itself.

The ceremony was held in the garden of the Beverly Hills mansion belonging to the Kardashians' best friends, Irving and Shelli Azoff. Kim and Kourtney were bridesmaids, also dressed in Vera Wang, and Bruce walked his stepdaughter down an aisle decorated with white roses. A 10-piece orchestra played during the ceremony and later Babyface sang at the reception in a marquee in another part of the property.

A film crew captured the whole day for *Keeping Up with the Kardashians* and the episode was the most watched in the history of the programme with 3.2 million viewers. During the festivities, Ryan Seacrest was overheard saying they were thinking of yet another spin-off, involving Khloé and Lamar.

Among the guests was the singer and actress Adrienne Bailon, who was Rob's girlfriend for two years and had been a regular on the show during that time. They had split unexpectedly, and Rob later admitted that he had strayed during their time together. She said, 'He strategically planned things out so that he could cheat on me, and that to me was disloyal.' She had a new boyfriend called Lenny Santiago, an executive with Roc Nation, by the time of the wedding, so there was little chance of them getting back together.

Rob lived with Kim in her condo for a while, before moving in with Khloé and Lamar. They had bought a

$4 million–dollar home together in Tarzana, an affluent neighbourhood not far from Hidden Hills. The house featured regularly on the show.

The beauty of *Keeping Up with the Kardashians* was that there were so many of them. Kim may have been the marquee draw, but her mother proved to be savvy when it came to pushing forward the rest of the family so they were all increasing the market value of the brand. There was money to be made individually and collectively.

Regardless of her sisters apparently enjoying the life she wanted for herself, Kim continued to work tirelessly. The poor reception of *Disaster Movie* didn't put her off acting altogether. She made her debut in a dramatic role on the small screen in *CSI: NY*. The prime-time CBS show, starring Gary Sinise, regularly attracted close to 13 million viewers, so once again it was excellent exposure for Kim.

She played a character called Debbie Fallon in an episode broadcast in December 2009, and looked the part of the femme fatale as she sashayed through the precinct in a fetching off-the-shoulder number and sporting an immaculate tan. This didn't seem very likely at Christmastime in New York, giving the game away that the series was filmed in Los Angeles.

Debbie Fallon turned out to be a cold and calculating murderess. In the episode, her partner in crime was played by the former beauty queen and MTV host Vanessa Minnillo, who was another survivor of *Disaster Movie*. In the very small world that Kim inhabited, Vanessa became the wife of Nick Lachey and the mother of his two children. The reviews for *CSI* were a little kinder than they'd been for her movie debut, although one criticised Kim's 'vampy smugness'. She has the problem facing many famous women who take on acting roles: you can never forget that it's her.

She tried a frothier role in *Beyond the Break*, a soap that followed the fortunes of four female surfers. Kim featured in four episodes playing Elle, the new girlfriend of one of the regular characters. Her character was mean-spirited – not something that came easily. Kim was subsequently linked to co-star Michael Copon. It was another one of her occasional insignificant dates, when nothing was going on, but it garnered some publicity – this time for the spin-off *Kourtney and Kim Take New York*.

Another one of these non-dates was with the Real Madrid soccer star Cristiano Ronaldo, which momentarily had the UK tabloids flickering with interest. Some gossip regarding the Chelsea player Wayne Bridge seemed nothing more than another photo opportunity. More genuinely, she started dating a black American footballer, Miles Austin, a wide receiver with the Dallas Cowboys.

They went together to an ESPY party in honour of Kim's friend Serena Williams in July 2010. She watched him play at the Alamodome in San Antonio, and confirmed they were dating. Any romance was short-lived, and lasted barely six weeks. She was finding it impossible to conduct a relationship while she was filming *Keeping Up with the Kardashians* for 12 to 16 hours a day. Perhaps she would have better luck in New York.

15

72 DAYS

————

You wouldn't have expected Kris Humphries' name to feature in a list of the 100 people most likely to date Kim Kardashian. He and Kim, superficially at least, appeared to have absolutely nothing in common. Reggie Bush, with whom she had evidently been very much in love at one time, was brought up in California, went to USC and lived in a bachelor apartment in Beverly Hills. He was a catch, a celebrity and seemed perfect for Kim.

Kris, though handsome, was born and brought up in Minneapolis, where his family still live. His father, William, is African-American. He has two elder sisters called Krystal and Kaela and so, like the Kardashians, they all had first names beginning with K. He wasn't known for enjoying the high life in New York, where he was living when he met Kim.

As a boy, he was a brilliant swimmer and, for 18 years, held the national record for the 50-metre freestyle in the boys' 10 and under age group. Only the legendary Olympian Michael

Phelps, who is the same age, was considered to be a better prospect.

At 12, he gave up swimming in favour of basketball. He was obviously going to be very tall, so he chose a sport in which he was likely to have a bright future and the chance to earn a fortune. Michael Jordan, the most famous player in the country, was regarded as the richest man in sport and a role model for youngsters everywhere.

Kris was a junior international, before a promising college career led to him being drafted by the Utah Jazz team at the age of 19. He then moved to the Toronto Raptors in 2006, to the Dallas Mavericks three years later and to the New Jersey Nets the following season.

When he stopped growing, Kris was 6ft 9in tall, which meant he was a full 1.5 feet (18 inches) nearer the clouds than Kim Kardashian. She is only just 5ft 3in – or even a tad smaller – and many people are taken aback by how petite she is when they meet her for the first time. 'She is *tiny*,' stressed the acclaimed writer Lynn Barber.

The height difference between Kris and Kim was probably the biggest in show business, although there were some well-known couples in the foot-high club, including her younger sister Khloé, who is 13 inches shorter than Lamar Odom, Will Smith and Jada Pinkett, and Sacha Baron Cohen and Isla Fisher.

Kim had been filming the spin-off series *Kourtney and Kim Take New York* when she was first introduced to Kris in the late autumn of 2010. The Nets' point guard Jordan Farmar, who is from Los Angeles and already knew Kim, invited them both out to dinner. She found Kris attractive, but was a little stand-offish, because she wasn't entirely sure she wanted to become involved with anyone new at that point. That, of course, made Kris very interested in her.

Kim seemed no more enthusiastic about basketball than she had been about football. She is surprisingly daring and is happy to try skydiving and snowboarding, but isn't so keen on watching dutifully from the sidelines. She was prepared to do that, however, if there was a new man in her life.

She flew in to Minneapolis after spending New Year in Las Vegas and watched the first half of the game between the Nets and the local Timberwolves from a courtside seat. She met Kris's family for the opening half and joined them for dinner at the city's elegant Grand Hotel on 2nd Avenue. The head chef had already gone home for the evening, but was promptly called back to cook for Kim and her party.

Life was about to change completely for Kris, who had been little known outside the sports pages. He literally came out of nowhere into the full glare of the *Keeping Up with the Kardashians* spotlight.

He never watched the show, which was a bad start. His girlfriend immediately before Kim, Bianka Kamber, a very exotic and attractive brunette, was a palliative care nurse in Toronto. She revealed that he had no interest in the show and would disappear to play a war game on his Xbox if she were enjoying an episode. 'He would say, "When you're ready to watch something that's a lot more educational and not a load of garbage, I'm in the other room."'

Their relationship suffered when he was transferred from Toronto to Dallas and finished just before he met Kim. Bianka praised her former boyfriend for being amusing, spontaneous and charming, but wondered how he had managed to attract the attention of Kim Kardashian, because he had 'no flirting skills whatsoever'. She added, 'Flirting to him was like burping and blowing it in your face or farting and then throwing the covers over your head.'

Such habits didn't seem to bother Kim, who was happy to talk publicly about her new boyfriend. Without a trace of irony, she said in January, 'He's a really good guy and I think that for once I've really taken my time. I've known him for months and have definitely tried to keep it low key.' They were married eight months later. Everything began to unfold in a similar fashion to Khloé and Lamar's relationship, even if it was just coincidence that both men were well-known basketball players.

In May, they went on the obligatory holiday to the Joe Francis villa in Mexico, where they were photographed. Apparently, Kris was happy to get some 'alone time', although the paparazzi were on hand to record the holiday and feature Kim in a breathtaking array of bikinis.

The courtship progressed in time-honoured media fashion, with rumours of ring shopping followed by a romantic proposal that would be shared with the television audience. By this time, Kris had overcome his aversion to *Keeping Up with the Kardashians*, at least temporarily, and allowed the television cameras to follow his every move.

Kim introduced him as her new boyfriend in the opening episode of series six. They were having a conversation in a New York restaurant, which appeared to have been cleared of all the other customers. He came across as normal and funny, although he did let out an enormous burp, which Kim tried but failed to match.

By episode 13, he was preparing to ask her to marry him. Kris Jenner opened the instalment with a classic remark to Kim, 'You actually got a keeper.' After asking Bruce for permission to ask her to marry him, her prospective son-in-law was supposed to propose at a family dinner. That didn't happen after he and Kim argued on the way there. It was already confusing and a little silly that mother and future husband were both called Kris.

Kim returned to her Beverly Hills home one afternoon later that month to discover Kris on bended knee in the bedroom. On the white carpet, he had written in rose petals: 'Will you marry me?' The room was bathed in candlelight and was very romantic, if appearing rather staged for maximum TV effect. Some have speculated that this was the work of a member of the production team.

Kris produced an enormous, dazzling diamond engagement ring that you might have expected to see on the finger of Liberace or Elizabeth Taylor. It was completely ostentatious and Kim clearly loved it at first sight. The 20.5-carat ensemble by Lorraine Schwartz was valued at a reported $2 million, it was the ring of a girl's dreams. The cost to Kris Humphries was almost certainly considerably less, especially taking into account the publicity the designer received. Kim had no hesitation in accepting his proposal.

The show's editors could manipulate the footage in any way they wanted to reveal tension between the groom and other members of the family. Even so, there remained a nagging doubt about their compatibility. Kim and Kris seemed closest during bouts of rough and tumble, in which he would lift her up and bundle her on to the bed. She was disgusted when he put one of his two small dogs on the kitchen counter. He remarked that she never cooked anyway, and she pointed out that she was a neat freak. This was absolutely true. She would only take a shower if the bathroom was absolutely spotless, so finding a dog sleeping at the bottom of her bed or pooping in her garden wasn't something she was ever going to enjoy.

Still, they pressed on with the wedding arrangements. They settled on a venue in the desirable and charming enclave of Montecito in Santa Barbara County, perfectly placed for guests to travel from Los Angeles or San Francisco. Described by local writer Richard Mineards as an 'Eden by the Sea', celebrities have long chosen to escape here from the faster-paced Hollywood. The place oozes charm, and residents like Oprah Winfrey, Jeff Bridges and Drew Barrymore can dine in the cosy restaurants untroubled by selfie-seeking fans.

The Kardashians hired, at a cost of $140,000, the scenic 10-acre estate Sotto Il Monte, owned by Frank Caufield, a venture capitalist. The venue was perfect for Kim's wedding, because she was very nearly following in the footsteps of Jennifer Lopez. When J.Lo and Ben Affleck were planning their wedding in 2003, they had selected the property as the perfect setting for the occasion. Kim needed no finer recommendation.

On her big day, everyone was asked to come in either white or black. Kim wore a classic Vera Wang ivory wedding dress that suited her hourglass figure. The gown had a tulle skirt, basque waist and Chantilly lace, and was matched with a pair of Giuseppe Zanotti shoes. The fashion writer Alison Jane Reid was unimpressed: 'It was a typical meringue and revealed far too much cleavage. It just looked fussy, over the top and unflattering.'

A smiling Bruce Jenner walked Kim down the aisle, which in this case was a long, white carpet. The ceremony was conducted by a minister from Minnesota, who read out their declarations of love for each other before declaring them Mr and Mrs Kris Humphries. It was perfect and nobody describing the dream wedding remembered that Kim had been married before. The bride didn't seem as relaxed as normal, however, suggesting she may have had misgivings.

Many of the celebrities connected with the Kardashians smiled appreciatively during the ceremony, before mingling at the reception. Babyface, Sugar Ray Leonard, Mario Lopez, Ciara, The-Dream, Kathie Lee Gifford, Eva Longoria, Serena Williams, Brittny Gastineau and Joe Francis were just some of the famous names who watched the couple take to the floor for their first dance – 'Angels' sung live by Robin Thicke.

The guest of honour was her 95-year-old grandfather, Art, the father of Robert Kardashian. He was in a wheelchair, but looked happy for her. She called him Poppi. His wife, Helen, had died three years before; he would pass away in December 2012.

Afterwards, Kim said, 'My one regret is that I wish I had more time to really enjoy the wedding, because there's so much going on that you're running around and now that I look, I'm like, "That day happened so fast".'

The residents of Montecito were, according to Richard Mineards, 'totally underwhelmed by the whole proceedings'. He recalled, 'I was constantly asked what the Kardashians were famous for.' The weekend upheaval, with helicopters from entertainment TV news shows clattering endlessly overhead, led to changes in local by-laws about people renting out their sprawling multimillion-dollar estates. Future would-be renters would have to go through a thorough legal process to get the necessary permission – if they got it at all. Montecito, the fifth richest postcode in the US (93108), didn't want a repeat of the Kardashian brouhaha any time soon.

The newlyweds were oblivious to that as they flew across the Atlantic for a honeymoon at the $3,300-a-night Hotel Santa Caterina on Italy's Amalfi Coast. The trip was a last-minute surprise gift from Kris, although there was time to ensure a photographer from the Splash agency was there to take pictures of Kim, in a revealing bikini, cuddling up to her new husband. She had been planning to go straight to New York after the wedding to start preparing for the new series of *Kourtney and Kim Take New York*, so she was genuinely taken by surprise.

Within weeks of their return, rumours began to surface that all was not well with the fledgling marriage. A clue to their differing outlook on marriage was provided by an episode of the reality spin-off. Kim is concerned when Kris suggests they move back to his home town.

She asks, 'How am I going to have my career and live in Minnesota?'

He replies, 'By the time you have kids and they're in school, nobody will probably care about you.'

Kim didn't reply, but you can imagine what she was thinking. The couple had moved into the luxury Gansevoort hotel in the Meatpacking District of New York, but Kris was seen apparently moving his things out of their suite just before her thirty-first birthday. After 72 days, she filed for divorce.

Kim issued a statement: 'After careful consideration I have decided to end my marriage. I hope everyone understands this was not an easy decision. I had hoped this marriage was forever, but sometimes things don't work out as planned. We remain friends and wish each other the best!'

It turned out they weren't exactly friends, as an acrimonious divorce dragged on for 20 months – far longer than they had been together as man and wife. It would later be revealed in the divorce papers that she never wanted to go on honeymoon.

Kim had the foresight to sign a prenuptial agreement. After her first marriage, she wanted just a few items back, including her Bible. On this occasion, she wanted to ensure she kept her fortune, then estimated at $22 million, although such figures do tend to be inflated in the press.

Speculation began immediately that the whole relationship, from start to finish, had been a stunt for her reality show. The media revealed that the couple had made a fortune from the fiasco, which reinforced the view that it had all been faked. Kim was reported to have earned $2 million from her nuptials, including more than $1 million in an exclusive picture deal with a magazine. She was also said to have been paid $90,000 for holding her hen party in Las Vegas at TAO, one of her regular haunts.

Kim defended herself vigorously in a blog that was posted on her website. It was a sad reflection of how she is perceived as a young woman who would do anything for fame. She wrote: 'First and foremost, I married for love. I can't believe I even have to defend this. I would not have spent so much time on something just for a TV show!'

She repeated an opinion of herself that others have voiced about her since she was a teenage girl: 'Everyone that knows me knows that I'm a hopeless romantic! I love with all my heart and soul. I want a family and babies and a real life so badly that maybe I rushed into something too soon … I felt like I was on a fast roller-coaster and couldn't get off when I know I probably should have.'

Kim realised that adverse public opinion could become a runaway train if left unchecked. Fans were fickle and could easily turn against you. Kris Humphries was jeered when he resumed playing basketball. Kim's emotional defence of her good intentions was intelligent and believable, but it wasn't enough to draw a line under her marriage.

Kris filed his legal response on 1 December. Surprisingly, he requested an annulment on the grounds of fraud. He didn't reveal the reason for pursuing this course.

Kim and Kris were simply a poor match. In a rather sad postscript, that amazing engagement ring was sold at auction by Christie's in New York in October 2013 for $749,000. Kim had returned it to Kris, and he had waited until their divorce was finalised before selling it. In an ironic twist of fate, that was also the month she became engaged again.

PART THREE

KIM KARDASHIAN WEST

16

THE COLLEGE DROPOUT

Kanye West was different. He was a sensitive, artistic and driven young man, brought up in a Chicago household by a mother who gave him the gift of self-expression. When Kim first met him, he was producing a track he had written for Brandy called 'Talk About Our Love' and they were recording at the Record Plant studio in Hollywood. Kim was working for Brandy at the time, and legend has it that she made everyone, including Kanye, a mug of tea.

He was already recognised as one of the most talented new names in contemporary music, but he had yet to become the enigmatic and controversial figure he is today. He wasn't from the street or from any sort of deprived inner city back-ground. He hadn't subsidised his teenage years selling drugs on street corners; he had worked for Gap and in telephone marketing.

When he first met Jay Z, he was wearing a pink shirt, a smart sports jacket, tailored trousers and Gucci shoes. He looked more like a preppy East Coast college man than an up-and-coming rapper. He recalled, 'It was a strike against me that I didn't wear baggy jeans and jerseys and that I never hustled, never sold drugs.'

Kanye Omari West was born on 8 June 1977, in Atlanta, Georgia. The name Kanye, pronounced Kahn-yay, didn't have any special significance for his parents, Ray and Donda West. It simply means 'the only one' in Swahili, and Kanye would be an only child. His middle name means 'wise man'. His parents liked the fact that their son had the initials KO. For the first three years of marriage, they were determined to concentrate on their careers and not have children. Donda changed her mind, however, and persuaded her husband that they should try for a baby.

Both of his parents were highly educated. Ray West was from a military family, had lived overseas and had been brought up in mainly white neighbourhoods. At the then predominantly white University of Delaware, he had become involved in politics and was elected president of the Black Student Union. Donda recalled that he was 'militant, fiery, passionate and, above all, very, very smart.' He spoke at rallies for the controversial Black Panther Party. Kanye observed, 'He was a military brat who grew up in Germany as a black kid among white folks. So he was looking for a place to fit in, to be part of a movement, a struggle. And they accepted him.'

After college, Ray followed his first love of photography, winning awards and setting up his own business in his home town of Atlanta. One of his regular contracts was shooting pictures for Spelman College, the liberal arts women's university. He met Donda when she worked in the public relations department of the historically black institution. She was subsidising her studies for a master's degree at Atlanta University.

They married three months after their first date. At first, they both took teaching jobs. Ray taught photography and media production at one college, while she taught English and speech at another. They both decided to pursue further education and lived in married quarters at Auburn University in Alabama, where he obtained a master's in audiovisual studies and media, while she studied for a doctorate in English.

Their marriage faltered after Kanye was born, with Ray apparently devoting too much time to photography and not enough to family life. When their son was 11 months old, they separated amicably. Ray would remain in Kanye's life, but his mother basically raised him as a single parent and was by far the most significant and influential person in his development.

Donda and Ray's son would grow up to be imaginative visually and verbally – an impressive combination of their talents. On 'Talk About Love', for instance, he wrote and performed the middle rap, produced the track and devised the concept for the video, in which he appeared in a cameo role alongside Ray J, with whom Kim had just made the sex tape.

When Kanye was three, his mother decided their life needed a complete change. Encouraged by a boyfriend, she secured a job at Chicago State University and moved to Illinois. Kanye was a precociously talented child with a mother thoughtful and intelligent enough to encourage her son in the way that she thought would best prepare him for the world. She wanted to ensure that he had high self-esteem and believed in himself. She wrote, 'I began teaching him to love himself. It's something I felt I must consciously do … As a black man and as a man period, he would need to be strong.'

Many of the values that Donda tried to instil in her son were the same ones that Kim's parents advocated for her: honesty, integrity and a strong work ethic. They attended church every Sunday at the Christ Universal Temple on South Ashland Avenue. She ensured he still saw Ray, spending summer holidays with his father and grandparents. Ray had become more religious-minded over the years and church was a compulsory event for his son whenever he visited. Sometimes they would speak on the telephone and say a prayer or two together before ending their conversation. Ray eventually gave up his job as a photographer and moved to Maryland to work as a Christian counsellor.

Donda's desire to build her son's confidence probably lay the foundation for what many perceive to be arrogance in the adult Kanye. His inner certainty allowed him to express his creative ideas from an early age. Even at three, he was thinking outside the box. His mother would tell him a banana was yellow, but he would draw one with his crayons and then colour it purple, because that's how he wanted it to look.

Kanye's self-confidence was evident when he sat an exam for elementary school. He was asked to draw a man, a task he found too dull and easy, so he told the examiners he would draw a man and put him in a football uniform. He passed the test easily and was accepted at the Vanderpoel Elementary Magnet School on South Prospect Avenue, which had a solid reputation for encouraging artistic children.

While there, Kanye began to take an interest in fashion and would sketch designs for the outfits he was going to produce when he had his own fashion label. Up until then, he had been quite happy to let his mother choose his clothes, usually from budget stores – on her salary, she had to be careful not to overindulge her child. She ignited his interest in the way he looked, however, by buying him his first pair of Air Jordans when he was 10. They cost $65, so it was an extravagant gift.

Donda broadened his education by taking him on trips around the US. They went to Washington, DC – not just to see the White House, but to tour the Smithsonian Institution as well. When they went to St Louis, they visited the zoo to have fun, but she wanted her son to appreciate the Gateway Arch, the awe-inspiring monument that had become the internationally recognisable symbol of the city. As a professor of English, she travelled abroad, but couldn't take Kanye with her. In 1987, she was offered a year teaching in China as part of an exchange between Nanjing University and Chicago State. She was going to turn down the opportunity before she was assured her son could go with her too.

China was an incredible experience for a young boy. Kanye would cycle eight blocks to school, where he was the centre of attention as the only black student. The others would come up and rub his face to see if his colour would come off on their hands. Stereotypically, because he was black, they wanted him to breakdance – fortunately, it was something at which he excelled. He was happy to oblige, but only in return for a lamb kebab. Even at the age of 10, he understood when he had something of value. He possessed an entrepreneurial spirit.

The one drawback during an adventurous year, in which he also travelled to Hong Kong and Thailand, was that his lack of fluency in the language held him back in class. He stayed in a lower grade until Donda decided to home school him. On his return to the US, he had to sit some exams to find his correct level of re-entry and performed so well that the school didn't believe the results and thought his mother must have helped him. He had to take the exams again with an invigilator standing over him. Once again, he excelled.

While he never got into serious trouble at school, he did embarrass his mother when he took a pornographic magazine in one day and got caught passing it around among his friends. When a teacher demanded to know where he had obtained the porn, he said he had found it in his mum's closet. She wanted the floor to open up and swallow her after she was summoned to the school and told what had happened. Kanye has admitted a healthy interest in sex from a young age, which included watching a hard porn movie on his VCR when he was 14. His unimpressed mother made him write an essay entitled 'The Impact of Watching X-Rated Movies on a Teenage Boy'. The project didn't dampen his enthusiasm for the opposite sex, but did teach him the benefits of proper research and preparation.

By the age of 12, he had become totally preoccupied with the way he looked. His mother, tongue in cheek, said he became Mr Style Guru. As a schoolboy, he even did his own washing and ironing to ensure he looked immaculate at all times. Once, when she gave him $200 to stock up on clothes for the new school term, he came home with just two shirts and one pair of jeans. Even then, his tastes were expensive.

He was also becoming obsessed with styling. Donda recalled, 'It was like a light went on inside of him and he poured the same kind of energy that he put into his art and music into putting outfits together and dressing well. It came without effort.' At 15, he even took over his mother's styling: 'He'd critique whatever I was wearing, whenever I had some place to go. Sometimes he'd be kind. Other times, cruel.'

At school, he formed a group called Quadro Posse with three friends. Kanye was responsible for the styling. He preferred everything to be coordinated. When they entered a school talent competition, which they won, he had decided that they all should dress completely in black. He was careful to make sure his shoes were exactly right, telling his mother, 'You can mess up a dope outfit with shoes.'

It's so easy to see that he and Kim are absolutely soulmates. If they had joined a dating agency, they would have been matched immediately and told to get married.

Kanye had moved on from Vanderpoel to Polaris High School in the affluent south-western Chicago suburb of Oak Lawn. It was demanding academically, but Kanye coped relatively easily. His teachers recall that he was prone to speaking first without thinking of the consequences of what he said. One of his teachers, Dr Carol Baker, recalled that he was easily distracted, often doodling, drawing or writing rather than paying attention: 'Back then I would have called it poetry, but it was really rap.'

His mother was determined that he receive the education he needed to be successful. 'She was the kind of mum who would pull him by the ear and drag him down the hallway if necessary,' said Dr Baker. 'I never saw her do that, but she was that kind of mum.'

One pursuit Donda was happy to encourage was Kanye's love of music. He was fiercely ambitious at a young age. His PE teacher Marilyn Gannon remembered him as a 'small kid with big dreams', who used to tell her almost daily that he was going to be the best rapper in the world. She invariably replied, 'OK, Kanye, you can get in line now.'

The characteristic that set Kanye apart from his contemporaries is an appreciation of all kinds of music. He used to impersonate Stevie Wonder at talent contests when he was a boy and often did well. He listened to proper singer-songwriters, like George Michael, Phil Collins and Michael Jackson. His favourite group was Red Hot Chili Peppers. Later, he became known for bringing many diverse elements into his music.

He wrote his first proper rap song at the age of 13. He was inspired by a favourite Dr Seuss book to compose 'Green Eggs and Ham'. He persuaded his mother to pay $25 an hour to give him enough time to record the song in a small basement studio, which was hardly high tech – the microphone was suspended from the ceiling by a wire coat hanger. Nothing from that version has ever been made public, but it was a start.

At 14, he bought his first keyboard with his own savings of $500 and the $1,000 his indulgent mother had given him as a Christmas present. From then on, he lived for his keyboard and the beats he could create on it. In mainstream pop music, a beat would be the instrumental track upon which the vocal would sit. In hip-hop, it would be the track, often using samples from other songs, on which the rap would be laid down. Kanye associated with a leading young hip-hop producer called No I.D., who took him under his wing after an introduction engineered by their mums, who both worked at Chicago State.

Like Kim Kardashian in Los Angeles, Kanye took on work as a teenager to afford the clothes he wanted, to run his battered Nissan car and to chase girls. He sold knives door to door and worked as a greeter outside a Gap store to try and encourage young black people to go inside. He made up raps to entertain passers-by: 'Welcome to the Gap. We got jeans in the back …'

On leaving high school, he won a scholarship to study at the American Academy of Art, but was more interested in his music. He changed to English literature at Chicago State, where his mum was now head of the department, but didn't enjoy that either. He dropped out of college, which was obviously a huge disappointment to his mother. Her concern was eased when he sold a set of beats to the well-known Chicago rapper Gravity for $8,800.

Donda took early retirement from her job to move with her son to New York, where there were greater opportunities, and took on the role of Kanye's manager. She was, in fact, a 'momager' before Kris Jenner took on that role for her children. He attracted the interest of Jay Z and made his breakthrough to the major league when he produced five tracks on the master rapper's 2001 million-seller *The Blueprint*. Practically overnight Kanye was one of the biggest producers in the US, but he was frustrated at being unable to perform his own material. Dapper and short of stature, he lacked the menace of the gangsta rappers who dominated the hip-hop scene at the time.

He continued to write, composing two of the tracks that would become Kanye classics, 'Jesus Walks' and 'Hey Mama'. The latter was a tribute to his mother, who had always given her son's well-being and happiness priority over her own personal relationships. Eventually Roc-A-Fella's co-founder,

Damon Dash, signed him as a recording artist and he flew to Los Angeles to make an album.

He nearly didn't finish it. After a late night at the studio, he fell asleep at the wheel of his rented Lexus and was fortunate to escape with his life. His airbag failed to open and his face smashed into the steering wheel, causing horrendous fractures to his jaw and nose. His girlfriend, Sumeke Rainey, and his mother were on the first flight from Newark to be at his bedside in Cedars-Sinai.

His relationship with Sumeke is the quiet one he seldom speaks of, but they dated for seven years and she hasn't used that fact to gain any fame since. She sang lyrics on an occasional song, but, more importantly, her father gave Kanye a box of old soul singles that he went through carefully and methodically, and used for sampling on his early recordings. He is also said to have told her dying father that he would marry Sumeke some day – something that didn't happen.

The number of people in Kim's story affected by bad road accidents is almost beyond belief. Khloé had her bad teenage smash; Kris Jenner's natural father was killed in one; Bruce's brother was another fatality; Lamar Odom's chauffeur-driven car was involved in a fatal accident in New York in 2011; Bruce himself would be involved in a crash in 2014, in which his Cadillac hit the back of another car, resulting in the death of its occupant. And then there was Kanye, who was lucky to be alive.

He was in hospital for two weeks, only able to take sustenance through a straw, as his shattered jaw had to be wired together. It could have been much worse. His escape was a life-changing moment, as his songs became more self-aware and honest. Up until that time, he had been trying to be unrealistically tough in both his lyrics and his music, because that was the fashion. He wrote and recorded a breakthrough song called 'Through the Wire', which he sang literally through gritted teeth.

He wrote it in the hospital and, as he usually did with his songs, simply remembered it. He didn't need to write the lyric down. He rapped about half his jaw being in the back of his mouth. He speeded up a sample of a 1984 big ballad by Chaka Khan called 'Through the Fire', which had originally been produced by David Foster. Kanye recorded it at the Record Plant studio with the wire still in his jaw. When Chaka agreed for her vocal to be used, she had no idea that he was going to speed it up and 'make me sound like a chipmunk'.

When the song was eventually released in September 2003, it was a top 20 hit in both the US and the UK. More importantly, it revealed that Kanye was the exception to the rule that producers don't make good rappers. The video, which he financed himself, won Video of the Year at the 2004 *Source* Hip-Hop Awards.

The track was the cornerstone of his debut album, *The College Dropout*, which sold 3.4 million copies in the US and gained him a reputation as one of the leading rap artists of his generation. It won Best Rap Album at the Grammy Awards, the first of 21 he has won, making him the most successful modern artist at the prestigious annual ceremony. The second single, 'Slow Jamz' with Twista and Jamie Foxx, provided Kanye with his first number one. The *New York Times* described *The College Dropout* as a 'concept album about quitting school, a playful collection of party songs and a 76-minute orgy of nose-thumbing.'

Kanye made the jump to the front pages of the newspapers in September 2005, during a telethon raising funds for the victims of Hurricane Katrina in New Orleans. He began with some home truths about the victims. He said that a white family would be portrayed in the media as looking for food, whereas a black family would be described as looting. He ended with a simple observation that was heard throughout the world: 'George Bush doesn't care about black people.' He hadn't planned to say it, but let an impulse rule his head. It would be the first of many controversial moments.

Donda West was proud of her son's outspoken honesty. Mindful of the battle against racial prejudice that she had witnessed all her life, she believed he had spoken the truth. She moved from the East Coast to the West to be with her son. First, she had been there to help him convalesce following his near-fatal accident; then she stayed on to look after his affairs. She was chief executive of West Brands, LLC, the parent company of Kanye's business concerns. She chaired the Kanye West Foundation, an educational non-profit organisation, which sought to decrease dropout rates and improve literacy. She was also the person whose opinion mattered most to him.

She died suddenly and unexpectedly in Beverly Hills in November 2007, the day after she had undergone cosmetic surgery, which included breast reduction and liposuction. She was 58. The coroner said that the final manner of death could not be determined, but stated that 'multiple post-operative factors could have played a role in the death'. His opinion, though, was that she died from some pre-existing coronary artery disease.

Kanye was devastated. Before she died, she had written a book entitled *Raising Kanye: Life Lessons from the Mother of a Hip-Hop Superstar*, in which she described her love and admiration for her son. The affection was mutual. He was devastated by her death.

He was in the middle of a tour in Europe and cancelled some dates, but a week later, in Paris, had to be helped off stage when he was about to sing 'Hey Mama'. He took time away to grieve, but returned at the Grammys in February 2008. This time he sang an emotional version of the song, and had the word MAMA shaved into his head.

Kim's father, Robert Kardashian, was a year older than Donda when he died. That sense of loss would be a common bond between Kanye and Kim. She said simply, 'I can really relate to his mother's passing. He can really relate to my father's passing.' Surely it was only a matter of time before they realised they were made for each other.

17

FANCY SEEING YOU HERE

———

The story of Kim and Kanye's love affair should be made into a Hollywood rom-com. The audience would be secure in the knowledge that they would eventually end up together, despite a series of relationships with other people that kept them apart for years. Her sister Khloé was always telling Kim that he should be her husband.

When they first met, she was involved with Ray J and technically married to Damon Thomas. Kanye, too, was attached – he was still with Sumeke. Their long relationship fizzled out when he moved to Los Angeles. She is acknowledged as a vocalist on two tracks from *The College Dropout*, but doesn't feature on the follow-up, *Late Registration*, a year later.

That album was number one in the *Billboard* charts and included one of his best-known songs, 'Gold Digger'. It sold more than 3 million copies in the US alone and was one of the 10 biggest-selling songs of the decade. In the UK, he performed for the first time at the Brits in 2006, using 77 female dancers wearing little more than gold paint and skimpy bikinis.

At the time of *Late Registration*, he was dating Brooke Crittendon, a production assistant at MTV. She seemed a refreshingly normal girl, who found it difficult dating a superstar: 'There was a lot of attention from other women. Kanye was very open and honest, but it ended up with me knowing too much. I don't want to be silly and say it wasn't cheating because I knew about it. But he wanted and needed me to be OK with certain things I wasn't OK with.'

Brooke revealed that Kanye wasn't the macho man he had set out to be in his music. Instead, he was a sensitive performer who liked to know she was standing by the side of the stage whenever he performed. Their liaison ended after one of an increasing number of rows, and Kanye went back to Alexis Phifer, a very pretty young designer he had dated briefly after Sumeke. She had been married for three years to American footballer Roman Phifer and had a young son called Jordan.

She and Kanye were together for three years and became engaged. He gave her a beautiful, large, square diamond ring by the New York-based Lorraine Schwartz. (She would also design the engagement ring Kris Humphries gave Kim.) They shared a passion for fashion – something clearly very important to Kanye in his search for a partner. Alexis moved into his home at the foot of the Hollywood Hills with views overlooking Hollywood Boulevard, but kept her design studio in downtown LA and went off to work every day. She was setting up her own label called Ghita, which she described as styles for 'the confident woman who doesn't mind showing a little of her sexuality'. Kanye never seemed to need the status of having a famous girlfriend, preferring to date unknown women most of the time.

He likes opulence and clothing. His dining-room ceiling paid homage to the Sistine Chapel, except it depicted Kanye flying among angels. His closets alone took up close to an entire floor. He clearly appreciated his fiancée's dress sense, crediting her with being the first person he would allow to style him. He said, 'Alexis was my original stylist. She helped me get fresh.' During their time together, Kanye began developing his own fashion label, called Pastelle. He spent three years on the project, but it never reached stores.

His mother Donda acknowledged Alexis as one of the family in her 2007 book and all seemed set fair for a wedding. Kanye still appreciated the curvaceous charms of Kim Kardashian, however. They were no more than friends, but he later admitted that seeing a photograph of Kim with Paris Hilton in Australia in 2006 reminded him that she had a great pair of pins.

In September 2007, a photographer caught them together at the grand opening of the Intermix boutique in West Hollywood. Kanye was with Alexis and Kim arrived with her younger brother Rob. Kanye is in the middle of a picture taken that night with Alexis on his right arm and Kim on his left. Intriguingly, in 2014 Kanye told the audience at one of his concerts that seven years earlier he had told Kim he was going to marry her one day.

She admitted, 'There was definitely a spark.' That spark was in evidence again in 2008, when they made the pilot of a hip-hop puppet show called *Alligator Boots*. This was like an X-rated *Spitting Image* and very funny if you liked that sort of humour. In the opening scene, Kanye and Kim share a stage with a deep-voiced randy bear puppet called Beary White, who serenades her with a romantic ode: 'Let me lay you down on my silky sheets and then come in close behind ya and then I'll show you my desire and put my penis inside your vagina.' Kim pretends to be outraged. 'Excuse Me!' she exclaims. Kanye was one of the executive producers, along with the television host Jimmy Kimmel. For some reason, Comedy Central decided not to commission it.

Throughout the show, Kim is a good sport, dressed as an outstandingly sexy Princess Leia, a dream costume for any *Star Wars* devotee with an interest in porn. For those with longer memories, Kanye was indulging in the same fantasy that Ross had in *Friends*, when he persuades Rachel to dress as the character. Kanye observed in the show, 'And I want to have, like, Kim Kardashian play Princess Leia, because you know Kim Kardashian's ass is so perfect.'

It may be with the benefit of 20/20 hindsight, but the pair do seem very relaxed in each other's company. The timing was always a little awry where Kim and Kanye were concerned. She said, 'We were both in other relationships and we kept our distance and that was really that.'

All was not well between Kanye and Alexis. He had struggled in their relationship after the death of his mother. Alexis was pictured arriving on the red carpet for a fashion event in New York without her engagement ring. A story in *In Touch* claimed the pair had argued when she discovered a naked picture of Kim on his mobile phone. Any thoughts of marriage were soon put to one side.

Kim was involved with Reggie Bush then, so she wasn't free. The next time they were seen at the same event was later that year, at the tenth anniversary party for *Flaunt* magazine in

Los Angeles. Kanye was now dating a shapely former stripper from Philadelphia called Amber Rose. He had seen her dancing seductively in the video for the Ludacris song 'What Them Girls Like' and decided he wanted to find out more. She was very distinctive, with buzz-cut blonde hair and a voluptuous figure, and stood out among the young women who generally inhabit hip-hop videos. Oddly, she shares the same birthday as Kim, 21 October, although she is three years younger.

She was at home in the Bronx, where her family lived in the projects, when she had a call on her mobile phone. 'Hi, it's Kanye,' he said. Amber, whose real name is Amber Levonchuck, had never met the rapper, so she hung up because she thought it was a prank call. He persisted, calling back until he persuaded her that he was genuine and wanted to fly her to Los Angeles to appear in the video for a song called 'Robocop'.

The video was never released, but Kanye invited Amber to the Grammys and bought her a Chanel bodysuit to wear. She explained why she fell in love with him: 'When I told him I was an exotic dancer, he was like "I don't care if you're a crackhead. I don't care if you're a prostitute. I just want to be with you."'

Amber moved to Los Angeles, where she and Kanye became one of the most striking couples in the music business. She signed with the Ford Models agency and said goodbye to her work as a pole dancer forever. She was with Kanye during his most controversial episode to date. At the 2009 MTV Video Music Awards, he charged on stage during Taylor Swift's acceptance speech for Best Female Video and took the microphone from her. 'Yo Taylor, I'm really happy for you and I'mma let you finish, but Beyoncé had one of the best videos

of all time. One of the best videos of all time!' He was refer-
ring to 'Single Ladies (Put a Ring on It)'.

It was a priceless moment. The audience at the Radio City
Music Hall in New York was dumbstruck to begin with and
then roundly booed him. His intervention will always feature
in the most shocking moments in music. Even President
Obama made an off-the-cuff remark about it, 'The young lady
seems like a nice person, she's getting her award and what's he
doing up there? He's a jackass.'

One can only speculate about whether Kim would have
prevented him from getting out of his seat in the first place.
Kim and Kanye have never admitted the extent of their feelings for one another in these early years, but the conspiracy
theorists enjoyed Kanye's contribution to 'Knock You Down',
a song by Keri Hilson. In his guest verse, he raps, 'You was
always the cheerleader of my dreams, To seem to only date the
head of football teams, And I was the class clown that always
kept you laughin', We were never meant to be, baby, we just
happened.' Obviously, the gossips assumed Kim was the cheerleader and Reggie was the head of the football team.

In February 2009, Kim and Reggie went to the Y-3 fashion
show in New York only to find Kanye there, practically beside
them in the front row. The actress Milla Jovovich sat between
Kanye, who looked slightly ill at ease, and Kim, who had her
arm locked around Reggie's.

The following year, Kanye and Amber Rose split up. He
was pleasant about it: 'It was an amazing time and it came to
an end.' She took a different view, later accusing Kim of
being a 'homewrecker' and her ex-boyfriend of unfaithful-
ness. She told the *New York Post*, 'He can't be faithful, and it's

not just with one person. He's just unfaithful with a lot of different women. I got to the point where I thought, my heart can't take it any more. I don't deserve this.' Amber was echoing the view of another of his former girlfriends, Brooke Crittendon.

According to Amber, Kim used to send Kanye salacious messages and photos. She claimed: 'They were both cheating on me and Reggie with each other … She was sending pictures and I was like, "Kim, just stop. Don't be that person."' Kanye subsequently denied this – when asked if Kim had sent him nude pictures while he was with Amber, he replied, 'I wish.'

When Kanye walked into the new DASH boutique in the SoHo district of New York in October 2010, neither he nor Kim was attached. She had temporarily relocated to the city to open the store and film the experience with her sister Kourtney for their spin-off show. Kanye didn't seem to mind the cameras when he flirted with Kim and gave them some advice about the shop. He also accepted an invitation to her thirtieth birthday party at TAO in Las Vegas. That was the glitzy, public celebration, but he also attended the private family party a few days later.

The great mystery about Kim and Kanye's love affair was why, after being thwarted for so many years, they didn't take this opportunity to begin a proper relationship. Perhaps they were each waiting for the other to make the first move, or maybe it was just a case of not having the time to devote to anything more than a casual friendship. Kim's work schedule for the first series of *Kim and Kourtney Take New York* was very demanding and that may have been a factor. In the best romantic-comedy tradition, they may simply not have realised what their true feelings were then.

One of the storylines for the series involved seeing if Kim could find a new man. Surprisingly, considering the rumours at the time, he turned out not to be Kanye but Kris Humphries. Kanye did help Kim with her ill-fated singing attempt, 'Jam (Turn It Up)', and appeared in the unreleased video in some steamy scenes.

Despite their obvious and natural chemistry, Kanye again took a back seat during her whirlwind romance and ill-fated marriage to Kris Humphries. He wasn't happy about it. Kim later revealed that he had expressed his interest, but she hadn't followed up, as she was being swept away on the roller-coaster that led to her wedding in Montecito. Kanye wasn't invited to the wedding, despite being continually described in Kardashian circles as a family friend.

Kanye dated a succession of attractive young women and there were even rumours that he had made a sex tape with one who bore some likeness to Kim.

At long last, Kim and Kanye's time had come. Kim made the first move to start an exclusive romance with Kanye simply by calling him. She finally admitted the obvious truth: 'I was always attracted to him.' She realised how hurt he had been when she went off and married Kris Humphries. 'I thought he was going to call me, since he knew that I was single again and he didn't. I knew what he was thinking. And so I called him and I said, "Hello. I thought you were at least going to call me or something."'

Just six weeks after she announced her split from Kris, Kim was seen in public with Kanye at an after-show party in Los

Angeles. He had been performing at the Staples Center with Jay Z, as part of their *Watch the Throne* tour, which saw the two superstars join together for a series of 57 dates that grossed $75 million. Kim attended the concert with Khloé, Scott Disick and her mother. They had seats right next to the stage, so Kanye was able to interact with them during the concert.

The party afterwards was held at the Beverly Hills estate of billionaire Ron Burkle. Kanye and Kim chatted with a very pregnant Beyoncé, who is married to Jay Z, but spent most of the night deep in conversation with each other. For once, stories that they had eyes only for each other were completely true. One eyewitness declared, 'Kanye was eating Kim up like she was a piece of cake. I think he was dying to kiss her, but there were too many people in the room.'

She continued to deny rumours that they were going out, which was hardly surprising, as her divorce was proceeding at a snail's pace. Before they were officially an item, Kanye's ex, Amber Rose, had become engaged to another rapper, Wiz Khalifa. Reggie Bush, too, had moved on to a new relationship and had settled down in Miami with a beautiful dancer called Lilit Avagyan, who bore a striking resemblance to Kim and, by coincidence, was Armenian.

In March 2012, Kanye invited Kim to join him for his Paris fashion week show. His fame had allowed him to pursue his interest for the past few years. He teamed up with Nike to release his own line of designer trainers, called Air Yeezys, a bow to the famous Air Jordan shoes he had loved so much as a child combined with his own preferred nickname, Yeezy. He designed a new shoe line for Louis Vuitton, as well as footwear for BAPE and Giuseppe Zanotti.

Since his Taylor Swift debacle, Kanye had spent much more time immersed in the world of fashion, especially after he cancelled a co-headlining tour with Lady Gaga in late 2009. Instead, he went to live in Japan to get away from the fallout. In Rome, he interned for four months at the Fendi fashion house, where he tried to interest them unsuccessfully in his design for a leather jogging pant. He also lived in Paris, which he loved and where he held two shows in 2011 and 2012.

In the romantic French capital, any reluctance Kanye had to begin a serious relationship with Kim vanished. She confessed, 'The magic happened.' Kim realised that the man she loved had been in front of her all along. She assured him that she was ready to make a commitment.

The show itself contained a lot of fur and very high, futuristic shoes. Kim wore a pair of Kanye West for Giuseppe Zanotti heels, made of calf leather and embroidered with pearls, which would cost $6,000 to buy and weren't exactly rainproof. She topped off her outfit with a striking white fur stole.

Both Kim and Kanye have become the number one celebrity target for PETA, the animal rights organisation, because of their love of wearing fur. Two weeks after Paris, Kim was flour-bombed at the launch of her new perfume, True Reflection, as she posed on the red carpet at the London West Hollywood hotel.

She had arrived looking flawless in a black blazer, blue blouse and leather trousers. A few minutes later, she looked as if she had been caught in an unseasonal snowstorm. Apparently, the female assailant shouted, 'Fur hag!' before taking aim. The fire department was called to determine what the white powder was and concluded that it was plain flour. After she had spruced herself up, Kim said, 'That probably is the craziest, unexpected, weird thing that ever happened to me. Like I said to my make-up artist, I wanted more powder ...'

Kim remains a target, although that was the most obvious physical attack she has received. At the start of her promotional tour for her book of selfies, *Selfish*, in May 2015, anti-fur protesters queued for seven hours to confront her. They held up posters and spoke to her in person.

Kanye, who probably wears just as much fur as Kim, went back to songwriting after the fashion show. He couldn't resist a dig at PETA in 'Theraflu': 'Tell PETA my mink is dragging on the floor.' The main focus of the track, which he retitled 'Cold', was that he mentioned Kim by name for the first time. 'And I'll admit, I had fell in love with Kim ... Around the same time she had fell in love with him'. Many took that to be about Kris Humphries, but it could just as easily be a reference to Wiz Khalifa, whom he also names in the song, if the 'she' is Amber Rose – it works just as well for both.

Kim and Kanye officially went public with their love affair in late April 2012, when they arrived hand in hand and posed for pictures at the annual artists' dinner at the Tribeca Film Festival in New York. She had already been spotted leaving his apartment one morning in the same clothes she had on the night before.

Privately, they were already talking of moving in together and starting a family. Two things needed to happen to make that possible. First, they needed to decide whose lovely house they were going to live in. Secondly, Kim needed to come off the pill, which she had been taking for 18 years. She told

Oprah, 'I want babies; I want my forever; I want my fairy tale. And I believe you can have what you want.'

The solution to the living arrangements was simple: they would both sell their homes and start afresh with something fabulous. Kim was happy to let hers go for $5 million – no more than she had paid for it, when taking into account the furniture she was including in the sale. Kanye's was a little smaller and worth a million or so less, but was probably more opulent. His house was fitted with a Crestron system, which allowed him to control the climate, lighting and music from any computer in the world.

In June, she splashed out on a black Lamborghini, costing $400,000, as a gift for his thirty-fifth birthday. Over the years, the men in her life, including Damon Thomas and Ray J, had all enjoyed driving the prestigious sports cars around the boulevards of Los Angeles. She could afford it. *Keeping Up with the Kardashians* had been recommissioned for three years by E! for a reported $40 million.

Kanye wasn't shy about publicity, but he had to get used to the media demanding a daily diet of Kim stories. She would post something on Twitter or Instagram to her millions of followers and the media would report what she said or did, thereby increasing the exposure. Her use of social media was masterful.

He had the last laugh, however. He surprised her by announcing that she was pregnant in front of a crowd of 5,000 fans at one of his concerts in Atlantic City on 30 December 2012. Kim, who was in the audience, had expected them to wait until she was showing, but Kanye always acts on impulse. He shouted into the mic, 'Stop the music!' and then pointed to Kim in the audience and said, 'Can we make some noise, please, for my baby mama right here?!'

The next day she confirmed the news on her website. 'Kanye and I are expecting a baby. We feel so blessed and lucky and wish that in addition to both of our families, his mom and my dad could be here to celebrate this special time with us.'

18

BODY CONFIDENCE

———

One of the first tasks Kanye set himself when he and Kim finally got together was to sort out her closet. Ironically, he decided to do for her what she used to earn a living accomplishing for others. Generally, he doesn't like being filmed for television, but on this occasion he was happy to let the cameras show him piling up the clothes he thought should go.

He wanted Kim to be more daring in her choices and not fall into the stereotypical look of a well-dressed Beverly Hills socialite. By the time he had finished, she literally had no clothes left; he had discarded so many of her favourite outfits. Though naturally a little upset, she trusted his judgement. She was in awe of his combination of creativity and certainty. Outside her room, dozens of pairs of barely worn shoes were dumped, ready for eBay.

She promised that everything would be prepared for online auction within the month and that some of the proceeds would go to the new church the family had founded, called the California Community Church. The pastor, Brad Johnson, had been given a fresh start by Kris Jenner after he had to leave his previous ministry following an adultery scandal. She discovered him working in Starbucks and asked him to lead the new church. They began holding weekend meetings in the ballroom of the Sheraton Agoura Hills Hotel, just a few miles from Calabasas. Church members donate either $1,000 a month or 10 per cent of their incomes. Kim chose to do the latter. Thanks to the financial support of the Kardashians and the congregation, a new purpose-built church is being constructed close by.

Kanye provided Kim with a whole new wardrobe, including some of the pieces from his Paris fashion shows, as well as other top-drawer designers. He pointed out, 'Look how dope this shit is.' Kim agreed it was the 'dopest stuff'. She tried on a long green dress with a generously plunging neckline, which met with his instant approval: 'It's like "I'm getting on best-dressed lists now, I'm stepping all into this territory".' When she tried on a busty black dress, he stroked her hips and told her, 'You look amazing.' He was obviously impressed with his girlfriend's body.

Kim is the perfect subject for a designer. She is and always has been stunning. As Alison Jane Reid points out, 'There is no denying Kim was born beautiful. At 13, for her eighth-grade graduation, she looks as if she has just stepped out of a Scott Fitzgerald novel, with her cute twenties bob, black eyes and full, rosebud lips. When she is with T. J. Jackson at her high school graduation, she has her hair up, which sculpts her face and shows off those cheekbones and sparkling, confident, look-at-me eyes to perfection. She is film star beautiful. Hers is a kind of old Hollywood beauty, like a young Elizabeth Taylor. Her features, a gift from the Armenian side of her family, give her enviable blue-black hair, peach-coloured skin and almond eyes. She has that kind of luminous, intense beauty that's impossible to ignore.'

Kim's body shape has changed so much over the years. As a young woman, she was petite and relatively slender, albeit with her much admired assets obviously on display. She has had to contend with many rumours that she has had her breasts or bottom enhanced by artificial implants. Her sister Kourtney happily admits that she first had a boob job in college and then some further work in 2009. At 5 feet tall, she was a slip of a girl growing up, whereas Kim always had curves. Her mother, Kris Jenner, is also not shy about the amount of cosmetic surgery she has undergone, including two breast ops and a facelift that she had prior to Kim's wedding to Kris Humphries.

Kim only admits to Botox. She has often commented that her breasts are completely real and quite saggy – something she first pointed out in her notorious sex tape. She has described her bottom as perfectly natural for a woman with an Armenian heritage. Many will never believe it is completely natural, however, and there will always be questions. She once tried to silence the rumours on *Keeping Up with the Kardashians* by having her bottom X-rayed, which proved there was definitely nothing foreign in there, but didn't disprove theories that she had her own fat inserted.

The problem for Kim is that her bootylicious derrière has become an essential part of her image and, consequently, her brand. Whatever she wears, we want to see how it shows off her behind. She is happy to fuel this interest. When she posted a picture of her rear squeezed into a tight pair of jeans, she added the comment, 'I think my butt looks too big in these jeans.'

It could be argued that Kim's greatest asset as a fashion role model for young women is not her boobs or backside, but her complete physical self-assurance. Alison Jane Reid observes, 'She has always had a great décolleté and has been flaunting it since her teenage years. It's a sign of her extraordinary body confidence. Her bottom definitely seems to have changed shape to the point of being quite out of balance and proportion to her tiny frame. There is a popular craze in LA to have this exaggerated, pert bottom and Kim seems to have been seduced by this. There are trainers and exercises that promise to help you achieve this look all over the Internet.'

Since Kim emerged into the limelight in 2007, she has been at the forefront of a style that has brought the overtly sexual into the mainstream. Years ago it is a look that would have been considered vulgar, but now it is socially acceptable and aspirational for young women and girls.

'The problem for Kim is that she is inconsistent,' commented Alison Jane. 'One moment, she looks like an icon and a female business entrepreneur. The next, she wears a pair of curtains to the Met Ball or a slutty latex dress that makes her look like Jessica Rabbit. When she nails it, she looks like a goddess, as she did in the sublime wine red dress she wore to the 2011 *Huffington Post* Game Changers Awards in New York. I love the fact that she isn't afraid to celebrate her voluptuous body, but then she often takes it too far.'

Being pregnant is always a challenge for a celebrity used to facing the cameras every day they step outside. Their choice of expectant wear is a target for fashion commentators. The 'pair of curtains' was, in fact, a specially designed Givenchy gown by Riccardo Tisci, a close friend of Kanye. Kim had modified it considerably to take into account her larger body shape. The jersey dress, with silver grommet detailing, was attached to long sleeves and a high neck. She wasn't completely covered, however. The dress split high at the sides to reveal her shapely legs.

The Met Ball, also known as the Met Gala, is generally regarded as the number one fashion event of the year. The official purpose of the night is to raise funds for the Metropolitan Museum of Art's Costume Institute, but in reality it is the night when a galaxy of celebrities try to outshine one another. The long-standing chair of the event is Anna Wintour, the legendary editor-in-chief of *Vogue*.

The theme of the night in 2013 was punk, but critics poked fun at Kim's dress, noting the matching accessories and describing it as a Mrs Doubtfire dress. The floral fabric seemed very old fashioned. Alison Jane observed, 'This would have been great on a supermodel, like her stepsister Kendall Jenner, but it wasn't a good pregnancy look. It really seemed as if she had just bagged the loose cover from her couch. Memo – never cover yourself in chintz when heavily pregnant.'

Tisci, the creative director at Givenchy, defended the dress: 'To me pregnancy is the most beautiful thing in the world, and when you celebrate something, you give people flowers. I think she looked amazing. She was the most beautiful pregnant woman I have dressed in my career.'

Kim also backed her choice. 'I thought it was so cool and it got a lot of criticism and I didn't care because I really loved it.' While her dress wasn't well received, it did garner by far the most publicity on the night. Kim's attitude has always been that it's better to be noticed than ignored. She and Kanye had taken to wearing matching outfits, but on this occasion he sported an elegant black Givenchy suit and crisp white shirt, matched with shiny black shoes – a sharp contrast to Kim's fussy ensemble.

The Met Ball was her last big public outing before she was due to give birth. She was fortunate to have avoided morning sickness, but did admit that being pregnant was a 'little painful'. Her sister Khloé was more direct: 'Her back hurts, her breasts hurt, her stomach hurts, her feet hurt, her head hurts, her eyes hurt, her nails hurt. And she cries all the time.' In fact, Kim was quite poorly during the pregnancy. On one occasion, she was taken ill on a plane and was told by doctors that she needed to throttle back on her work commitments.

Kimye, as the media had named the couple, prepared for the arrival by buying a new family home, although palace would be a better description of the 10,000 square-foot property in a gated Bel Air community, where their neighbours included Jennifer Aniston and Joe Francis. Set in three-quarters of an acre, the house was so large, it had an elevator to access the five bedrooms and seven bathrooms. It was built in the Tuscan style that Kim liked, but Kanye was intent on remodelling and began a huge redevelopment that practically meant pulling down the house and starting again. There was little chance it would be ready by the time their first child was born.

Kim decided that she wasn't going to be filmed giving birth on *Keeping Up with the Kardashians*. Kourtney, who now had two children, had already done that successfully and apparently easily, and Kim didn't want millions of viewers watching her push her daughter into the world. She hinted that she intended to be a touch more private in the future. She did, however, share early on in her pregnancy that she was expecting a girl.

Kanye spent much of Kim's pregnancy away from home, recording a new album in Paris, where he always felt so inspired, and returning by private jet when he was required for doctor's appointments. The cast of the reality show never saw him. Bruce Jenner confided that he had met him only once, while his son Brody, who had joined the cast for the ninth series, had never met him. Kim likes Paris, so she would travel over to stay at his loft apartment above a hotel while he concentrated on recording. The result was the critically acclaimed album *Yeezus*.

He made it back to Los Angeles for the baby shower, but arrived, hidden underneath a hoodie, when it was nearly all over. This wasn't a cosy gathering of a handful of guests in the lounge, but a full-blown occasion, bigger than most weddings. The white-themed party was another Kardashian event held in the gardens of the Azoff home in Beverly Hills. A series of marquees was erected, so that guests could dine alfresco while keeping out of the sun. Kim wore a voluminous, flowing white gown and kept cool, thanks to a security guard walking beside her with an open parasol shielding her from the brunchtime sun.

Thousands of dollars of white bouquets and table arrangements were shipped in as more than 50 guests, including Mel B, Kelly Osbourne, Nicole Richie and Kimberly Stewart mingled and waited their turn to wish the mum-to-be the best of luck. All the women wore white garlands in their hair to match the dress code. Kendall Jenner, who had grown up before the eyes of a television audience, stood out, as any top model should, by wearing all turquoise.

Very few men braved the day. Lamar Odom and Scott Disick dutifully arrived together. Kim's nephew, Mason, wore white and looked the image of his father. Kanye clearly didn't want the photographers to take his picture on this particular day, although his reluctance to show his face may also have had something to do with him ending his association with Irving Azoff. The Live Nation company had promoted his *Watch the Throne* tour with Jay Z, but apparently Irving and Kanye didn't agree about how his career should progress.

Inevitably, Kanye's prolonged absence in Paris led to whispers that all was not well with the relationship. On top of that, Kim had to deal with a kiss-and-tell story in which a Canadian model claimed to have slept with Kanye after a concert in Atlantic City the previous summer. She also alleged a meeting took place in October in New York, where he kept an apartment. Considering the high profile of the Kardashians, there have been relatively few exposés over the years. The most graphic, as far as Kim personally is concerned, was when a porn star called Julian St Jox alleged he had a threesome with Kim and another woman – a porn actress – at a swingers' party in Culver City when Kim was 20.

The rumours were well wide of the mark, as Kanye prepared to be based full time in California by quietly listing his Manhattan bachelor apartment for $4.5 million. He intended to take family life seriously when his daughter was born. He instructed removal men to ship his most precious possessions to Los Angeles.

His move coincided with the news, a week after the baby shower, that after many months Kim was finally divorced. Apparently, the lawyers reached a settlement in April that put an end to nearly two years of legal jousting. Kim and Kris had both signed a prenup, but the prolonged proceedings were due to Kris demanding an annulment rather than a straight-forward divorce. In the end, agreement was reached before she was due to give birth, which was a huge relief to her. In any self-respecting rom-com, the heroine takes a wrong turn before realising where true love lies and, unfortunately for all concerned, the marriage to Kris was Kim's.

She was supposed to have six weeks before the delivery date, but that didn't happen. Instead, 12 days after becoming a free woman again, she was rushed to her birthing suite at the Cedars-Sinai Medical Center, complaining that all was not well. She needed to go into emergency labour, because she was suffering from pre-eclampsia, a condition that can affect women in the latter stages of pregnancy and result in soaringly high blood pressure. The only way to cure it is to deliver the baby, so Kim gave birth five weeks early, on 15 June 2013, to a girl weighing 4lb 15oz. Kanye made it to the hospital in time, although he waited outside during the emergency delivery. Sweetly, he couldn't contain his excitement: 'When I walked in to see her, Kim was holding the baby. I said, "Oh my God, you're a natural." Kim said, "I know, it's so weird."'

The expectation was that they would name the child something beginning with K, and Kaidance was an early favourite. Speculation ended when news was leaked that she was going to be called North, which led to much guffawing in the media. One humorist suggested the child was going to go straight to the top … and a little to the left. According to Kris Jenner, the choice had nothing to do with points of the compass. Instead, Kim explained to her that the significance of North was that to them it meant highest power, and her birth was the highest point of their life to date. Kris said, 'I thought that was really sweet.' Mostly, Kim and Kanye called their new daughter Nori, a neat combination of their middle names – Noel and Omari.

Their new home wasn't ready. They were still choosing the furnishings, including gold fittings for the four luxury toilets, a Swarovski-encrusted fridge-freezer and six special edition beds similar to the ones in the best suites at the Savoy Hotel in London. The new family moved into Kris Jenner's house in Hidden Hills. She and Bruce spent most of their time at a property they still owned in Malibu, which gave Kim and Kanye some privacy – although they employed a nurse to make sure their premature baby suffered no problems in her early weeks.

Three days after North was born, the album *Yeezus* was released and went to number one in both the UK and the US, as well as another 29 countries worldwide. June was turning out to be a very good month. They decided against negotiating a fee for the first pictures of their baby. They didn't need the money, as *Forbes* placed them fifth among the highest-earning celebrity couples, with $30 million – still some way behind top-ranked Jay Z and Beyoncé, who had collected $95 million the previous year.

Instead, Kanye was a guest on the season finale of Kris Jenner's new talk show and proudly showed a picture of his child on screen. He spoke movingly of his love for Kim and North: 'Now I have two really special people to live for, a whole family to live for; a whole world to live for.' Disappointingly for Kris, who up until this point seemed to have a Midas touch on TV, the show was cancelled by Fox after six episodes – even a rare interview with Kanye couldn't save it.

Now that the baby was thriving, her parents could think about marriage. Kanye didn't disappoint. He met Kris and told her confidentially that he was going to propose. She loved his grandiose plan, and persuaded him to allow them to film the moment for *Keeping Up with the Kardashians*. He agreed on the basis that nothing would be shown immediately. He intended to make his move on Kim's thirty-third birthday. Only Kris knew what was really going on. Everyone else in the family was told that he had a big surprise planned for Kim's birthday and they needed to be at the AT&T Park, home of the San Francisco Giants, on 21 October.

On the night, Kanye led a blindfolded Kim out into the centre of the ballpark. Fireworks lit up the sky and a 50-piece orchestra serenaded her with her favourite Lana Del Rey song, 'Young and Beautiful'. When he told her to remove the blindfold, he was down on one knee, with the widest smile on his face and his arm outstretched with an engagement ring in his hand. Above, fireworks spelled out 'Pleeease Marry Meee!'. Kim, who thought it was going to be an extravagant birthday party and genuinely didn't know what was going to happen, couldn't conceal her delight, as she shouted yes and took her new fiancé in her arms for a loving kiss. In the rom-com film of their lives, *When Yeezy Met Kimmy*, this was the perfect ending, without a dry eye in the cinema.

Two people were conspicuously absent from the big night: Lamar Odom and Bruce Jenner. When asked, Lamar would only say that he had something to do. Bruce, however, had quietly split up with Kris and it seemed inappropriate for him to join the celebration.

After becoming a mum, Kim worked hard to lose the 50 pounds she had gained during pregnancy. It paid off, because in December she looked back to her fashionable best at the *Hollywood Reporter* Women in Entertainment breakfast in a mustard silk dress and coat that matched her newly dyed blonde hairdo. Kanye had always been an advocate of mono-chrome outfits, using all one colour to create a striking effect.

Now that she was seeing more of him, they were able to confer every day on her outfits. She stopped using a stylist all the time, preferring to share the task with him. If she was going to a shoot, then he would often show up to give his opinion and input some ideas. She said simply, 'He is my best stylist.'

As a preface to their actual wedding, Kim fulfilled a long-term ambition when she appeared on the front cover of *Vogue* for the first time at the beginning of May. She said it was a 'dream come true'. For the shoot, she wore a Lanvin wedding gown, with her engagement ring, another creation by Lorraine Schwartz, prominently displayed. Kanye stood behind her and held her in his arms. Annie Leibovitz, one of the finest and most prestigious photographers in the world, had taken the sort of understated shot that always seems to work best for Kim.

She looked beautiful. Would her own wedding dress look as good later in the month when they married in Florence? Kanye has a great affinity with Europe and he wanted his wedding to be across the Atlantic. He might well have settled in Paris permanently if he had chosen to pursue a career exclusively in fashion.

Their wedding celebrations began on a Wednesday in Paris, at Givenchy, where presumably Kim was having a final fitting for her wedding dress. The next day, she chose a pearl-covered outfit from Balmain couture to pose with her girlfriends in front of the Eiffel Tower and the Louvre Museum. In the evening, her closest female friends joined her for a special dinner. Her mother's best friend, Shelli Azoff, proposed a toast that gave an emotional insight into the kind of woman Kim is behind the glamour of her celebrity image. Shelli said, 'I am incredibly proud, and always have been, of who you are as a human being, as a person. I am incredibly proud of how smart you are. I am incredibly proud of how kind you are. I am incredibly proud of where you are today and I love you very much.' Kim beamed.

On Friday, Kim and Kanye joined their guests for a brunch hosted by the legendary designer Valentino in the gardens of his seventeenth-century Chateau de Wideville, just west of the capital. In the evening, there was a private tour of the Palace of Versailles.

On Saturday, 24 May 2014, they were married in Florence at the sixteenth-century Forte di Belvedere, next to the Boboli Gardens, with views across one of the most beautiful settings in the world. It was perfect. One hundred white doves were released into the sky as they exchanged their vows. As Kim walked down the aisle on the arm of her stepfather, she heard the sound of one of her favourite singers, Andrea Bocelli, singing 'Ave Maria'. She looked up and, amazingly, he was actually there in person, performing for her at her wedding. He continued with 'Con te partirò' during the service. Later, at the reception, John Legend, a good friend of Kanye, sang his soulful ballad 'All of Me'. Rumours that Beyoncé was going to perform proved to be untrue, as neither she nor Jay Z attended.

Kim couldn't have looked lovelier. She had three wedding dresses ready, but on the day chose a sublime couture gown by Kanye's friend Riccardo Tisci for Givenchy. Alison Jane Reid enthused, 'It was a demure lace and pearl embellished work of art that fitted and flattered her body like a second skin. Most importantly, the dress is flattering from all angles.

'The dazzling white of the gown gave her a look of extraordinary radiance and contrasted brilliantly with her dark hair and black eyes. For once, Kim didn't flaunt an ounce of flesh and she looked luminous, elegant, timeless and as regal as a royal bride.' For many, Kim's dress outshone Kate Middleton's Alexander McQueen gown when she married Prince William, simply because it wasn't as safe and successfully walked the fine line between demure and sexy. Alison Jane explained, 'The Givenchy gown works because it shows the line of her body, while the flesh stays covered. This is a great fashion conceit – to give tantalising hints at what lies beneath.'

This time the wedding wasn't filmed for *Keeping Up with the Kardashians*, although the reality show was there for all the build-up. E! no doubt helped with the bill. Both Bruce and Kris Jenner gave speeches at the dinner afterwards. Bruce wasn't the centre of attention on this day, but he soon would be.

19
CAITLYN

Kim kept the biggest Kardashian family secret for more than a decade. She had arrived home unexpectedly and found her stepfather wearing a dress. Apparently, she was so taken aback that she ignored his efforts to explain, ran straight out of the house and never mentioned what she had witnessed to anyone. She said later that she thought it was something she wasn't supposed to talk about.

Nobody spoke about Bruce's gender or cross-dressing issues in the Kardashian or Jenner households. He insisted that when he met Kris he was 'a good solid B cup' because of his hormone treatment. She doesn't agree with his version of events, maintaining that there was nothing obvious, just a hint of man-boob.

The first time the public had an inkling was when Robert Kardashian's widow, Ellen, revealed that Bruce was a secret cross-dresser in an interview with a tabloid magazine in January 2012. She claimed then that his first wife had confided in her at a drinks party.

Ellen said that Chrystie Crownover, who had remarried and was now called Chrystie Scott, had told her that she discovered what was going on when she returned from a trip and realised he had gone through her clothes. He had even clipped an elastic band to one of her bras, so he could fit into it.

Surprisingly, the revelation didn't lead to a public clamouring for more information. Perhaps they didn't believe that the Olympic hero liked to wear female clothing around the house. It seemed so far-fetched, especially as it hadn't featured in any episode of *Keeping Up with the Kardashians*.

The story said that Kris Jenner had always known about it. The suggestion in the ground-breaking *Vanity Fair* interview was that she had set some rules, which meant he could only indulge in cross-dressing when he was away from home. She denied this.

A man dressing as woman is largely a subject of comedy in modern culture, with films such as *Tootsie* and *Mrs Doubtfire* becoming box office success stories. In the UK, there is a long tradition of hugely popular entertainers, including Dick Emery, Les Dawson and Paul O'Grady (Lily Savage), relying on cross-dressing to get a laugh. The implication as far as Bruce Jenner was concerned was that, even if it were true, it was just a bit of eccentric fun.

The Jenners' marriage had been going downhill, practically ever since the cameras invaded their lives. Bruce felt he was being sidelined in his own home, as Kris seized the opportunity to build an empire that left him on the fringes. They argued all the time, seemingly wanting different things from their lives.

Bruce hated the way he had become unimportant. He told *Vanity Fair* that gender issues weren't the principal reason for the breakdown of his marriage: 'Twenty per cent was gender and 80 per cent was the way I was treated.' Her opinion was that he never fully explained his gender dysphoria until after they were divorced.

The rumours that all was not well had been in circulation for months before the Jenners finally split in June 2013. Bruce stayed in Malibu, where he had always preferred to live. Kris moved back permanently to Hidden Hills and shared the house with Kim, Kanye and baby North.

Bruce and Kris issued a joint statement: 'We are living separately and are much happier this way. But we will always have much love and respect for each other. Even though we are separated, we will always remain best friends, and, as always, our family will remain our number one priority.' The statement, which yet again emphasised the importance of family, had the air of something dictated by Kris.

Bruce decided that now was the time to move forward with his gender transformation, although he had no plans to go public with his decision before the divorce had been granted. It's easy to forget that Bruce and Kris had been married for more than 20 years. In her autobiography, published two years before, in 2011, she had acknowledged Bruce for 'twenty years of unwavering love, happiness and support'.

While Kris was announcing to the world that they had a 'pretty fabulous' relationship after their separation, he was intent on embracing his female identity fully. He made an appointment for a tracheal shave, a common process for transgender women, which reduces the size of the Adam's apple. A surgeon makes an incision in the throat and slices off part of the cartilage to achieve a more feminine appearance.

Unfortunately, in December 2014, he was seen leaving a consultation in Beverly Hills, and a story appeared online that he was planning the procedure, which is often one of the first steps towards gender reassignment surgery. It was nearly the final straw for Bruce, who had lived a lifetime of agony. He contemplated suicide, using a gun he kept in the house: 'I've been in some dark places.'

A week before Christmas, his divorce from Kris was finalised. There had never been a prenup agreement, so, basically, they each kept their own assets and existing contracts. Both had become extremely rich over the years, although Kris was by far the wealthier of the two, thanks to her business acumen.

She kept the family home in Hidden Hills and agreed to pay Bruce $2.5 million, but no spousal support was involved. Bruce had by now bought a new $3.5 million home in Malibu. They divided up the vehicles. She had the Bentley, a Rolls-Royce Ghost and a Range Rover, while he kept a Porsche Coupe, a Cadillac Escalade and the Harley-Davidson motorcycle that he had always loved.

The appearance of the story about his tracheal shave meant he needed to tell his children his plans as a priority. He was no longer in control of the time frame. He discovered that his four elder children already knew of his struggle with his gender identity. Chrystie had told Burt and Casey 20 years before and they had kept his secret, as so many had in this story, because of their love and regard for him.

Linda didn't tell Brandon and Brody until after the first stories started to appear about the cross-dressing, but it gave them an insight into their father and to some extent explained why he had found it difficult to maintain a connection with them. That was about to change for his four eldest children. For the first time in many years, they would feel they were genuinely part of their father's life, as he became the person he had always wanted to be – a woman of poise and grace called Caitlyn Jenner.

The Jenner side of the family readily accepted his frank admission about how he wanted to live his life in the future. His daughter Cassandra, in particular, bonded with her father during a girls' night at the house in Malibu, when he was finding his feet with female company in a social setting. When he first told her, she asked him what she should call him. He replied, 'I'm Dad. You can call me Dad.'

After he had told all his children individually, he underwent an exceptionally painful 10-hour procedure called facial feminisation surgery, which involved reconstructing the contours of his face to give him more recognisably female features. He also had breast augmentation.

Bruce decided it would be best to move out from under Kris's management umbrella, and hired a new team to mastermind his public revelations. A masterful campaign took shape under the watchful guidance of Alan Nierob, a long-standing executive at Rogers & Cowan, who had helped to suppress a story about Bruce's cross-dressing as far back as the 1980s.

Nierob decided the journalist Buzz Bissinger could have three months' access for a *Vanity Fair* article, in which he would reveal Bruce's new identity for the first time. The accompanying pictures would be taken by Annie Leibovitz.

The world became aware of what was happening to Bruce for the first time in April 2015, during a two-hour *20/20* special with Diane Sawyer, *Bruce Jenner: The Interview*. It was filmed at his Malibu home and watched by 16.9 million viewers. He told the distinguished broadcaster, 'To all intents and purposes, I am a woman.' He also told her that this would be the last interview he would ever give as Bruce Jenner.

The programme was universally praised for handling a difficult issue with humanity and frankness. Diane didn't avoid asking the questions that needed to be answered for the public to understand what Caitlyn was going through. That included clarifying the issue of his sexuality. He told Diane that he was heterosexual, had never been with a man and wasn't gay. This was an issue of gender, not sexuality. He understood that it was confusing for some people to understand that sexual orientation and gender identity aren't the same thing. He said of his own sexuality: 'Let's go with asexual for now. I'm going to learn a lot in the next year.'

Bruce also admitted that he had downplayed the extent of his true nature to Kris, and was generous in his appreciation of his third ex-wife: 'I loved Kris. I had a wonderful life with her. I learned a lot from her.'

The Kardashian side of the family didn't appear in the broadcast. Their involvement would come later in episodes of their reality show. Bruce did reveal, however, that Kim had been by far 'the most accepting and easiest to talk to about it'. She had said to him, 'Girl, you gotta rock it, baby. You gotta look good.'

Up to that point, Bruce hadn't got on particularly well with Kanye West. They weren't close. It was the superstar, however, who held the most enlightened view in the Kardashian camp. He had an enormous influence on Kim's ability to accept what was happening and persuade the rest of her family to do the same.

During the Diane Sawyer interview, Bruce spoke about the role Kanye had played. 'He said to Kim, "Look, I can be married to the most beautiful woman in the world and I am. I can have the most beautiful little daughter in the world and I have that ... But I'm nothing if I can't be me. If I can't be true to myself, they don't mean anything."'

Khloé found it most difficult to process the news. Bruce said she had taken it hardest. She had been most obviously affected by the death of her father and seemed the most sensitive of the children.

At times, Bruce was emotional and a little tearful as he explained that his brain was much more female than male. That was where his soul was, and what he had tried to explain to his children. He told Diane, 'I'm saying goodbye to people's perception of me and who I am. I'm not saying goodbye to me. Because this has always been me.'

The response to the broadcast, particularly among celebrities, was supportive and positive. Elton John said, 'It's an incredibly brave thing to do, especially when you're older.' Lena Dunham observed, 'I think it's an incredibly powerful and brave move to disclose anything about your gender identity or sexuality in such a judgemental society. The interview is going to mean a lot to a lot of young people.'

His family tweeted their love and support. Kim used the hashtag 'ProudDaughter' and wrote in Kanye-like terms: 'Love is the courage to live the truest, best version of yourself. Bruce is love. I love you, Bruce.' Kris Jenner said, 'Not only was I able to call him my husband for 25 years and father of my children, I am now able to call him my hero.' The most touching reaction came from Rob Kardashian: 'You have always been a role model to me and now more than ever, I look up to you. LOVE YOU!!!!'

The one voice that jarred with the prevailing mood belonged to Kris Humphries, who tweeted, 'Man, I'm glad I got out when I did.' After a night's sleep, Kris hastily apologised for his ill-considered remark, which proved an interesting contrast with the attitude of Kanye, the man who replaced him.

Another two months would pass before the *Vanity Fair* issues hit the news-stands, revealing that Bruce was no more. 'Call me Caitlyn' proclaimed the cover, which featured her wearing a one-piece white swimsuit. The picture, a throwback to old-style Hollywood glamour, is already an iconic image. Caitlyn looked astonishing for a woman of 65, an age when you normally collect your pension and a free bus pass.

It hadn't been easy for Caitlyn to choose her new name. She considered both Heather and Cathy, before settling on a name she had felt an affinity with since childhood. It would have been unbearably twee to have spelt it with a K and, in any case, the choice was made more complicated by the fact that her son Brody's girlfriend was the blogger Kaitlynn Carter.

The most seized-upon revelation in *Vanity Fair* was Caitlyn's claim that she hadn't been treated well by her former wife. She said Kris had become less tolerant, controlled the money and had mistreated Bruce. It was strong stuff. Caitlyn said, 'A lot of times she wasn't very nice.' Kris was, by all accounts, 'beyond distraught' after these remarks.

Inside the magazine, the photographs were as glamorous as the cover. Caitlyn reclined on a sofa in a black Hervé Leger top and skirt. She sat in her dressing room in an Agent Provocateur corset. She posed confidently behind the wheel of her Porsche, a $180,000 gift from Kris, in a scarlet dress by DKNY. She compared the shoot with winning Olympic Gold in 1976: 'That was a good day. But the last couple of days were better.'

The *Vanity Fair* exclusive was empowering for the transgender community. One of the most powerful effects was when 18 transgender people posted their own '*Vanity Fair*' covers, introducing themselves to the world, proclaiming 'Call me' followed by their new name. Some commentators pointed out that not everyone had the money to afford the treatment and surgery that Caitlyn had undergone. They also might not be able to afford high-end designer dresses to look as good as she did.

Kim met Caitlyn for the first time when she was invited to attend the Leibovitz photographic sessions. She observed, 'She's beautiful and I'm so proud that she can just be her authentic self. I guess that's what life is all about.' Under Kanye's influence, Kim has been able to approach important issues in a sensitive and intelligent manner. She drew attention to the plight of the many transgender men and women who didn't have the family support Caitlyn enjoyed: 'There's such a high suicide rate in the transgender community, which is heartbreaking.'

Kim had touched on an issue that would become Caitlyn's cause in the coming months – the treatment of transgender men and women, particularly the young and vulnerable, in society. Caitlyn began a series of blogs to highlight the ordeals of people fighting for survival in the world. She wrote, 'Many trans teens are bullied and abused in high school. It's just horrendous.' In a second blog, she told the heartbreaking story of a 14-year-old trans boy in San Diego, who had been unable to cope with the pressures and had committed suicide.

Caitlyn drew further attention to the plight of the transgender community when she received the Arthur Ashe Courage Award at the 2015 ESPYs in Los Angeles. She received a standing ovation and delivered a powerful speech, which harked back to the hundreds of motivational speeches she had given as Bruce Jenner.

She said, 'All across this country right now, all across the world, at this very moment, there are young people coming to terms with being transgender ... They're getting bullied, they're getting beaten up, they're getting murdered, and they're committing suicide ... Trans people deserve something vital. They deserve your respect. And from that respect comes a more compassionate community, a more empathetic society and a better world for us all.'

The stirring speech pointed to a future role for Caitlyn. It seemed incredible that this was the put-upon dad figure from *Keeping Up with the Kardashians*. She had managed to hide his true self for more than 400 episodes.

Her own television series, *I Am Cait*, premiered 10 days later on E!. It was another Bunim/Murray production and apparently the Jenner children decided not to take part in what they feared was just another entertainment show. His 95-year-old mother Esther featured, however, and poignantly referred to Caitlyn as Bruce throughout: 'It's overwhelming. I knew he was going to be dressed as a woman. I think he is a very good-looking woman, but he is still Bruce to me.'

Kim and Kanye were also involved. Kim bonded with Caitlyn over her wardrobe. They went off together to investigate her clothes and Kim told her which outfits looked chic and which had to go – presumably on eBay. The Queen of the Closet Scene hadn't lost her magic touch when it came to styling.

The rapper told Caitlyn that her transition was 'one of the strongest things that has happened in our existence as human beings who are controlled by perception.' Kanye, who seldom features in his wife's reality show, praised the way Caitlyn had overcome so many hurdles: 'You couldn't have been up against more. Like, your daughter [Kendall] is a supermodel, you're a celebrity, you have every type of thing, and it was still like, "Fuck everybody, this is who I am."'

20

DOUBLE THE POWER

———

Kim works just as hard today for *Keeping Up with the Kardashians* as she did when it started 10 seasons ago. She has been up for six hours by the time filming begins at noon. She wakes at 6a.m., checks North's baby monitor by the side of the bed and then her emails on her phone. She gets tired, but is never hungover, so she hasn't lost the knack of springing out of bed to face the day.

After popping into her daughter's bedroom to say good morning, she is straight into her jogging gear for a run along one of the many trails that twist around Hidden Hills. It's scenic and safe, although many of the residents do like to ride their horses first thing in the morning. If she doesn't fancy leaving the house, she can make do with an hour in the home gym.

They never moved into the mansion in Bel Air, which they have been renovating since they bought it at the beginning of 2013. It seems likely they will sell it quietly when a potential buyer comes along who will ensure a tidy profit. Instead, they both seem to have settled on Hidden Hills as a better place to raise their family. Living at her mother's house reminded Kim how much she enjoyed the quiet of the gated and guarded community.

Kanye often preferred to keep away from the madness of *Keeping Up with the Kardashians* and stay at his old bachelor home at the foot of the Hollywood Hills, which has been on the market for five years. That unsatisfactory arrangement changed when they finally bought a family property to move into in August 2014.

The fully landscaped three-acre estate was previously owned by Lisa Marie Presley, and reportedly cost them just under $20 million. It boasts eight bedrooms, 10 bathrooms, eight fire-places, two swimming pools, two spas, tennis courts and a vineyard, a rose garden, an acre of lawn and a gated motor court. For good measure, there's an entertainment pavilion and a separate, secluded guest house – and they bought the house next door for a miserly $2.9 million to guarantee their privacy. The main, stone-fronted manor house is actually a new-build in the French country style. This may be what the snobs of Beverly Hills and Bel Air call the suburbs, but it's undeniably grand even for someone brought up in Tower Lane.

They can easily afford this luxury. Kim could write the cheque from her own earnings alone. Rich list figures often seem to be plucked from thin air, but *Forbes* suggests that from 2014 to 2015 her income has risen from $28 million to $53 million. Much of that increase is due to the success of her iPhone and tablet game, *Kim Kardashian: Hollywood*, which launched in June 2014. It's a brilliant concept. You create your own Kim Kardashian-like character and see yourself rise to fame and fortune. Within nine months, it had become a huge hit, with an estimated 28 million downloads and 11 billion minutes of play.

The concept of being able to update the game in real time came about by accident. Kim put a picture of herself in a bikini on Instagram the day of the launch, when she was on holiday at Joe Francis's Mexican estate. Fans immediately thought it was part of the game and started to update their app with the swimsuit she was wearing.

The characteristics of the game mirror Kim's own lifestyle and progress. You can customise your look from literally hundreds of style options, just as Kim does when her make-up and hair team descend on the house every day at 10 a.m. to prepare her for filming. It normally takes about an hour and a half. If she has an early meeting in Los Angeles, then she will forgo her morning run and be in the 'glam room', as she calls her dressing room, at dawn to be fashioned into Kim Kardashian. Her make-up artist will have hundreds of brushes and blushes ready to contour her face into her now iconic look. The result is somewhat futuristic, and one that suppresses individual beauty in favour of a flawless mask, but it is very much of the moment.

Kim has a lot of meetings because her projects are on a conveyor belt, whizzing by like the prizes at the end of a game show. They either generate publicity and greater fame or cash in on it. The inspired 'Break the Internet' campaign was part of the former, based around a nude photo shoot for *Paper* magazine, in which she posed with a champagne glass balanced on her butt. Other front and rear shots were great fun and cheeky. They seemed much more brazen than the more innocent days of *Playboy*. It was just the image boost she needed before she starred in the 30-second commercial for T-Mobile's Data Stash, which premiered during the 2015 Super Bowl.

Kim is careful to build her diary around the reality show rather than try to squeeze it in between other business meetings, pet projects or family time. The Kardashians, on the other hand, made a sort of Faustian pact to live their lives as if they were the cast of *The Truman Show*, the famous 1998 comedy-drama starring Jim Carrey. The main character is unaware that his life is a carefully constructed reality television show, broadcast to millions around the world. The Kardashians are well aware that they live in a constructed reality show. Kim has even made the connection to the movie herself in trying to describe what her life is like. When they are filming, they often don't stop for lunch. One camera crew breaks and another comes in, so they never stop rolling and can capture Kim eating what her chef has prepared that day.

'They are consummate performers,' observed Kevin O'Sullivan, TV critic of the *Sunday Mirror*. 'They know what to do in front of the camera to an excruciating extent. Sure, the Kardashians play to the cameras, but there is innately something about them that makes them born reality television stars. Their lives would be car crashes with or without the prism of reality television. I firmly believe Kim would go out and marry someone for 72 days whether or not she was on telly.'

The success of the show was never better illustrated than in February 2015, when the Kardashians signed a new four-year deal with E! reputed to be worth $100 million. They were already the highest-paid stars in reality television and this reinforced their status. The figure is probably inflated, nevertheless they do make an absolute fortune. The show will be even more female dominated than before, with the six women taking the limelight: Kim, Kourtney, Khloé, Kendall, Kylie and their mother, Kris Jenner.

All the major events of the family's lives are chronicled. Everything is shared. No storyline could ever match the journey of Caitlyn Jenner from Olympic champion to the most famous transgender person in the world. The tenth series of *Keeping Up with the Kardashians* will be her last, although crossovers with her own show, *I Am Cait*, will almost certainly continue. The publicity surrounding Caitlyn's transition has understandably eclipsed everything. The emotional struggle of Kris Jenner, whom she was married to for 23 years, was largely forgotten, as viewers became absorbed in which swimsuit Caitlyn would choose for her first dip in a pool as a transgender woman.

Khloé Kardashian observed that her mother was probably the most 'jarred' by what had happened and was left wondering if her life for all those years they were together was still validated. She was questioning, according to Khloé, whether Caitlyn was ever truly in love with her. Whatever her private thoughts, Kris has been very supportive of her ex-husband in public: 'I think that someone following their dream is truly inspirational to a lot of people … You have to do what makes you happy.'

At the age of 58, she embarked on a new relationship with a music executive, Corey Gamble, whom she met in August 2014 in Ibiza at the fortieth birthday party for Riccardo Tisci,

Kanye's great friend and the designer of Kim's wedding dress. Corey, who is 24 years younger than Kris, comes from Atlanta, the same home town as Kanye.

Corey is very stylish and stands out from the crowd, with his diamond earrings and shaven head. For the first time, Kris is following the lead of her famous daughters and dating a handsome and fashionable African-American. He works for Justin Bieber's manager, Scooter Braun, and is usually part of the superstar's entourage around the world.

Kris and Corey were seen enjoying dinner dates back home in Los Angeles and he was her plus one for Kim's thirty-fourth birthday celebrations, which were held, as usual, in Las Vegas. A year later, they are still a couple, despite him being younger than Kim. Her children have found it interesting, to say the least, watching their mum date again after all these years.

On one occasion, when Kim and Khloé popped round to their mother's house, they heard the banging of the headboard coming from Kris's bedroom, a sign that vigorous sex was being enjoyed. The two sisters kept as quiet as possible, waiting for them to finish, so they could have a cup of tea and a visit. When everything went silent, they expected to see their mum walk into the kitchen. Instead, the headboard started banging again, as they went for round two. Kim and Khloé had heard more than enough and crept away.

Kris and Corey flew to Europe in June 2015 for a romantic break, but also to support Kendall Jenner, who was one of the catwalk stars of Men's Fashion Week in Paris. They sat in the front row at Riccardo's show for Givenchy and watched Kendall and Naomi Campbell vie for attention in daring outfits that seemed to have nothing to do with men's fashion.

Kendall and Kylie were youngsters when *Keeping Up with the Kardashians* was first broadcast in October 2007. Kendall was 11 and Kylie just 10 when they made their debut as refreshingly normal, sometimes sulky girls. The elder one grew up to be a stunningly attractive girl who dreamed of being a model: 'I would sit at home and have my friends take pictures of me on my little Canon camera that my mom gave me for Christmas.'

While she can't yet match Kim's following on social media, the gap is closing. When Kim broke through the barrier of 27 million followers on Instagram, Kendall had more than 20 million.

She has used her online presence to generate interest in her modelling career, which began at the age of 14, when Wilhelmina Models signed her. In the early years, her mother helped guide her career, but in 2013 she joined The Society management and moved into the runway world of high fashion. Their biggest coup to date was landing her the contract as the face of cosmetics giant Estée Lauder. The company shrewdly allowed her to make the announcement on Instagram and Twitter, thus immediately hitting millions of young women within the right age demographic. The slight irony in choosing Kendall is that, unlike Kim, she rarely looks like she's wearing any make-up.

The media, which can't bear the fact that she never seems to have a steady boyfriend, have tried to link her with Justin Bieber, Harry Styles, Lewis Hamilton and the bisexual model Cara Delevingne.

Much of her personal branding, which has been set up by her mother, consists of joint ventures with her more controversial sister Kylie. It very much follows Kim's blueprint for commercial success with her personal clothing and jewellery lines.

Kylie, meanwhile, admitted on an episode of *Keeping Up with the Kardashians* that she had lip-fillers, which was no surprise to anyone who could see how much her face had changed recently. She also had to contend with rumours that she had a boob job at 17, claims that she firmly denied online.

Most controversial is her ongoing relationship with Tyga (Michael Ray Nguyen-Stevenson), the Vietnamese-Jamaican rapper. He apparently met her for the first time when he was the guest artist at Kendall's Sweet 16 party. She was 14 and he was 21. At the time, he was with his fiancée, a hip-hop model and former stripper called Blac Chyna (Angela White), and the pair had a little boy, King. Kris and Kim, resembling an expensively dressed aunt, were both at the party, looking obviously out of place, as the latter politely thanked the shirtless Tyga for coming.

Neither Tyga nor Kylie confirmed anything more than a friendship. Kris Jenner was diplomatic when asked about it. Tyga lived in the same neighbourhood as Khloé, she said, and he and Kylie shared many mutual friends. It became slightly harder to conceal their true feelings when Kylie became 18 in August 2015 and he gave her a white Ferrari worth $320,000 as a birthday present.

He parked the car, tied with a red ribbon, outside the Bootsy Bellows nightclub in West Hollywood, where Kylie, with a new blonde hairdo, was celebrating with her friends and family, including her father, Caitlyn Jenner, who was meeting Tyga for the first time.

When Tyga and Blac Chyna were together, they were very good friends with Kim and Kanye and were pictured out with them. She even appeared in an episode of *Keeping Up with the Kardashians* during the ninth season. To make matters even more awkward, she is now best friends with Kanye's ex-lover, Amber Rose.

Both Kylie and Kendall's ongoing storylines in real life already reveal just how much more mileage there is left in the Kardashian family reality show. Kim and Kourtney are mothers in their mid-thirties, so it's important that the younger women can bring fresh material and new characters into the family's world.

Kourtney has, for some time, ensured that the show takes second place behind her three children in her list of priorities. As well as Mason, aged five, she has Penelope Scotland, who was born 8 July 2012. She gave birth to a second son, Reign Aston, on 14 December 2014 and, by an unusual twist of fate, he shares Mason's birthday. She has always been single-minded and decided early on that she was always going to be home to put her children to bed and she wasn't going to work weekends.

The roller-coaster of her relationship with Scott Disick has been one of the main threads throughout the years of the show. They always seemed a step away from getting married. He first proposed during an episode of *Kourtney and Kim Take New York* in 2005. She said no. When asked about their status at the beginning of 2015, he said, 'If it's not broke, don't fix it.'

By July, it was broke and they split up. He had struggled over the years with bouts of heavy drinking and partying. Kourtney once recalled that their fights always appeared fresh and new and kept playing on her mind, because, instead of being forgotten about, they were endlessly on repeat on the show. He had three bouts of rehab, culminating at a centre in Costa Rica, but he checked out after only a week.

The final straw came when he was pictured in Monaco at the beginning of July 2015 in the company of Chloé Bartoli, a celebrity stylist and old flame. They appeared affectionate, but you never know when that's just for the benefit of the photographers. It was enough for Kourtney, however, and she threw him out of their house in Calabasas. Fortunately, he already had another home in Beverly Hills.

Following the breakup, Scott was seen partying in Las Vegas and Calgary, while Kourtney posted pictures online of herself with her sons and daughter. She sought legal advice about custody of the children, but reports suggested she would be happy with joint custody. Scott isn't part of the new TV deal, but is already rumoured to be in talks with E! for a new reality show based loosely on the theme of *Entourage*. Nobody is still sure what he does for a living. He seems to invest in a variety of businesses but earns most from his celebrity appearances. Scott has always been one of the more interesting people in *Keeping Up with the Kardashians* – a show not blessed with strong male characters.

Kevin O'Sullivan explained that reality shows, like the most popular soaps, are based on strong female characters, usually headed by a matriarch. If Kris were in *Coronation Street* or *EastEnders*, she would be the landlady of the Rovers Return or the Queen Vic. 'These shows are about strong women and weak men revolving around them. That's why the Kardashians are like they are. Stupid men are exposed as idiots by strong women. This is the DNA of all soap operas and, leading on from that, of all reality shows, because women, mainly, watch the shows. All women in these programmes are ultimately winners, and all men are ultimately losers.'

While it would be no surprise if Scott and Kourtney rekindled their relationship in season 11, for the moment at least the men on the show are becoming thin on the ground. Robert Kardashian, makes such infrequent appearances that he gets paid by the individual episode. He seems to hate the goldfish bowl in which the other Kardashians happily go about their daily lives.

Of course, his insecurity, his growing bulk and his lack of desire to be filmed all featured on the show. He missed the Christmas celebration and couldn't face being a much-photographed guest at Kim's wedding to Kanye. Apparently, he flew to Europe before realising that he didn't want to be pictured so heavy, and caught a flight straight back home. When they discussed their worries about him on the show, Kim observed, 'He obviously has some kind of depression.'

He has always been in the shadow of his glamorous sisters, although he did far better than Kim on *Dancing with the Stars*, finishing runner-up in 2011. Kris found him enough commercial deals to become a millionaire, but he is nothing like as successful as his sisters, who have all manner of clothing shops and brands on their CV. Rob had to make do with his own sock line, called Arthur George.

He dated Rita Ora for a moment or two in 2012, but that quickly became nothing and he hasn't had a serious relationship since Adrienne Bailon, which ended in 2009. He may return to the show on a more full-time basis in the future, because it clearly needs a regular male character, but they may well build up roles for Corey and Tyga.

Kim has been surprisingly unsympathetic towards her kid brother, believing the family is being overindulgent. She acknowledged that he doesn't feel comfortable appearing on the show because of all the weight he has put on, but said: 'Do I think he smokes weed, drinks beer, hangs out and plays video games with his friends all day long? Yes.' Rob was reportedly furious that she spoke about him and was said to have blocked her from his phone. A few weeks later, however, relations appeared to have thawed again when he shared a picture of Kanye and North on Instagram and subsequently went for a hike with Kim, which she tweeted about as 'the hardest hike ever'.

Rob, now 28, still lives with Khloé in the house she bought after breaking up with Lamar Odom. She filed for divorce in early December 2013, after a turbulent year that included her husband's alleged battle with substance abuse and his arrest for driving under the influence – she herself had a DUI during the first series of the show. She also had to contend with various women coming forward to claim they've had affairs with the basketball player. Unsurprisingly, they sought marriage guidance, but that failed to provide any solutions.

Khloé is the most extrovert and emotional of the Kardashians. She is also extremely popular with people she meets every day in restaurants and stores. In the show, she plays the volatile sister, Kim is the sweet one and Kourtney is the thoughtful sibling. This represents only one aspect of their personalities, but it's the trait that has been developed to give them an individual identity on the show.

Khloé has had more than her share of the drama – not least in the question of her parentage. It's become almost a game online to speculate who her father might be, with suggestions ranging from O. J. Simpson to Lionel Richie and her mother's hairdresser, Alex Roldan. In one episode of *Keeping Up with the Kardashians*, Kris had a DNA test to prove that her daughter wasn't adopted, but it proved nothing about her father.

Both of Robert Kardashian's other wives, Jan Ashley and Ellen Kardashian, have claimed he told them he was not Khloé's dad, which wasn't very helpful to her. It's really a Prince Harry syndrome. Conspiracy theorists will always believe he is James Hewitt's son on the spurious grounds that he has red hair. Khloé has never looked like her older sisters, but in terms of biology, their comparative looks are completely irrelevant.

After her split from Lamar, Khloé became involved with rapper French Montana (Karim Kharbouch), but it turned into nothing more than a friendship. She offered him support after her best friend and fellow rapper Chinx was the victim of a drive-by shooting in New York. French, the CEO of Cocaine City Records, had himself survived being shot in the head outside a recording studio in NYC in 2003.

Khloé has since been linked to James Harden, who is a star basketball player like Lamar. He's 6ft 5in, is nicknamed 'The Beard', for obvious reasons, and plays for the Houston Rockets. He also won an Olympic gold medal with the US basketball team at the London 2012 Olympics. Khloé has been pictured supporting him courtside, but it's early days to see if anything will come of it.

Her divorce proceedings have been as drawn out as those of Kim and Kris Humphries but reports suggest they finally signed the papers in July 2015. She still talks to him as often as she can. She remains very gracious about him, telling *Complex* magazine, 'Lamar is genuinely one of the best people I've ever met and everyone says that when they meet him … He's had a really hard life.'

Since the breakup, she has concentrated on working out and looking her best for her first time on the cover of *Complex* magazine, emulating Kim from 2007. She has never looked so good. Ironically, she managed to keep her marriage problems entirely secret during the filming of *Keeping Up with the Kardashians*. Like Caitlyn's gender issues, there are some things that are too too private to share with millions of viewers.

For once, Kim's wasn't the biggest story in the Kardashian world when she announced, at the beginning of June 2015, that she was pregnant with her second child, a son. The iconic cover of *Vanity Fair*, featuring Caitlyn's first picture as a woman, overshadowed it. Kim didn't mind; she was just grateful that after some fertility worries she was able to conceive. She and Kanye had been having sex a 'thousand' times a day to ensure conception. It evidently worked.

The demands of a second child seem unlikely to slow Kim down, especially as her brand continues to flourish and now, in effect, has double the power, because she is married to such a famous man. Intriguingly, she has become an executive producer on *Keeping Up with the Kardashians* for the new season – a sign perhaps that she intends to step away from the limelight a little, despite her brand relying so much on a daily diet of exposure.

At first, Kim seemed almost too eager to please, too quick to be influenced by a very talented man. Since her wedding, however, her fashion and lifestyle choices seem inspired. Husband and wife find time every day to speak to each other – not just about their own lives, but about what's going on in the world. And they support each other.

Kim was a step behind her husband when he was the star attraction at the 2015 BRITs. He performed his single 'All Day', surrounded by what the *Guardian* described as a 'Greek chorus of 40-odd men in black tracksuits and hoodies, two of them holding giant flame-throwers.' It was a theatrical tour de force. He was upholding the Kardashian edict of making sure you are part of the conversation. In this case, he was the *only* conversation at the usually tepid awards, hosted by Ant and Dec.

Kim made sure she got in on the act by presenting the Global Success Award to Sam Smith for his number one UK single 'Stay with Me'. She shouted 'Wassup, London!' not entirely convincingly, but was dressed breathtakingly. She showcased the Kardashian Wests' now preferred monochrome in an all-black Julien Macdonald jumpsuit that barely covered her generous chest and looked as if someone had attacked it with a pair of scissors. After Sam had been ushered off stage, she had the chance to take a selfie with the grinning hosts, which was neat publicity for her book, *Selfish*.

She was also at Glastonbury at the end of June, when Kanye was a controversial choice to headline the festival. Kim looked

uncertain as she arrived by helicopter in the middle of a
Somerset field in unsuitably high heels. While her sister
Kendall danced away with Cara Delevingne, she watched
proudly from the wings as her husband performed. Some wise
guy in the crowd tried to dampen the excitement by producing a banner showing a scene from her sex tape in which Ray
J's penis was perilously close to her mouth, presumably to try
to distract Kanye or provoke a reaction.

The *Daily Telegraph* pointed out: 'Kim Kardashian made a
sex tape in 2003, and despite becoming a billionaire business
woman with one of the world's strongest brands, finding love
and becoming a mother, we are still somehow totally unwill-
ing to let go of something that she did when she was 23 years
old and that she presumably thought would remain private.'

Kanye took his turn to support his wife in Armenia in April
and the following month, when she once again braved the red
carpet at the Met Ball in New York. Kanye, she admits, has
given her a new confidence in fashion, but more importantly
has convinced her that it is acceptable to experiment, even if
you don't always get it right. He has moved her away from
treating fashion as a commercial opportunity.

This time her dress, by Peter Dundas for Roberto Cavalli,
was a total success. Alison Jane Reid enthused, 'As a perfect
celebration of a woman's form, and the art of the couturier,
this earthly bird of paradise dress is a masterpiece. It is a
glorious, trembling, unabashed homage to the glory of
sensuous curves and the ability of well-placed exquisite
embroideries and precision engineering to reveal and conceal
at the same time. This is how you do sexy Kim Kardashian –
in lace, not latex, and fluttering, shake-your-tail feathers. I

think a gown like this does wonders for voluptuous women the world over.'

Kim then had to return to the day job, dressing around her pregnancy and ringing Silicon Valley every day to talk about the latest ideas for her app, now her principal money-spinner. All her businesses so far have relied on the success of *Keeping Up with the Kardashians* for their oxygen.

Reality television is now an acceptable genre. Kevin O'Sullivan observes, 'The Kardashians are artistically under-rated. This family is not just going in front of the cameras and being filmed. They are putting on a performance. There is a dazzling brilliance about the Kardashians. It may be staged and slightly ridiculous, but, by Christ, they are doing it well. They are the first and the best.'

At the heart of that brilliance is Kim, a consummate profes-sional in all she does. She continues to be derided as devoid of talent, as if winning a television dance contest would in some way legitimise her success, huge wealth, lovely home and a family that loves her. If what she did were easy and everyone could do it, there would be a million Kim Kardashians out there, but there aren't. There is only one.

LAST THOUGHTS

————

The car park at the Sheraton Agoura Hills is full. I'm here, like everyone else, for the 11a.m. service of the California Community Church. When Kris Jenner founded the church in 2010, it was called the Life Change Community Church, but was rebranded three years later. It's the Kardashian personal place of worship, although you aren't going to see them in the front-row seats every Sunday. The last time they came en masse was for the Easter service. Everyone wore white, including Kim, Kanye and baby North.

Kim attends occasionally, usually with her mother, and, in particular, when it's been a bad week, as it was when she decided to split from Kris Humphries after only 72 days of marriage. After a trip to hear Pastor Brad Johnson speak, she tweeted that she 'needed that'.

I was expecting a Californian experience of Botox and gospel, but it is surprisingly cool. There's coffee and cake before we get underway and everyone is happy to welcome a new face. The Kardashians are invariably fashionably dressed when they turn up, but the regular congregation doesn't overdo it. Pastor Brad is wearing an extra-large T-shirt and has very white celebrity teeth, but he is funny, likeable and self-deprecating. He talks about his grandson, but there isn't a grey hair on his head.

There's no church organ being played by a local piano teacher here. Instead, a house band with a good sound system plays tight God-rock. Of course, the lyrics have a happy-clappy slant and flash up on a big screen: 'Sing Holy, Holy, Holy' and 'Beautiful One I Love', but it's a perfectly pleasant introduction to worship.

The idea of the church is to promote a sense of community in an area where it's hard to get to know your neighbours, because everyone values privacy and security so highly. One idea, projected on the screen, is called 'Dinner for Eight', in which one member of the congregation hosts a getting-to-know-you supper for seven others. Another initiative is for a women's weekend retreat costing $230. They won't be going to a remote part of the Nevada desert or the Rockies, however. It's in Malibu. My overall impression is that this church could be a slimming club or a Women's Institute gathering – an informal and relaxed way of getting out of the house and meeting people who share a common bond – in this case, using God to find meaning in their lives.

Kim told Piers Morgan, when he interviewed her in 2011, that she gave 10 per cent of her earnings to good causes – partly to the community church. She confirmed that she had given away millions. As well as the church, she supports a charity called Dream Foundation, a national organisation, based in Santa Barbara, which grants wishes for terminally ill adults, aged 18 or over. 'It's not just about giving away,' she said. 'It's about finding something you really connect with. So when I find something like the Dream Foundation, it makes it so much more meaningful.' She also donated the financial worth of her wedding gifts from her ill-fated second marriage to the charity.

Sometimes Kim will be moved to give to something in the news. In November 2013, she donated the profits from an eBay auction to the International Medical Corps (IMC) to aid those affected by the deadly Typhoon Yolanda, which killed thousands of people in the Philippines. She tends to change the beneficiary of her eBay auctions, depending on what has caught her eye.

She started supporting the Children's Hospital Los Angeles seven years ago and, as well as regular donations, continues to find time in her schedule to pop in unannounced to visit the sick patients. Sometimes Kanye or her sisters will go with her, but often she is quite happy to slip in by herself and sit at a bedside.

When she arrives, she has presents such as iTunes gift cards or beauty products. All the children, of course, want to have a selfie taken with Kim Kardashian and sometimes she posts them online for them. At other times, she will just chat or help a young girl to do her nails.

Her guiding light here, as in so many areas of her life, is her father, Robert Kardashian, who died from cancer: 'I remember what it was like when my dad was going through it. You see the kids that are so strong. They feel so helpless. You want to do anything to help them.'

The cynical will always believe that celebrity charity is all about tax advantages and publicity. That may be the truth where some well-known names are concerned, but not Kim Kardashian. Just because she has built her brand around a frivolous TV show doesn't mean she lacks a social conscience. When all the extravagance and opulence of her baby shower during her first pregnancy was over, she quietly arranged for all the presents to be packed up and sent to a children's hospital in Chicago, the city where Kanye grew up.

Variety reflected the improved perception of Kim by naming her in their list of five Inspiration Impact Honorees at the Power of Women lunch in New York in April 2015. She was recognised for her support of the children's hospital in LA. Perhaps her next book will be entitled *Selfless*.

While her father remains the biggest influence on Kim's character, Kanye has empowered her to be a stronger woman. Her sister Khloé acknowledges the difference he has made: 'What I love about Kanye is he wants to build her up instead of take her down ... She finally has someone who wants to elevate her and make her like this queen and beautiful princess that she is.' Kanye is firmly in the camp that believes celebrity can be used to make a difference, to project one's own ideas, and one should never be frightened of being passionate about something.

His support was clear during her first visit to Armenia in April 2015 with the mission of bringing the anniversary of her mother country's genocide to the world's attention. This was Kim Kardashian, selfie queen, meeting the prime minister of a country to talk about something that really mattered. It's part of a gradual process over the past year of making Kim more serious. The Armenian trip raised awareness of one important issue, but there have been others.

She was the initiator and executive producer on a documentary called *#RedFlag*, which aimed to heighten awareness of mental health issues. The premise of the film, which was shown on the American channel HLN (Headline News), was that social media could help people who were distressed. She was hoping to break down the taboo of mental illness. She wanted to let social media users, particularly youngsters, know that it was OK to admit to an issue with their mental health and understand that they weren't alone, there was assistance available to them. Kim explained her motivation: 'I have so many friends who have suffered from depression and other mental illnesses. And because I've never experienced it, I don't understand it. I wanted to really inform myself because it's not something you can snap out of.'

The newly serious and enlightened Kim has been able to accept and support Caitlyn Jenner and share her concern at the treatment of transgender people. Her relationship with Caitlyn has changed: 'We're definitely closer and I understand her a bit better, and her struggle.' She wasn't particularly happy with her remarks about Kris Jenner in the *Vanity Fair* article, however, and told her that she didn't need to bash the family on her way up. For the moment, there is an overwhelming public love affair with Caitlyn Jenner and her brave decision to reveal her transition, but it will be interesting to see if that changes in the future, as people become more accustomed to treating her like any other celebrity.

People who think Kim can't be taken seriously because she posts naked pictures of her famous rear online are confusing the brand with the person. Kim Kardashian, in my opinion, is a product just as much as a chocolate bar or a smartphone.

You need to be highly visible to be successful. If you are the CEO of one of these concerns, you want to get on the Tube and see people eating your snack or playing a game on your make of mobile. If you are Kim Kardashian West, you are the CEO of the Kim Kardashian brand and you want to see it everywhere – in magazines and newspapers; you want to smell the perfume on a young woman going to work and recognise that it's yours or see a piece from your jewellery collection dangling on her wrist. It's part of the job description to promote the product, which, in this case, just so happens to be herself.

A problem Kim has as a brand is: how can she be judged to be successful? If you are an actress, you can win an Oscar or an Emmy. A musician like Kanye will win applause for taking home a Grammy or a BRIT Award. As a brand, Kim's success can best be measured in financial terms. By that yardstick, she is doing fantastically well, with a current net worth estimated at $85 million, which, combined with Kanye's $130 million, gives them a family fortune of $215 million, but that figure is rising rapidly. It will greatly increase in the next year, thanks to the new E! deal and her *Kim Kardashian: Hollywood* app.

The first question she was asked, when she was interviewed at the prestigious Code/Mobile conference in Half Moon Bay, California, in the heart of Silicon Valley, was: 'Why do people not take you more seriously?' In her reply, she expressed her frustration about this, but admitted, 'I think when people hear that I might have gotten success off a reality show they take that as a negative.'

That is certainly true. If reality TV programmes were a sport, they would be in the Olympics by now, but for some reason they aren't considered an acceptable genre in which to excel. There are so many bad ones that I can't see why you can't be applauded for being good at it. 'I don't think reality TV gets the respect it deserves,' she said firmly. If there's one question she hates, it would have to be: 'What do you do?'

Kim and the entire cast continue to emphasise the importance of family at every opportunity. She loves the fact that her job involves the people she cares about most. They are a raggle-taggle bunch who can't seem to sustain proper relationships. Hopefully, Kim and Kanye will break the mould and not fail. Absolutely anything and everything happens to this family – the rest of us might have at least one thing in common with them, but the Kardashians take everything to the extreme, and that's part of their appeal.

Should I ever return to that hotel in Calabasas, I hope that I can catch up with the receptionist who wondered about the point of Kim Kardashian. I would tell her why I think she should be applauded for what she has achieved. Kim is always going to get those who will sneer at the sex tape and the role that it played in her subsequent career. She just has to live with that, but I don't suppose she loses any sleep over it.

This time next year I expect we will see Kim and Kanye walking along a Calabasas mall with their two children in their arms. Goodness knows how she will manage to fit in being a mum of two with her already ridiculous schedule. I remember reading a week in the life of Kim back in 2012: Paris one day, Los Angeles the next, then New York for the *Late Show with David Letterman*, home to Los Angeles for a day, on to the Ivory Coast in Africa for a mobile-phone launch and then Paris for Fashion Week. That's changed a little because of North, but she still works all the hours she can.

When Piers Morgan asked Kim what she put down under occupation on her passport, she said she usually made up something, like teacher. There are so many real things she could list – TV star, businesswoman, entrepreneur, model, photographer, mother. She is all these things and many more. In our modern world, there is something that she could choose that, for me, best reflects her position in society … I think she should just put down 'fame'.

KIM'S STARS

It can be so easy to become accustomed to good fortune. Kim has the birth chart of someone destined for enormous success. Jupiter, planet of royalty and excess, stands proud at the Virgo Midheaven, the highest point of her chart, and its godly rays protect and enlarge many areas of her personality and life. Jupiter bestows confidence and optimism, allows a sense of control over one's destiny and promotes growth beyond the limits many endure in their lives. However, as a double dose of cosmic luck, a tight link between Jupiter and its starry opposite, Saturn, planet of restrictions and limitations, suggests Kim is someone who will never take things for granted. There is always fear wherever Saturn sits. In this chart, the fear is of public failure – one of the many spurs that will motivate her to give of her best.

This placement of Saturn and Jupiter in discerning, perfectionist Virgo warns us that she will not accept anything second-rate, either in those upon whom she depends, or indeed herself. Kim also knows how to read the world – she is astute, savvy, with an eye for detailed analysis of situations

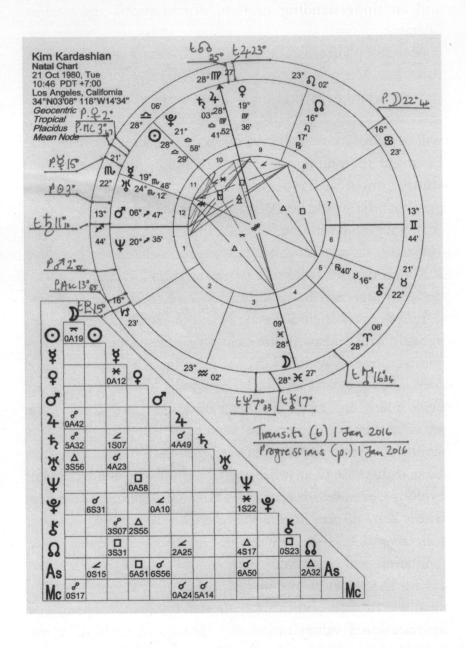

and an understanding of how organisations and people operate.

Mercury, planet of commerce, communication and mischief, rules her Midheaven, so a natural environment for Kim's success would be within the media or, indeed, big business. A tendency to overanalyse might seem like indecision, but this will be offset by an ability to think far ahead of her time. She has a gift for pulling disparate factors and people together, creating order. Such is her inherent instinct and skill for enterprise that she would be an enormous asset to any international corporate establishment.

Success is one thing, reputation another. Kim's career accomplishments will make her a commanding figure; nonetheless, there will be occasions when she may feel undermined, her power eroded. Mars, planet of assertion, in the sign of Sagittarius and awkwardly placed, suggests potential shortcomings, one of which is ever-expanding goals and a level of consequent dissatisfaction. But perhaps, more importantly, there will be occasions when she struggles to define and ask for what she wants, as opposed to what others want. Then this inability to steer her own course may result in actions that make little sense to anyone and behaviour that is emotionally explosive, even self-destructive. Things will fall into place best when Kim directs her very great gifts into fighting for a collective cause – this is when her courage will flow and her reputation will be assured.

Kim has a very strong instinct for speaking the truth. Her ideas will often be radical and her views won't be constrained by traditional values unless she wholly believes in them. Indeed, her inclination for holding nothing back will supersede any bond of loyalty, even to herself. Clearly then, this gabby gift to the gossipmongers will sometimes trip her up. Ultimately, however, as detailed later on, it is likely to be her greatest strength.

With her Sun, the planet of identity, in the harmony-loving sign of Libra, Kim will have acted as a mediator and peacemaker between her siblings and parents. She may have performed the role of emotional caretaker and will be highly sensitive to those within society who are excluded. It is likely she will have developed both humour and resignation in this role as go-between and there will have been times when she needed all of her mercurial skills to extricate herself from some hidden agendas. With Uranus, planet of sudden change, rebellion and independence, influencing the area of her chart linked to siblings, her relationships will be marked by unpredictability – periods of disconnection, followed by closeness. With the sign of Scorpio implicated, bonds will sometimes be affected by suspect motives, rivalry and manipulation, but she needs her siblings and loves them very much. As part of an extended family, Kim will be matchless at promoting genuine friendships; that is, relationships of equality, tolerance and fairness. She will work through her own wounding to give practical and kind support.

Kim's father will have had an enormous impact upon her, revealed by the dominant placement of the patriarchal planets Saturn and Jupiter. The position of this first planet will act as a spur, either by exciting a need to live up to her father's success and expectations, or by burdening Kim to achieve a failed paternal ambition. Her achievement would thus be perceived as redemption of the family reputation. Jupiter, king of the gods, is associated with ethics and integrity, so Father would have modelled these virtues and handed on to her an appreciation of the divine – a sense of religious identity or set of beliefs that will have made a huge impact on her. She will carry them with her all of her life.

Looking at any of the planets taken to signify Father – Sun, Jupiter, Saturn – it is clear they all link awkwardly to the Moon. The latter, being the planet that symbolises Mother in a chart, suggests an inherent tension between the parents. Kim's Moon in Neptune, sign of unconditional love, suggests a compassionate mother, but one who was unavailable at times, perhaps uncertainty around her own primary relation-ship creating emotional distance. Her importance to Kim is enormous, although there may be a blurring and confusion around the role she plays – often she will be more like a sister. It is likely, though, that Kim will place her on something of a pedestal.

The awkward link between the Sun and Moon once again, at a personal level, spells out a message. Kim's uncertainty in integrating what she needs with what she wants and defining her own agenda will cause inner discomfort. Compromising and adjusting will be the pattern activated by an overdevel-oped need to please others. The main arenas in which this will play out will be those concerning her image – the face she presents to the world – and her partnerships.

Neptune, planet of glamour, illusion, victimhood and sacri-fice, is placed prominently in Kim's chart at a point called the Ascendant. She is highly sensitive to others and this instinctive speed-reading of their needs allows her to respond in a way that will ensure her acceptance and popularity. With a partner, a guardian figure or even the public, Kim's compliance will ease her journey through life, but the path could be a slippery one. Kim is someone who charismatically embodies ideals of femininity, not least those defined by commercial values, so her own desire to live up to the expectations of others can undermine her. The real question is whether a certain naivety and her desire for fame have been exploited; whether those who should have protected her have occasionally let her down. Awareness is everything if patterns are not to be repeated.

Kim will look foremost for a partner who is companionable and mentally stimulating. Gemini, sign of the twins, marks the chart area associated with partnerships, suggesting an attraction to those who are adaptable, flirtatious, fun-loving and, above all, easy communicators. She will enjoy arguments, not least because they are a way of clarifying her own views and ideas and are a means of learning. Discussions could become very heated, however, if she uses her perceptive insights in a manipulative way. At an emotional level, Kim can be an instinctive strategist, able to play the victim or innocent party to great advantage – perhaps something she learned as a defence mechanism early on.

Kim's Sun, a symbol of men in her life, is linked to Pluto, shadowy planet of power. It is likely her father was a figure of potency, somebody exposed to the darker sides of human nature and society in general and able to deal with the grittier aspects of life. Perhaps through his experience Kim learned about confrontation and ways of dealing with it. Friendship in marriage will be vital for her, but there will also be a desire for magnetism and strength – the type of individual you don't ignore. Most importantly, acknowledging her own very great need for independence will help her to choose wisely; otherwise, she is likely to pick someone who will give her that freedom when she least expects it.

Looking ahead, Kim will shortly experience a number of important planetary transits. Jupiter, planet of good fortune and hope, links to Venus in November 2015. This will be a time when she will enjoy being the centre of attention and her current relationships are harmonious. Any relationship that starts now will be one in which the balance between freedom and love is easily achieved. She will want to surround herself with beauty, but should be careful not to squander resources.

This will be followed by a period of responsibilities in January 2016, as Saturn, planet of restrictions and authority, crosses the Ascendant. This really is the beginning of a new cycle for Kim, one that feels initially constraining, but will lead to greater maturity, realism and status. Kim will need to complete what needs to be finished, so that life can be simplified, cutting away excess and all distractions that are not conducive to her development over the next seven years. Relationships that aren't strong and worth fighting for may not last – she will know they no longer belong to her future.

This is an important period for her, because it presents a time when she can put up proper boundaries and take greater control of her life, possibly something that will feel very alien to her. To have Neptune on the Ascendant in the birth chart is a mixed blessing. At its best, Kim can give expression to collective feelings and images. She embodies modern femininity for countless women, who admire the way she has used her looks and brains to build a successful public presence. She is open about her sexual nature. She is powerful. All of this is of vital importance when women in many areas around the globe are subjugated, abused, even culled at birth, creating a psychic wound in the world. The openness with which she deals with the emotional realm is another important validation of the feminine. At a personal level, however, there may have been some cost, and this transit of Saturn will provide her with the chance to be discerning and more selective both in whom she chooses to trust and in the way she allows the public access to her.

Kim's ascendant sign, Sagittarius, the centaur, also hints at the way this resourceful woman may develop. The symbol is part animal, part human. Thus, early on, one may be driven by instinctual needs – greed, the need for attention or whatever – but could begin the lengthy journey towards the noble ideals and lofty vision of the philanthropist, given a supportive birth chart and a heavy Saturn transit. As mentioned earlier, perhaps Kim's greatest asset is her instinct and ability to speak the truth and one day this will be employed for the greater good. Meanwhile, Kim will continue to experience worldly success.

Later in September 2016, Jupiter reaches the very top of her chart, an augury of prosperity, and spends approximately a year highlighting her achievements. There will be some conflict between her home and public life, possibly coming to a head in July 2016, when she experiences an awkward link between Uranus, planet of rebellion, and natal Uranus in her chart, associated with her siblings. This could be a period of family tension. This transit will reccur in August 2016 and again in April 2017 and will mark out the steps of growing independence and individuation for her.

Finally, in February 2016, the planet Pluto, moving forward, will wield an influence on her personal finances and her values. Pluto is the planet of breakdown and regeneration, so she may have to deal with a period when her resources are reorganised. Perhaps more importantly, there will be a major and irrevocable change in the way she thinks of and uses her assets. Eventually, there may be a shift away from an emphasis on material acquisition in her life towards a greater endorsement of moral and spiritual imperatives. In the words of another fashionista, 'There are people who have money and people who are rich' (Coco Chanel).

Madeleine Moore
August 2015

LIFE AND TIMES

21 Oct 1980: Kimberly Noel Kardashian is born in Los Angeles, California. She has a sister, Kourtney, who is 18 months older. Her parents are businessman and former lawyer Robert Kardashian and his wife, Kristen Houghton. The family lived in a private cul-de-sac in Beverly Hills called Tower Lane.

June 1984: Younger sister Khloé is born. The children lead an idyllic and privileged existence surrounded by cats, dogs, rabbits and birds. For a time, both Madonna and Bruce Springsteen are neighbours.

March 1987: Her brother Robert, known as Rob, is born. Kim goes to the Buckley School in Sherman Oaks, where she meets Paris Hilton, Nicole Richie and Kimberly Stewart.

April 1991: Is a bridesmaid at the wedding of her mother Kris to Olympic champion Bruce Jenner four weeks after Kris's divorce is finalised.

June 1994: 'Auntie Nicole', Nicole Brown Simpson, is murdered. O. J. Simpson is subsequently charged and Robert Kardashian renews his licence to practise law to join his defence team. The trial causes much tension within the family.

Oct 1994: Celebrates her fourteenth birthday at Neverland, the famous Santa Barbara ranch of Michael Jackson. She has started dating his nephew, T. J. Jackson, who would be her boyfriend throughout her high-school years.

Oct 1996: On her sixteenth birthday, Kim is given the keys to her first car, a brand-new white BMW 318 saloon. She has to sign a contract with her father that she will be responsible for any repairs – and promptly drives into the back of another vehicle.

Nov 1995: Kendall Jenner, Kim's half-sister, is born. She is given the middle name Nicole in memory of her mother's dead friend.

Aug 1997: Kylie Jenner is born. She is the last of Kris Jenner's six children; the eldest, Kourtney, is now 18.

Jan 2000: Gets married in Las Vegas to record producer Damon Thomas without telling her family. She is 19. It proves to be an unhappy marriage.

July 2003: Her father tells the family he is suffering from oesophageal cancer. All four of his children attend when he marries Ellen Pearson at a ceremony at his house in Encino.

Sept 2003: Robert Kardashian dies, aged 59. Kim gives an address at the funeral at Inglewood Park Cemetery.

Oct 2003: Now separated from Damon, she makes a sex tape with her well-endowed boyfriend, Ray J, a hip-hop artist and actor. They fly to Mexico the next day to celebrate her twenty-third birthday.

Feb 2004: Her divorce from Damon is finalised. She receives $56,000 in the settlement and the return of an inscribed Bible, a gift from her father, which she had left behind at their house.

Jan 2006: Opens a Myspace profile under the name of Princess Kimberly. Says she is in a relationship (with Ray J), is straight, Christian and would like children some day. Acquires 856 friends.

May 2006: Goes to the movies in Calabasas with singer Nick Lachey and has her picture taken by the paparazzi. Publication of the pictures gets her noticed for the first time.

July 2006: Accompanies Bruce Jenner to the ESPY Awards at the Kodak Theatre in Hollywood and meets American football star Reggie Bush, but it takes months for him to ask her out. On their first date, they go to a car wash and Chipotle Mexican Grill.

Dec 2006: Spends the run-up to New Year in Sydney with Paris Hilton, who has flown to Australia to choose the face of a new beer. Kanye West sees a picture of the two young women on Bondi Beach and knows he wants Kim to be his girl.

Feb 2007: Announces she is suing Vivid Entertainment in a right-to-privacy lawsuit over the distribution of her sex tape.

April 2007: Settles her suit with Vivid after reaching an agreement with the company. *Kim Kardashian Superstar* reportedly becomes the biggest-selling sex tape of all time. Filming begins for the Kardashian family's reality TV show, focusing on Kris and Bruce's sixteenth wedding anniversary celebrations.

Sept 2007: Attends opening of the Intermix boutique in West Hollywood and is pictured with Kanye West and his girlfriend, Alexis Phifer. Kim later admitted 'there was definitely a spark' between them.

Oct 2007: *Keeping Up with the Kardashians* begins on E! and, including repeats, draws an audience of more than 13 million during its first four weeks. Less than a month after the premiere, the family starts shooting its second season.

Dec 2007: Appears on the front cover of *Playboy* magazine. The shoot was documented in an episode of the reality show and Hugh Hefner helped to select some nude shots for inside the magazine.

March 2008: Plays the love interest in video for 'Thnks fr th Mmrs', a song by rock band Fall Out Boy. Shares billing with a bunch of chimpanzees, who she says were 'scary'.

Aug 2008: Makes her feature-film debut in the ironically named *Disaster Movie*. The critics hate it and Kim is nominated for a Golden Raspberry Award (Razzie). Says her ambition is to be a Bond girl.

Sept 2008: Is the third contestant voted off season 7 of *Dancing with the Stars*, despite being paired with reigning champion Mark Ballas. Judge Bruno Tonioli called her rumba colder than Siberia.

Dec 2009: Guest stars in an episode of *CSI: NY*, playing a femme fatale called Debbie Fallon. She turns out to be the villain.

Feb 2010: Watches Reggie Bush and his team, the New Orleans Saints, claim the Super Bowl in Miami by defeating the Indianapolis Colts. She invades the pitch afterwards to give her man a congratulatory kiss. Launches her first perfume, Kim Kardashian, at TAO nightclub in Las Vegas.

March 2010: Splits with Reggie for a second and final time. She buys a $4.8 million Tuscan-style villa in Beverly Hills, with swimming pool, Jacuzzi, movie room and a waterfall in the garden.

July 2010: Unveils a wax statue of herself in Madame Tussauds, New York. She wears the same pink Hervé Léger dress as the figure and exclaims, 'I think she's pretty hot.'

Nov 2010: Demonstrates she never turns down an opportunity by opening a new toilet facility in Times Square, New York. She doesn't go inside to be the first to spend a penny. Poses dead in a coffin for the Digital Life Sacrifice in support of a World Aids Day campaign. Watches new boyfriend Kris Humphries play basketball for the New Jersey Nets.

Dec 2010: Is officially the top-earning reality TV star with $6 million. She launches the premier Kim Kardashian Signature Watch Collection. Distributes hundreds of toys at Children's Hospital Los Angeles on Christmas Day.

March 2011: Releases her first and only single to date, a dance song from The-Dream entitled 'Jam (Turn It Up)'. The record is not a success, despite being for charity, and Kim doesn't pursue a pop career. The video, directed by Hype Williams and co-starring Kanye West, is never released.

May 2011: Walks into the bedroom of her Beverly Hills home to discover boyfriend Kris Humphries on bended knee, holding out a 20.5-carat diamond ring, worth a reported $2 million. 'Will you marry me?' is spelled out in rose petals on the floor. She says yes.

June 2011: Kim is named Entrepreneur of the Year at the *Glamour* Women of the Year Awards in Berkeley Square Gardens, London. Has bum officially X-rayed to prove that she hasn't had butt implants.

Aug 2011: Marries Kris Humphries in a lavish ceremony in Montecito, California, which is filmed for *Keeping Up with the Kardashians*. He surprises his new bride by taking her for a quick honeymoon on the Amalfi Coast.

Oct 2011: A two-part special, *Kim's Fairytale Wedding: A Kardashian Event*, airs on E! and is a big ratings success. The first night attracts 4.4 million viewers; the second night 4 million. Kim files for divorce after 72 days of marriage, citing 'irreconcilable difficulties'.

April 2012: Kim is a guest at the White House for the Correspondents' Dinner. Arrives hand in hand with Kanye West at the Tribeca Film Festival in New York.

Nov 2012: Launches a new clothing line for curvy girls, the Kardashian Kollection, at Dorothy Perkins in London. She and her sister Kourtney are accompanied by an entourage of 47.

Dec 2012: At his concert in Atlantic City, Kanye stops his song 'Lost in the World' and points at Kim. 'Can we make some noise, please, for my baby mama right here?!'

May 2013: Fails to please everyone in her Mrs Doubtfire dress at the Met Ball. The theme of the night was punk, but critics thought her outfit from Riccardo Tisci for Givenchy resembled a pair of curtains.

June 2013 Finally divorced from Kris Humphries after divorce proceedings that lasted seven times longer than her marriage. The marriage is dissolved, not annulled, as he had asked for.

Her first baby, North West, is born a month prematurely at the Cedars-Sinai Medical Center in Los Angeles. Nori, as she is called, weighs 4lb 15oz. The *Keeping Up with the Kardashians* cameras are not invited to the birth. Kim's mother and step-father separate after 23 years together.

Oct 2013: Kanye's birthday surprise for Kim is to take her blindfolded to the AT&T Park in San Francisco and pop the question, with an orchestra playing her favourite song, 'Young and Beautiful' by Lana Del Rey. The message 'Pleeease Marry Meee!' lights up the night sky. Kris Humphries sells the engagement ring he gave her for $749,000 at Christie's in New York.

March 2014: Wins the Razzie as Worst Supporting Actress for her role in *Temptation: Confessions of a Marriage Counselor*, written and directed by Tyler Perry.

April 2014: Realises a long-held ambition to appear on the cover of *Vogue*. The picture, with Kanye, is taken by Annie Leibovitz. Kim tweets, 'This is such a dream come true!!!'

Aug 2014: She and and Kanye buy a $20-million estate in Hidden Hills, boasting 10 bathrooms, eight bedrooms and two swimming pools. They purchase a $2.9-million property next door to ensure their privacy.

May 2014: Kim and Kanye marry in the most romantic setting, Forte di Belvedere, on a hilltop overlooking Florence, Italy. The cameras aren't invited and her beautiful Tisci-designed wedding dress is kept hidden until the big day. Her brother Rob doesn't attend, nor does stepbrother Brody Jenner. Andrea Bocelli sings 'Ave Maria' as Bruce walks her down the aisle. The not-so-secret honeymoon is in Ireland.

July 2014: *Kim Kardashian: Hollywood*, a video/mobile game created by Glu Mobile, is an instant hit, with 28 million downloads and 11 billion minutes of play in the first six months.

Sept 2014: Kim is named *GQ* magazine's Woman of the Year at the Royal Opera House in London.

Nov 2014: *Paper* magazine features Kim on the front cover and inside, with nude images of her famous rear end, and the inspired marketing tag 'Break the Internet'.

Jan 2015: Premieres her 30-second commercial for T-Mobile's Data Stash during the Super Bowl. She is filmed taking selfies and says, 'It's your data. Keep it.'

Feb 2015: Joins her family in signing a deal worth a reported $100 million with E! for another four years of *Keeping Up with the Kardashians*. The show is now broadcast in 160 countries. Presents a prize to Sam Smith at the BRITs in London and introduces her husband Kanye West's performance.

April 2015: Visits Armenia for the first time with Kanye, North and Khloé. She lays flowers at the Genocide Memorial in Yerevan and meets Prime Minister Hovik Abrahamyan. They journey on to Jerusalem, where North is baptised. Named as one of *Variety*'s Power of Women Inspiration Impact Honorees for her charitable work. Both Kim and Kanye make *Time* magazine's list of the 100 Most Influential People in the World.

May 2015: Wears a show-stopping Roberto Cavalli bird-of-paradise gown to the Met Ball. Her book of selfies, *Selfish*, is published and becomes a bestseller on both sides of the Atlantic. Announces she is pregnant with her second child. Meets Caitlyn Jenner for the first time at her photo shoot for *Vanity Fair* magazine. She says, 'She's beautiful.'

June 2015: *Forbes* places her thirty-third in their Celebrity 100 list of the world's highest-paid celebrities, with annual earnings of $52.5 million. Watches Kanye perform on the main stage at Glastonbury.

Aug 2015: Has combined following on Twitter and Instagram of 77.8 million and rising. The population of the United Kingdom is 63.5 million.

ACKNOWLEDGEMENTS

Just for a change, I wanted to begin by saluting the brilliant work done by the astrologer, Madeleine Moore. She has written birth charts for all my best-known books and they have never been less than fascinating. In the case of Kim Kardashian West, however, she has excelled herself. She may be one of my dearest friends, but she never sees the manuscript or discusses the subject with me beforehand. I am always amazed and delighted if some of what she reveals reflects the story I tell. I couldn't put down the pages about Kim – a powerful woman who can make a difference.

On the subject of unsung heroes on Team Sean, thank you to Jen Westaway, who somehow manages to transcribe my interview tapes, even when it's quite clear I am chatting over a nice lunch in a very noisy restaurant. Once again, Arianne Burnette has done a marvellous job copy-editing the text. My researchers, Emily-Jane Swanson, Jo Westaway and Alison Sims have been terrific and they, like me, are in awe at just how much Kim Kardashian has achieved in her 35 years.

Special thanks to my old friend Kevin O'Sullivan, the best television critic in the country, for his insight into reality television, and *Keeping Up with the Kardashians* in particular. On that subject, Elliot Mintz, the former media consultant for Paris Hilton, was fascinating. I loved his stories of clubland with Paris and Kim. Alison Jane Reid was as incisive as ever regarding Kim's fashion. Good luck with your website: http://www.ethical-hedonist.com/

Congratulations to my agent, Gordon Wise at Curtis Brown, on deservedly being named Agent of the Year at *The Bookseller* Awards of 2015. I always knew he was the best agent in the business and now it's official. Thanks also to his assistant, Richard Pike, for dealing so expertly with far too many enquiries from me.

In Los Angeles – and Calabasas – I enjoyed meeting a number of aspiring actresses and singers working in bars, restaurants and hotels while they pursued their dream. Many people in LA preferred not to be named when they talked about Kim, because it's a very small world out there. Thank you, and I won't forget that I owe a lot of lunches. It was great to see Gill Pringle, Katie Hind and Richard Mineards while I was there. Thanks to Cliff Renfrew for putting me up and sharing an excellent meal at Carousel, the Kardashian's favourite Armenian restaurant. I can see why – the food is excellent.

There's a superb team at HarperCollins backing me up. Sincere thanks to my editor Kate Latham for her enthusiasm and expertise; Georgina Atsiaris and Mark Bolland for project editing; Anneke Sandher and Martin Topping for their breathtaking cover design; Virginia Woolstencroft for looking after

ACKNOWLEDGEMENTS

publicity; and Kate Elton for overseeing the whole project. Finally, a special word for my publisher, Natalie Jerome, who first suggested that Kim would be a great subject for me. I hope you are enjoying your time with the new baby.

You can read more about my books at seansmithceleb.com or follow me on Twitter @seansmithceleb and facebook.com/seansmithcelebbiog.

SELECT BIBLIOGRAPHY

Beaumont, Mark. *Kanye West: God & Monster*, Omnibus Press, 2015

Behan, Pam with Sara Christenson. *Malibu Nanny: Adventures of the Former Kardashian Nanny*, Minnesota Girls Press, 2013

Billieon, Maxwell and Ray J. *Death of the Cheating Man: What Every Woman Must Know About Men Who Stray*, Strebor Books, 2012

Cohen, Nadia. *Kim & Kanye: The Love Story*, John Blake Publishing, 2014

Crawford, Byron. *Kanye West Superstar*, CreateSpace Independent Publishing Platform, 2014

Jenner, Bruce and Phillip Finch. *Decathlon Challenge: Bruce Jenner's Story*, Prentice-Hall, 1977

Jenner, Bruce with Mark Seal. *Finding the Champion Within: A Step-By-Step Plan for Reaching Your Full Potential*, Simon & Schuster, 1999

Jenner, Kris. *In the Kitchen with Kris: A kollection of Kardashian-Jenner family favorites*, Gallery Books/Karen Hunter Publishing, 2014

Jenner, Kris. *Kris Jenner ... and All Things Kardashian*, Simon & Schuster UK, 2012

Kardashian, Kourtney, Kim and Khloé. *Kardashian Konfidential*, St Martin's Press, 2011

Schiller, Lawrence and James Willwerth. *American Tragedy: The Uncensored Story of the Simpson Defense*, Random House, 1999

Simkin, Ryan. *Flash! Bars, Boobs, and Busted: 5 Years on the Road with Girls Gone Wild*, 4 Park Publishing, 2010

West, Donda with Karen Hunter. *Raising Kanye: Life Lessons from the Mother of a Hip-Hop Superstar*, Pocket Books, 2007

PICTURE CREDITS

Page 1: (top) Mirrorpix; (middle left) Mirrorpix; (middle right) Mirrorpix; (bottom) Ron Galella Ltd/WireImage.

Page 2: (top) Maureen Donaldson/Michael Ochs Archives/ Getty Images; (bottom) Donaldson Collection/Getty Images.

Page 3: (top) Splash News/Corbis; (middle) Lawrence Schiller/Polaris Communications/Getty Images; (bottom) Fred Brown/AFP/Getty Images.

Page 4: (top) John Shearer/WireImage; (middle left) Johnny Nunez/WireImage; (middle right) Michael Tran/ FilmMagic; (bottom) Chris Graythen/Getty Images.

Page 5: (top) PhotoNews International Inc./Getty Images; (middle) Chris Polk/FilmMagic for Bragman Nyman Cafarelli; (bottom) Splash News.

Page 6: (top) Jeff Vespa/WireImage; (bottom) Jeff Kravitz/ MTV1415/FilmMagic.

Page 7: (top left) Mark Davies/Getty Images; (top right) Rob Loud/Getty Images; (bottom) Richard Bord/ Wireimage.

Page 8: Stefanie Keenan/WireImage for PMK.

Page 9: (top left) John Shearer/WireImage; (top right) Denise Truscello/WireImage; (bottom) Startraks Photo/Rex Shutterstock.

Page 10: (top left) Denise Truscello/WireImage; (top right) Mark Cuthbert/UK Press via Getty Images; (bottom) Neil Mockford/Getty Images.

Page 11: (top) Ethan Miller/Getty Images; (bottom) Paul Archuleta/FilmMagic.

Page 12: (top left) Jennifer Graylock/FilmMagic; (top right) Jonathan Hordle/Rex Shutterstock; (bottom) Steve Granitz/WireImage.

Page 13: (top) Christopher Polk/Getty Images for BET; (bottom) Marc Piasecki/GC Images.

Page 14: (top left) Pascal Le Segretain/Getty Images; (top right) Trago/Wireimage; (bottom) Pascal Le Segretain/Getty Images.

Page 15: (top) Gonzalo/Bauer-Griffin/GC Images; (bottom) Kevin Winter/Getty Images.

Page 16: (top) Karen Minasyan/AFP/Getty Images; (bottom) Dimitrios Kambouris/Getty Images.

INDEX

284